ALL THE WAY
TO SECOND STREET

ALL THE WAY
TO SECOND STREET

A Memoir

Nancy Casey

LOGWOOD STONE

*For Kim ~
In celebration of
the girls we once
were and
the women
we have
become.
Peace
Nancy*

Published by Logwood Stone Moscow, Idaho
Inquiries should be directed to publisher@logwoodstone.com

Book design by Robert and Erik Jacobson
www.longfeatherbookdesign.com

Some names and locations have been altered or obscured to
protect the privacy of individuals.

BIOGRAPHY AND AUTOBIOGRAPHY/Women
FAMILY AND RELATIONSHIPS/Parenting and Motherhood—
Anger—Interpersonal Relationships
HISTORY/United States/20th Century—State and Local/West

ISBN: 978-1-937203-00-9

www.AuthorNancyCasey.com

ALL THE WAY
TO SECOND STREET

Visiting the Old House

… what good are notebooks?
— "Life During Wartime"
    David Byrne and Talking Heads

Tuesday, January 26, 1993

Last Saturday I checked on the Old House, the place in the valley where Robb and I lived when the kids were tiny. We say its name a certain way. We don't put the accent on the word "house" the way you would lean on the second word if you were saying "old friend" or "old shoe." The weight goes on the first syllable—as it does when you say "small house" or "wrong house." The Old House.

I was with my friend Diane. We're teachers. We drove through the valley on our way back from a high school in Coeur d'Alene where I'd done a workshop on a notion called "writing across the curriculum." The idea is—if you write about what you are trying to learn—no matter what the subject—even if all you can manage to say at first is how little you understand, the very process of writing will draw clarity forth. About three-quarters of the way though my introduction, I looked at the math teacher, and the coach, and thought, *This is the kind of thing English majors always say.*

By the time we finished the sinuous two-lane ride from Coeur d'Alene and turned into the valley, it was dark. The road got muddier as we climbed, and after rounding the curve that begins the final, harrowing, quarter-mile ascent, I accelerated through slush—left, right, left again, up, up—like driving a boat, I always thought. I knew we wouldn't get stuck. I can gauge the condition of the road at the turnoff, down by Delbert's barn where there's a light, and decide then if I need to put chains on or not.

"Tell you what," Diane proposed as I swung around in a wide curve, crisscrossing the other tire tracks on the flat in front of the house, and coming to rest facing downhill in the slush and the mud. "If there's someone there, let's not go in."

"Fine with me," I said. It was already late. I did want to know if Stan and Marsha were living there again. They had been caretaking it for several years, but moved to an apartment in Frederick last spring after a bad scare from Stan's emphysema. Stan had called the day after Christmas, though, wanting to know if they could move back in. He said all they would have to do would be to get some firewood together. He said he wasn't ready to sit in a recliner and watch TV until he died.

So I did want to know if they were there now, or if they weren't, if the house had been vandalized yet, but I could do without a visit. I go back there to look and remember. I don't much enjoy seeing or talking to the people I knew.

The windows of the house were dark. None seemed shot out. The headlights reflected on the wet glint of the shake shingles and flashed white on Marsha's kitchen curtains.

"Somebody is living here," said Diane with certainty, but I knew she was wrong. This the first spot where you can turn around after the road gets slick and steep. That's the reason for all the tire tracks. There were no footprints, however, no path to the door. Even if someone was living here, they hadn't been home for a while.

I told Diane I just wanted to run inside to see what it looked like, and began to pick my way towards the gate in awkward mincing steps. Melting snow seeped into the sides of my pumps, spiking my arches with cold.

A truck rumbled downhill in low gear towards me. I didn't recognize the dark 4 x 4 rig until it stopped. Jack Matthews, a trapper from the other side of the ridge, was collecting his dogs after looking for cougar all day.

"There's five of 'em have crossed up above this winter," he said, "Caught one a bit ago."

I wondered sarcastically what he does once he catches them, but I didn't pursue it. I didn't want to be standing there in my little skirt and nylons, so stupid as to not know what "catch" means, or so silly to think that some creatures should be left alone.

I dashed inside—or tried to. Stan had redone the porch door and the latch was different. The tomcat was still there. Poli comes up and feeds him now and again. It's a foil to make the place look more used. The cat probably watched the thieves carry out the stoves last summer, the very same way he was watching me.

Climbing the stairs, I felt stumbly and disoriented. How could my body not know this porch? I used to be smug when people teetered on the slanted, uneven steps. Even on cloudy, moonless nights like this one, even with armloads of schoolbooks and groceries, I sailed up those two short flights. Now I was hesitating like a visitor.

Maybe I needed more resolve. Or more remembering. Maybe Stan had changed the steps. I touched the wall for balance, making my gingerly way to the door.

I will skip the reverie on the faces of small children at that door. Let us not revisit occasions when I looked past its windows, held it open for someone, or crossed the threshold in either direction. This isn't even the same door.

I struck a match in the kitchen and the flame lasted long enough for seeing that the place seemed undisturbed since my visit in September. No need to grope my way across the living room or into the bedroom to check on the residual clutter that inhabits all abandoned houses. There was no sound of dripping, no evidence that the roof was caving in. From up on the hill in the tangle of the old garden last September, I had noticed how the green asphalt roofing looked rippled and bare.

It's not that great of a house. No one wants to live here, and it's foolish to try and maintain it from a distance as some sort of shrine. It will fall down. That will be okay. I am finished with this house.

When I got back outside, Jack asked if I got the letter he sent last year wondering if the place was for sale. It's the timber he's after. I told him no. Not now anyway. These trees sustained me when I lived here. No need to mow them down.

"Are you ready?" asked Diane. I strode to the car and hopped in, still trying to show Jack that I was oblivious to the slush.

"Are you sure you want to go?" Diane pressed.

All that was left to do was take one long drink of that gleaming hulk of house crouched there above the road on a January night, and remember what that house holds for me.

”Whenever I see you here, you look so small,” Diane said, and then became quiet, as if respecting some silence I should need. So I didn't give voice to any of the vivid burbles triggered in a few glances by the myriad things that had changed and things that were still the same.

Diane talked first. "Are you okay?"

So many stories. They all begin the same. "Once…"

Of course I am okay. It's not this house that haunts me. It's the way I don't know the name of the experience I had when I lived here. Visiting the Old House is not what makes me know that. Visiting the Old House isn't sad. Writing this is sad.

Nancy Nugent

Believe shall be a boat.

—The Wise Cow
A visit to William Blake's Inn by Nancy Willard

SUNDAY, NOVEMBER 23, 1980
ROYAL OAK, MICHIGAN

I wonder how many people go into the drug store at 11 Mile and Main, buy a six-pack of Miller and a carton of cottage cheese, then ponder over junk food—no, that's no way to start a new life. Pay $4.69 and refrain from saying, *I just left my husband, my home, walked out, ditched, deserted, and you think I'm just some lady buying cottage cheese and beer.* People who say stuff like that are weirdoes.

I am sitting here drinking that beer, hoping it will make me sleep because I have a big day tomorrow. I have to stand up in front of the branch office and babble Office Systems. I can do it, too. I can do a lot of things.

I wonder if I am screwing up.

Friday afternoon, talking with Iris in the bar. When I said that Dominic was never going to change, never, ever going to get it, she said, "That's right, you know." Nothing left to say. I went to the bathroom and had it out with myself in the mirror… *If you sleep here tomorrow night, you are a coward.*

Well, I slept there Saturday night, but that's not where I am tonight.

What a funny little room this is. The lady so sincere and enthusiastic, "It's real nice, ain't it?" Well, it will do. It will certainly do. $112.50 per week for one and a half rooms and a refrigerator. A refrigerator with four beers in it and a pint of large curd cottage cheese. You'd think it would have occurred to me that I didn't have anything to eat it with.

Leaving. Dominic said, "I'm sorry I can't look at you." And repeated that I still hadn't explained to him why I was doing this. That's the problem. I've told him so many times and he still doesn't understand.

I didn't know what to say. I was scared to say anything, lest he remember it forever.

I packed like I was going on an IBM trip for a week. That part wasn't hard. When the suitcase was zipped and closed, and I was standing there looking stupid, looking for an alternative that wasn't staying or going, he said, "Just remember…" *I love you? I care about you? The oil needs changing?* "Never mind," he finished.

His face in the tiny window of the front door as I backed out of the driveway. After that it was driving down Woodward Avenue in the dark. Familiar.

Last Wednesday when I asked him what he thought I was like, he told me I was talented, witty, and brilliant. I wanted to snap at him. *Five years of marriage and that's all you can say?* Then he added, "You are also very selfish."

I am so fucking selfish. But then, who are we supposed to look out for? Even all of the love-thy-neighbor stuff is in response to the question, "How can I save my soul?"

Hard as I tried, I couldn't get the silly alarm clock to click over to the "set" position. I could make the radio play. Moreover, I had already set the alarm once, to make sure it was going to work. It did. And then it didn't. I flipped on the TV, turned the UHF dial round and round, but it never moved off 25. I tried the clock again, and it popped out of the "set" position every time. On the second attempt to get the UHF dial to move, to my surprise, it did. It looked like I would be able to watch the last episode of *Cosmos* on 56 after all.

The dial stopped at 50. Static.

I kept my fingers twirling the knob gently and methodically. It had worked before, so surely it would work again. Twirling the knob is what you do to change the channel. If you do everything you're supposed to do, surely it will all be okay. Sometimes you have to hang in there a long time before you get results, but keep plugging. I watched the tendons ripple across the back of my hand, strong criss-crossing piano fingers swirling the knob while the fucking number stayed the same. Foiled by a television. Tricked by an alarm clock. Even mechanical devices are out to stop me, show me how the world isn't waiting before my big toe right now.

Is this a dumb thing I'm doing—have done? Is this caterpillar spinning a cocoon or walking across the expressway? Will I become a butterfly or puree de caterpillar?

Dominic and I had so much, especially lately. Or did we? So much what? House? Cabin? Job? Potential? Lately it has been neat, comfortable and better only because he is struggling so hard to try and understand me. But that's not enough. He's struggling, but not understanding at all. The comfort of his effort has been enough to make me complacent with it—willing to watch *Cosmos,* read a while and drink Cognac until Sunday night disappears, when really nothing fundamental was changing. Doing this in February, however, could have made more sense than pulling it four days before Thanksgiving.

Dominic doesn't understand me. That's only half of it. What do I understand of Dominic? Dominic is strong to a fault.

Imagine a relationship where love—not convention, duty or dependence—is what binds. Sometimes they love hard, sometimes hardly at all. Ebb and flow, good times and bad, sickness and health, the whole shot. A connection made of love can thin, but it won't break if someone falls.

I don't know if that's possible, but that's what I want. And if it's not possible, I just threw away the most reasonable facsimile.

That's what I was thinking while I made circles with the TV knob. How stupid could I be? I could be drinking coffee and brandy, hooking the rug, and watching 60 Minutes. I could be home, where I belong.

I don't think home is there anymore. I've been chipping at it for some time, but tonight I destroyed it. It will never be the same. That could be tremendously good or simply bad. Whichever, it's done. Embrace the uncertainty—and watch emptiness rush in.

What I have done is history. What I should do is the direction I wish I had. What I am doing amazes and perplexes me. Sometimes it seems completely out of my control.

If the alarm set once, it would set again. If the channel incremented from 25 to 50, surely it would make it to 56. I gave the TV a break and tried the clock radio. It clicked in place.

A brief interlude in the bathroom. A slight scare when the toilet threatened not to flush.

I attack the remaining mechanical holdout, resolutely spinning the channel-changing knob…until I give up.

MONDAY, NOVEMBER 24, 1980

Each time I told someone, I learned something.

Kate was the first person I told, and a rush of emotion came out with the words as I heard them the first time. She scared me. She squirreled her face and said, "Well, you don't look so happy about it now." It's possible I've made a huge mistake. I can still change my mind.

During that conversation, I realized how big a role my own selfishness played—first in the conquest and now my lack of pain. Why have I never been burned—"gotten it in the ear"—ever? What have I missed?

Wilson struck the head of one nail after another—how this is probably a "right smart" thing, a deliberate step towards change and growth, almost exciting. The predictions about pain—how it would come like I'd never felt it before, and then get worse. He cautioned my tendency to entertain myself with personal drama, even said I could be back at home quite quickly, quite soon, if I decided that. "Don't rush into anything or out of anything. Think of what you have."

This evening, on the phone with Iris: the details are different for everyone, what's the same are the ups and downs. She made the perfect friendly gesture and suggested we go out for dinner on Thanksgiving.

I met Joann for a drink after work. If nothing else, your sister will give you insight on your upbringing. "Did you see a priest? Marriage counselors are pro-divorce. Priests tend to be much more positive." A lecture about the dangers of burying myself in my job. My job is satisfying, hers isn't. That's why she truly needs a husband like Peter. So—if you want a happy marriage, get a rotten job?

She warned that by the time she steps off the plane in Dallas Wednesday afternoon to spend Thanksgiving with Mom and Dad, they better already know. That's fair.

TUESDAY, NOVEMBER 25, 1980

Calling my parents. I didn't know *that* would be the phone booth. The man at the desk said "the door down the hall" and when I opened the door I thought it was just a closet for the wheelchair. I didn't see the phone on the wall until I looked in the hallway for a different door, couldn't find one and came back in.

The wheelchair seat was low, low. Elbow on my knee, head in my hand, curtain of hair, the receiver heavy against my jaw. In the dark I'm in a story with too many symbols, a cripple in an isolation box, hammered by voices piped in from a subdivision in Dallas.

"Have you found yourself? Are you happy now?"

"No, I'm not happy. But I wasn't happy before, either. I guess the only difference is that now it's public."

"Who have you told???"

They searched accusingly for The Answer.

- Is it your job? Take a leave of absence right now! No job is worth this.
- You should be having children. You need to start a family.
- Believe me, there's things I know about you. You use vulgar language and you haven't been going to Mass.

So determined to mash every bit of rebellion in me, every feeling, every curiosity.

- Swallow your pride! Pack your bags and go home! Tonight! *Lions! and tigers! and bears! oh my!* How many times did she say that? As if once she heard it come out of her mouth she just had to hear it again. And again. It was like being whipped with a strand of leftover spaghetti.

- There are good times and bad. If you ask God for the grace to get you through the bad times, he'll give it to you.

- Don't you even *think* about getting used to being on your
  own because I *know* you, you *throw* yourself into everything.
  Go back to Dominic before you even *start* to enjoy being alone.
  Swallow your pride...!

The judgments.

- You failed.
- You've ruined our Thanksgiving. *(Oh! the mess!)*
- You have so much and you are just throwing it all away.

Nowhere to run, nowhere to hide. Certainly nowhere to sit down and decide.

I feel like never talking to them again. Maybe they'll improve. Give them time. It's a shock.

My shock: I didn't seem to let them down so much as make them angry. They didn't try to understand at all. They let *me* down.

It's not fair for me to turn away in the face of how I am hurting them. I have a responsibility to accept it. I expected the conversation to wend into thickets of pain and confusion, but also I expected us to be kind to each other because of that. I thought it was going to end up with one of them, probably Dad, after Mom had done most of the talking, saying, "We don't understand this at all. This is terrible. But you're still our daughter. We want you to be happy. Let's talk in a few days."

I thought they'd say that. I really did.

WEDNESDAY, NOVEMBER 26, 1980

"Two eggs, please, with hashbrowns and coffee."
"You mean you want the Special?"
"No."
"Well, there's the Special," and he points to the sign. I read what's written on the window, slowly, because from the inside, it's written backwards. "Seven days a week, 2 eggs, bacon or sausage, hashbrowns, toast, $1.39."
"That's exactly what I want."
"You want anything to drink with that?"

Everyone seems to have a name for what I want. Seven days a week. And it's cheap, too. Only I don't recognize it when it stares me in the face.

Something hurts.

Joann sang a tune of how before she got married, she had great periods of uneasiness about it. She could calm herself down by going to church and praying. Praying helps put it into perspective.

Perspective. Is that what you get when you sit in church all afternoon so you don't have to figure out what to do with yourself? Ignore your feelings until they go away and can't tempt you? Perform a lobotomy on yourself lest you risk a sniff of the bark of the tree of knowledge of good and evil?

The void in me. The thing that hurts so, the thing that makes me nervous at times—shaky, antsy, sarcastic, mouthy. The void.

Place a pebble in an empty jar. When the jar is still, there's but one little spot that isn't empty. Now shake the jar. It's is just as empty, but the one full spot is moving, moving all the time. No one spot can call itself empty, but the jar is never full. The whole system—shake, shake, shake— it makes one hell of a clatter. Wise cracks in the bar. Sarcasm. Wit, cuts, zing, laugh. *My god, Nancy, whatever got you going?*

Nothing, absolutely nothing. I am just running around trying to fill it with something.

Just like I could have bitten the edge off my glass in the bar on Wednesday night, I could bite the edge off my coffee cup here, in Spence's restaurant.

I really don't know who I am. I've always tried to find out by asking other people. Act something out, see how they think I am doing. The owner of this restaurant thinks I'm doing badly. He wants me to get my feet off the chair.

Lots of times I've done a good act and folks are pleased, really pleased and call me a good lady. Other times, I'm not so sure what the crowd wants, then I get nervous, because I don't know what to do. I'll look at the group around the table in the bar and ask myself what they need. Puns? Heavy food for thought? Gossip? Word origins? A scientific conundrum? Used to teach all that stuff, you know. Size 'em up and let it fly. Seldom do I shut up and take in whatever it is I need.

You can't know what you need, until you know what you are.

Much as I disagree and am angered by what my parents said, there's always the possibility that maybe, just maybe, they're right. That they know what I need and I don't. And if I'd listen to them, I'd be happy. One thing for sure, if I'd listen to them, *they'd* be happy

The problem with you, Nancy, is you're too damned stubborn to ever admit you're wrong. The problem with being born stubborn, though, is that no matter how hard you try, how deeply you look, how sure you might feel, you can never be right. If you don't do what they say, clearly you are stubborn. They are not stubborn, so if they were wrong, they would have capitulated by now. But they haven't, so they're right. Yup, and you're stubborn. In the face of your stubbornness, they will pray for patience. God gives them the patience to wait for you to stop being stubborn. He wouldn't do that if they weren't right.

Thursday, November 27, 1980

Thanksgiving Day phone call—Mom:

- Walking out and not facing it.
- Your marriage vows don't change
- We're going to Mass. I hope God hears our prayers and makes you go back.
- You can't turn your back on what God wants and he wants you to go back.
- I talked to Dominic last night, and he wouldn't even say anything against you.
- Go find Dominic and go up to the cabin. Right now

Dad on the phone next:

- You are making the biggest mistake of your life.
- You are hurting yourself. Even more, you are hurting Dominic. I don't know how he puts up with your crap.
- You better come to your senses…

Then they put Joann on…

It was like running the gauntlet or getting gang-banged. When one got tired of working me over, there was always someone fresh, ready to grab the phone and start in on me anew. While the others basted the turkey and blended up another round of whiskey sours.

FRIDAY, NOVEMBER 28, 1980

A week since I made the decision.

Monday was and wasn't hard. Was and wasn't strange.

Tuesday was harder. I can't remember for sure what I did all day. Talked to Wilson. He didn't mash me back, but neither did he cheer the drama. *Slow down, Lady.* Even today my mind is racing back and forth, asking me if I want to be in the single slot or the married slot, the career slot or the working mother slot. Each slot is a trap.

Finding an apartment or house or room or flat. I don't know. It's a kind of commitment, or plan. So is staying in this motel another week. Not to decide is to decide. To do it is to spend some money on a security deposit and rent. To be wrong is to throw a little money away.

Thoughtcrime. I am committing Original Sin. It is very frightening.

MONDAY, DECEMBER 1, 1980

Begins a week.

Begins December.

Begins the season to be jolly.

Begins my lease.

Wilson offered to give me some kitchen stuff. I'll take that, but not a couch or posters for the wall. I want to live in an empty apartment. I want to hang stuff on my walls, but I want to see something and choose it, say, *I want to look at that all the time.*

Iris says my desire to live in an empty place says something: empty house, empty person. Bad? Yes, but good to the extent that the truth can't be bad. Empty person—or just a person with nothing to show? Nothing for the public view, anyway. Something's there, but I hide it? I won't show it until I'm sure what it is? Until I'm sure that I like it?

Funny, whatever it is, I couldn't show it to Dominic.

TUESDAY, DECEMBER 2, 1980

What a day. Every day is a trip. Or at least a leg of the journey.

Wilson said that after I left the bar, they said I was a "survivor." Survivors are dangerous people to come up against. They throw old women and children out of lifeboats.

"Nancy, be strong," he said. How do you tell strong from stubborn? Now I wish I would have asked him—*be strong and do what?*

I was very sad in Sears and in Penney's and in Meijer Thrifty Acres and in McDonald's. I felt lonely and very alone because…well, I don't know. I just did, that's all

A bathroom rug. It doesn't matter that they didn't have any gray hand towels to match. Hand towels are basically for company, after all. Don't really need much beyond bath towels for myself.

I don't really feel much like writing when I get sad. Sadness touches the emptiness. Is it sad because there's nothing there? Do I not feel like writing because to write one must look, and I don't want to look? Do I not want to look because if I look I can see the problem, and if I can see the problem, I can derive a solution? I don't want a solution? A solution would be a decision, and I don't like decisions. Not to decide is to decide. Can you decide you don't know what to do yet? Do you have to promise when you'll know?

What kind of a decision did I make when I decided I was leaving? When did I make it? At the cabin? In the bathroom at the bar? Sometime earlier? Was it a decision not to work on our problems anymore? Then I must be lazy. People who've had everything handed to them tend to be that way.

WEDNESDAY, DECEMBER 3, 1980

Kate says Dominic is lost, very much in love with me, wants me to be happy above all else. And I stand a terrible risk to lose him. She made me feel as though I'd done something awful: thrown away all this without trying hard enough.

I have always liked and admired Kate. Like me, she is always bumping into one unanswerable question after another. Unlike me, she's arrived at some justifications, selected her course, and wants to get on with life. Kate stuck it out. But I'm not Kate. She's afraid the course she didn't take might make someone happy.

She could justify her own situation if she could convince me to stay in one like it. Instead of forcing me, like my family is doing, she twists my own words into reasons for me to go back and do things as she's done them. She seems so earnest, desperate to make me see that the only road to happiness starts where she is.

The arguments she has are good ones. Do they apply universally?

Don't, Kate. Don't do this to me. Don't do this to yourself. Please recognize that we have much in common and use that as a base from which we can help each other out. Recognize that we aren't carbon copies of each other. The argument that worked on you is working. Just stop there. Don't insist it work on me.

THURSDAY, DECEMBER 4, 1980

For Christmas, I could go to Kate's, or Joann's. Not Dominic's. What about Nancy's?

Nancy's? Where's that? Is it the 3 x 6 rectangle between a bathroom and a linen closet where she sleeps in an apartment on Galpin Street? Would it be the desk with her name on it in the desk-ocean on the 21st floor of the Renaissance Center? This morning it could have been her briefcase, it was so organized. What kind of a home changes size and moves from place to place?

A spaceship in a black hole does not recognize the event horizon until long after it's been crossed. How do you stay sane?

To claw your way out of the abyss, you must have some kind of absolutes to serve as handles and grips. If they all pull off or turn to silly putty, you are in a vortex whose sides are smooth as glass. To get out then, you have to fly.

What is a belief? It's what we choose to think when faced with ideas which cannot be proved or disproved. In other words, when we don't know and can't find out, we think what we want to think. We believe. It feels better than not believing.

Friday, December 5, 1980

Talk about living in a box. You compare your marriage to a shrinking crate, and run away to a cell the size of an air mattress. Because everywhere else in this apartment is in complete view of the busy sidewalk. If someone saw you, what would they see?

A weirdo.

Saturday, December 6, 1980

There are things I need here. Shelves to put my clothes on. I knew I needed those. I knew I needed curtains. The seed needs. I think I like this place.

I understand why it was so hard to buy groceries last night. It hadn't occurred to me that I had a kitchen, much less what food I would eat in it. How startled I was to pull open what I had remembered as an empty kitchen drawer and *yikes!* The orange tray full of silverware from Wilson leapt at me like a jack-in-the-box. I slammed the drawer. I'm going to accept this place gradually. I've done enough for one day.

Last night before I ordered a second drink, I looked around the bar and asked myself what, what, could possibly happen to surprise me if I stayed there. I went to Penney's and picked up the curtains.

I pretended I was going to the bathroom and left without telling anyone I was leaving or say why. If I told them the truth, they would try to talk me out of it, like I was breaking the rules. Friday night = bar = fun. Curtains = chore = no fun. A discussion would lead to the revelation of an uncomfortable truth: hanging out with that same circle of faces is boring.

Penney's was hushed and antiseptic as a computer room. It was pleasant to walk the aisles like it was a museum, wander quietly and just look. I slowed down, smiled at people. I know how to pay for curtains. Nobody thought I was brave. Or bad.

With curtains now on all the windows, I can go everywhere. It's like a gymnasium in here. A too-big, echo-y space.

The hallway seemed really tiny last night. Now I'm a dot in the corner. Me, a pallet, and a clock. I wonder how long it will be before the occupied spot grows. It's okay to be ready, but don't force it.

Line of least resistance lead me on.

SUNDAY, DECEMBER 7, 1980

Consider Adam. Consider God. Who is the more greedy, vain, and weak?

Things I was very happy to be reminded of last night...

- It's not boring or sad to be alone. Once I'm alone, my first impulse is to find someone else or to go somewhere, but once I get past that initial jitter, I discover I am actually in pleasant company
- What I need is often very close, but sometimes I have to pause and allow myself to see it, instead of cutting a wider and wider circle frantically looking for it.
- Because I am a person who continuously acts and changes roles for the crowd I'm in, I tangle into a confused jumble if I can't renew myself by being alone for a while.
- Right now I am in some combination of good shape and bad shape.

MONDAY, DECEMBER 8, 1980

Poor ol' God. Makes a creature in his image and likeness and gets mad at what he sees. Invents a rule, baits a trap. Doesn't the smartest being in the universe have anything better to do all day?

Sometimes he dabbles in immaculate conception.

TUESDAY, DECEMBER 9, 1980

If Adam brought sin and Jesus came along to fix it, why aren't we back in the Garden of Eden?

Maybe it's more a case of Adam choosing to learn, grow, and become fully himself. He took a step on his own. God, who can't tolerate that, banishes Adam from what he loves.

Jesus said to renounce violence and vengeance, to abide in God-is-love. God watches while they string him up.

It's hard to please this God.

The truth never changes. It is our perception of it that shades and grows. Stories do not *tell* the truth, they reflect it. We are not trying to understand the stories so much as use them to understand the truth.

WEDNESDAY, DECEMBER 10, 1980

Make up a system, any system at all. Make up the words and their definitions, all the rules of behavior. Knit fragments together with logic and see what can be explained. You don't have to come up with it all right away. Take your time. Fiddle with the rules and definitions to improve your system however you like. No matter what you do, a few things will always be true:

- You can always use the words of the system to ask a question the system can't answer.
- If you follow all the explanatory paths, sooner or later you will come to a contradiction.
- These problems of not-knowing start when you invite the parts of the system to consider themselves.

Bertrand Russell and Kurt Gödel nailed all that down before I was ever born. Now what?

Thesis. Antithesis. Sisyphus. Human understanding is not a system.

To keep a system intact in the face of questions and contradictions you must label certain people stubborn.

Galileo. Now there's a stubborn old man. It wasn't until he was pained and threatened that God gave him the grace to overcome his stubbornness and admit that the earth was flat. I don't claim to be Galileo, but dammit, I'm not stubborn. When you're stubborn, you're rigid, not wilted. I would like to fit inside a system. It's easier. But to fit, one should change, not break.

This writing is an escape. I wonder if I should stop.

THURSDAY, DECEMBER 11, 1980

The task of the authorities is to keep people in line. The Church keeps people doing what "good people" do, what the saints would do. The saints did this, the saints did that. The Church tells us all about it, leaving out the critical fact—the saints did the things they did because they were in touch with the meaning and purpose of their lives.

FRIDAY, DECEMBER 12, 1980

I don't want to be a shining example of how the system works. The system doesn't work and I don't want to bear the responsibility for every questing soul who looks at me and the trappings I've collected and assumes, deduces, concludes, infers, *sees* that the system works and is reassured.

I don't want to go back amid sighs of relief and clucks of delight that my momentary aberration is ended. Sorry, gang, I *am* the aberration. You can mash me, bend me, even break me or snuff me out, but you can't undo the fact that I did it. And now that I've done it, I *am* it.

You are so sorry I have turned my back on my faith. I turned all right. Instead of standing in line with you, casting sidelong glances at knowledge and goodness and evil, I turned and I am looking, making you afraid and sorry. Afraid I'll say what I see. Afraid that if you see what I see you'll be sorry.

Gouge out that eye…

SATURDAY, DECEMBER 13, 1980

The magic word in the Garden of Eden was "yet."

Adam was doomed. The whole time he didn't eat the fruit, he hadn't eaten it *yet.*

And God said, "Just don't throw me into that briar patch."

SUNDAY, DECEMBER 14, 1980

Dominic's house. I can be here until eight o'clock while he is at the cabin. I have twenty more minutes. I feel like Goldilocks.

Take my stuff without leaving a trail. I don't want him noticing anything and drawing conclusions. I wouldn't want to curl up in a chair and be comfortable here. It could remind me of—what? Of how comfortable it was? Yeah. How nice it was to have furniture to plop onto and a stereo to listen to. The tuck of the afghan around my feet on the gold couch, watching *Mash*. I'll do just fine here on the basement steps. I can see the boxes of Christmas ornaments under the ping-pong table.

I don't pine sentimental for the Dominic-and-Nancy Christmas tree. I don't want to arrange the little ornamental things and people, call him in to see, get a hug because I am so cute.

I guess my dad was right. I don't even care about Christmas.

I wish there was some way Dominic could understand how much I do miss all the things we would do together. Go to the cabin. Take walks. Read to each other. Sunday evenings. We had so many pleasant after-noons together last winter doing nothing.

The time he drank too much champagne at the campfire and got sick. That evening I had a theory he was really upset about us, but nothing was ever said. I built the campfire. Dominic dropped his first hot dog into the fire, got the second one safe in the bun and poured champagne all over it, thinking it was a cupful of onions. We laughed so hard. But there was something pathetic in not being able to roast yourself a hot dog.

Poor Dominic. Poor Nancy. Poor us. Two basically very nice, very outwardly compatible people. One emotional, temperamental—nasty sometimes. The other stern and very kind. Both headstrong. Both wanting distinct things. Same or different? Can't tell. They've never been able to make that clear enough to each other to find out.

All that could be lost. The one who knew you when. Looking back on a life that grew solid and deep beneath you.

Looking back and wondering what a little passion might have felt like.

MONDAY, DECEMBER 15, 1980

Kate, who all this year teetered on the edge of my act, has withdrawn. Kate, who has a husband, two children, a station wagon and a dog. Kate, who is logical and quick, whom I respect, admire, and envy.

Kate, how do you know so fucking much? You sound just like my mother, except you spout it in new vocabulary. *Using the intellect to cre-ate feelings…the immaturity of chasing the imaginary…the wisdom of* *elders...abusing my gifts...*Because you were open and rebelled longer, your world is larger, more patterned and crisscrossed than my mother's.

I never thought of you as one of those who, with a wrench of will, would curve her universe and let it snap shut.

TUESDAY, DECEMBER 16, 1980

We do live in the Garden of Eden. Power and pride are the forbidden fruits.

Very sad.

WEDNESDAY, DECEMBER 17, 1980

Christmas is terribly close. Didn't have anything to do this Christmas anyway. Christmas is the time you spend with the people who love you.

With Dominic's family I could go from room to room avoiding conversation, eventually and grudgingly meandering into the kitchen where I belonged. We'd drink Manhattans and play bridge after dinner. Right when we call it a night, his mother would wake up refreshed from her snoring couch-nap and sulk because everyone abandons her once she's rested from all her hard holiday work.

At their house, everyone is civil. The talk is dull, but they all seem to like each other.

THURSDAY, DECEMBER 18, 1980

I can't let myself get trapped in the crossfire of my mother's leading, loaded questions. *I hear you've been writing. What's that all about?* I dare not plug a single sentence into the network. Taking one of them into my confidence is the same as taking them all in. They deal my words out like chits. *Don't tell Nancy I told you this.* The tidbits from which they craft their weapons.

They are not to be trusted.

When she asked about the writing, I ignored it like a fart. Next she would whine, "Is it helping you *understand* anything?" while thinking—*Boy would I like to get my hands on that!* Then it could be just like high school. All those people who were so busy reading about me—diary, mail, the zipper pocket of the purse—if only they had taken the time to get to know me instead of creeping through evidence, confronting and shaming me with what they found. Sorry, gang, you only got away with that once.

SUNDAY, DECEMBER 21, 1980

I am afraid. Afraid of what a divorce would do, would feel like. Over this weekend, I have gradually arrived at the realization that it could very well be in the cards. I keep running through my alternatives. There must be more, but there seems to be only divorce or going back to Dominic.

What's palatable?

MONDAY, DECEMBER 22, 1980

Lessons of history. From the Romans, we learn it's impossible to control an empire you cannot communicate with. From the dinosaurs, mastodons, and the giant moose with the ten-foot antler span, we learn that development in a direction which is easy, fun, and seems natural could be the very cause of your demise. From the Greeks we learn we are the center. From England we inherit common law. From everyone we have culled technology.

Who will teach us how to respect and love?

Not my father.

On the phone, he ran the usual routines: pronouncement, self-flagellation, lashing out. He was apoplectically angry when he said, "I'm calling you because I love you and it would be decent of you to get in touch with me whether you call or use a postage stamp!" This is a guy who, when we lived in the same house, could go weeks without talking to me.

It's important not to get tricked into saying what I'm thinking. When they don't understand, more words to confuse them are not going to help.

It was mean of me to tell him to mind his own business. His disapproval of my going to a party was a little funny, a little cute. His suggestion that Dominic might already be interested in another girl reflected his fears as well as his desire to get under my skin. He was prying when he asked about my writing. He was mean to say, "Oh, I didn't think you knew you had a family." He was foolish to say, "If you don't want to talk to me then why don't you just hang up?" It was mean of me to take him up on it, but a lot less mean than all the responses that came to mind.

I'll have to put the word out that I've quit writing.

From our parents we learn how not to raise a child.

TUESDAY, DECEMBER 23, 1980

The whole second part of yesterday evening was the best, after I crawled into the car and realized I was too drunk, even after a hamburger, to drive home.

I went up to the office. The slightest alteration in the co-ordinates is exciting. Someplace *where* you belong, but not *when*. A little sideways step in spacetime. Sitting at Thurman's desk, freighters on the river and Lynyrd Skynyrd on his stereo.

Later, lights out, rolling to a stop at the curb and walking through the old neighborhood. Crunchy ice. Sound of traffic on Woodward. The house so utterly indistinguishable from the version of itself with me asleep therein. Maybe I was curled and dreaming inside, and what loitered on the street was a transparent cartoon that had stood up and walked away from my sleeping self.

SATURDAY, DECEMBER 27, 1980

The unstable nucleus broke down. Scatter shots of alpha, beta, gamma. Leaving only a hydrogen atom and the other piece.

Have I thrown away all that I was raised for? If I was raised to be a kicking leg in a chorus line, yes. If I was raised to put my brain in neutral and my left front wheel to the tracks and come shining clean from the car wash, yes. If I was raised to play all the roles that give the others the warms and the fuzzies…

Oh screw them all. Let them find a robot, an actress, a puppy to start over with. All I want is to live, and they think I am as good as dead.

This would be no worse if you had been killed. That's what my mother had to say to me on Christmas day. She could cover a strychnine suicide with food poisoning after a few years. The complete me-of-myself must not exist in their universe.

I broke the rules and they've thrown me out of their hearts.

I'm going to keep a low profile for a while. Friendly, impersonal letters. Keep in touch, but don't get close. No more phone calls. They destroy the possibility of communication.

The tears? It will never be like it was before.

SUNDAY, DECEMBER 28, 1980

Sunday night foray into the hushed canyons of Meijer Thrifty Acres. Now I have records and FM music. *Deacon Blues* and *Sara, the poet in my heart.* Books. *Gödel, Escher, Bach* and *Even Cowgirls Get the Blues.* All arranged on my fifty-dollar étagère.

I can eat all the pasta with all the butter and all the garlic and all the salt I want, now and for the rest of my life.

All the private pleasures of the body. Nobody's business but my own.

MONDAY, DECEMBER 29, 1980

They allow wide-eyed curiosity and random concatenation of ideas until you hit the age of reason—six. After that—*you should know better!*—all mistakes damage your soul. In high school and college you learn the last of the right answers and how not to ask certain questions. By the time you are done, every inconsistency is resolved or forgotten.

I earned all the intellectual badges of achievement, hung every star on my transcript. The applause fades and it's time for the next thing—husband-following and childrearing. Forsake books for needlepointe and canning. Concern myself with the order of my home and the color of my furniture, not the order of the universe and the spectra of receding stars.

We all know you're smart, Nancy.

I'm not showing off. Neither path is wrong. As long as the pieces fit.

They have no interest in my real happiness. What matters to them is that this thing they built is broken. They are so sure they have the glue to put the pieces back together. They still think the pieces go together.

THURSDAY, JANUARY 1, 1981

Suddenly I found myself alone in what had been a chatty laughing party an instant before. Seconds to midnight. Ten, nine, eight. The random mingle begins to exhibit order. The couples pair like chromosomes anticipating mitosis. Arms tendril around waists. Stroke of midnight. First smooch of the new year.

If you have a date.

FRIDAY, JANUARY 2, 1981

No resolutions.

SUNDAY, JANUARY 4, 1981

Religious "facts" become more interesting after they are undermined by science. Resurrection, transubstantiation, burning bushes.

Why have a messiah? You can't save anyone who doesn't want to be saved.

Using scripture to find truth is like using twitching sticks to find water.

SATURDAY, JANUARY 17, 1981

It wouldn't be so frightening if I didn't like all of the changes in me so much.

SUNDAY, JANUARY 18, 1981

Coming up the Manistee River Road, I felt a twinge of disappointment. I was arriving. The trip, the plans, the cautions and predictions— all that was over. Ahead: a week alone with myself. Why reluctance?

Walking the trail into the cabin—heart-thumping paranoia. Carnivorous life forms in the pillows of snow. A world made strange by moonlight—purple sky, blue-black pines, distinct shadows painted on the sparkling snow. I was scared to death of everything from muggers and bears to discovering Dominic's body somewhere. A terrifying, keening silence. Thrums of wonder. Incredible how the world could be so beautiful and so eerie.

I hope it's clear like that tomorrow night. Being outside in it is so frightening. I have to keep doing it until I can see it for what it is, not all the bugaboos I imagine it could be.

MONDAY, JANUARY 19, 1981

The day dies he landscape takes over, laying a calm that is the same in summer dusk and on winter afternoons. The moon rises between the tall trees across the river and I gasp at the reflection in the water. The mist puffs and rises, the river covering itself for the night.

Taking pictures today was fun. Trying to see in black and white. I had never looked at the ground like that. Tracery of tracks—deer, birdies, skis, snowmobiles—and shadows. Snow is not white.

TUESDAY, JANUARY 20, 1981

Encased in a bullet-poof armored limousine, the ingoing and outgoing presidents ride. President Nixon was the first to have bullet-proof glass protect him and the occupants of the stand from which he would take the oath of office. Crowds line the streets to witness a pivotal moment in history.

The pivotal events of a life are private. They will not be replayed on television or explained on the radio news. Nobody will tell us they matter. We have to learn that ourselves. Outside, the world will wave and flap about what we should think is important. Making it difficult to recognize that things inside are important too.

The manhole covers are cemented shut. Police are on top of all the buildings and pointing rifles out of strategic windows. Inauguration is the only history they want made today. This inauguration has about as many surprises as Sunday Mass.

I will now turn off the radio. When I turn it on again, the hostages will be free, we will have a new president, and nothing in history will care that I didn't listen.

If you cross-country ski at a leisurely pace for one and a half hours, how far have you gone? Far enough to see things in the moonlight. Far enough for my butt to get cold and my feet to get numb, my legs tired, my shoulders sore. Far enough for my breath to condense into crystals on the front of my shirt and in my hair. Far enough to stop being scared.

Not a single star stayed inside tonight. However, most had to compete with the moon, and although they shouted and drummed and created the greatest stir they knew how, the moon out-commotioned them and truly owned the sky. It even tried to capture the ground by spilling shadows all over it. That moon will play and sing until dawn, then cry squatters rights when the sun obliterates its artwork, cleaning the canvas for its own strokes.

I followed the same trail as yesterday afternoon's trek, because the deep, crusty snow is unnavigable under the moon shadows, and because

I went there yesterday, and last winter, and spring, and summer, and fall. It is the way I always go along the river.

What if I left a note at the yellow trailer compound? "Do you remember the day Ronald Reagan was inaugurated? That was the day I skied across this very deck sometime between 9 and 11 p.m., when the moon glared so bright you could read. I read and ignored your 'Private Keep Out' sign. Sorry.

"I know you've seen spring and summer afternoons from your swing and you've swum in the river, been inebriated around campfires. You've watched the creeping calm of sundown and the habits of ducks. The loud canoeists and the solitary ones. The silent fishermen. Thunderstorms and summer rains, frost. Tonight I got ahead. I saw the snow, the pines, the river, the shadows, and the softness of the still night. I didn't mean to invade your privacy. I merely took what was offered, and with no one to share, I scarfed up as much as I could."

I stood at one of those bends in the river where a few white pines of substantial stature make me jealous of the lumberjacks for what they saw. They had to see it to obliterate it, didn't they?

They needed money, right? They also liked being outdoors and feeling that macho camaraderie that comes from being physically fit, exhausted, drunk, and horny—alternately, simultaneously and with enough erratic rhythm to keep it interesting. Not the reason why they mowed down 300-year-old trees in the prime of their lives, but the reason why it was fun.

The moon hums gray bass notes as it opens its glance downstream. Stars tumble and play triangle notes all over the snow and in the frosted branches. At the foot of the pines, snow-covered sedge is a carpet of swamp through which the vein of river flows. Upstream, needle-nosed spruces lay their shadows over the sedge like tomorrow's blue jeans.

I was rapt, absorbing beauty with senses I didn't know I had when I heard it. A motor. Upstream. North. Snowmobiles. Snowmobiles are wintertime motorcycles. Discovery by a snowmobile gang of course means robbery, rape, mutilation and chain-whipping, so the sound strikes fear into the heart of every moonlit petunia on skis within a 50-mile radius.

It couldn't be snowmobiles, it was too loud. It was a freight train with an engine the size of a house, barreling down the river, laying tracks before it as it went, enveloping the banks in its god-awful roar and turning them into warehouse districts behind the caboose. Why rape a petunia when you can rape the river's whole supporting tissue?

The roar filled the universe and held—until it disappeared to the southwest. Airplane.

It occurred to me I hadn't spoken a word since I got gas in Midland. There've been some gasps—at the moon's reflection, and at a particularly elegant white pine yesterday. A bit of singing with the radio, but no utterances made of words aimed at communication have escaped these lips. I wonder if I can forget how to talk by Monday.

WEDNESDAY, JANUARY 21, 1981

In the *Dancing Wu Li Masters* last night, I read a two-paragraph, perfectly lucid description of Boyle's Law. When you heat up an "empty" closed container, the air molecules inside increase their kinetic energy and bounce harder, faster, off the container walls, increasing the pressure. I remember spending two hours one Sunday afternoon arguing with Dominic about that. At first he asked questions as if he was trying to understand it, or like he was helping me bring the concept to clarity. But he didn't care about Boyle's Law. He was just enjoying the way he could ask questions that would trip me up.

He used to be a lot more romantic.

THURSDAY, JANUARY 22, 1981

When I was sixteen, I could have written the essentials of my autobiography. Certain details would be left to chance and surprise—like what college I would attend, who I would marry, the sexes and spacing of my children, where I'd live. No place in the story would it matter if I knew how to think.

I liked being an interesting tale for my mother to tell at bridge club—or to hold back in quiet superiority, listening to other mothers' problems. After the pomp of the Junior Miss pageant was over, the winner was the only one who didn't have a date. What teenager in his right mind wants to hang out with a mini-clone of his parents?

No wonder, now that I should be an adult, I'm acting like a kid. I missed the first swing through childhood. I should be pretty well caught up by the time I'm forty, but by then it will be too late. Too late to make my biography honorable again.

I remember playing golf once with Dominic. Playing bad as ever and not minding it, enjoying the weather and the walking, thinking I was having fun, only to have Dominic angry at me. He picked up my ball and slapped it into the palm of my hand. "Here. Now walk."

Saturday, January 24, 1981

Every tree is a story, a testimony to the passage of time. A tree moves gracefully, responding to and expressing its surroundings. Its dance is slow and measured, twisting and stretching inside the natural rhythms it helps establish. At every moment of its life, a tree is complete, yet it continuously becomes.

You've got to know your trees. Know them in summer for what they support: leaves, birds, insects. Know their conduction of saps and juices, their chemical timetable. Know them when they stand cold and naked in the snow, alive. Know them as silhouettes against the moon and the sunset. Know your trees. They are one of the living threads of which the earth is woven.

Sunday, January 25, 1981

Last day. Many things to do.

There is no event to describe. Not even a process. I didn't flip bits, didn't add memory or registers. Something shimmered between the cycles and the scales fell from my eyes.

Two types of experiences here this week: activities and encounters. Activity filled the hours—letters written, fires built, books read, food eaten, skis skied upon. Encounters, which occurred on their own schedule, and in the absence of rational thought, were between myself and the world of all possibilities. I started out shaking with imaginary fears and am ending inside the luminosity of wonder.

This afternoon, on the final tour of the ski trails, I slipped outside the bounds of linear time and into the dance of the trees. A jack pine, cones a-dangle, chittered like a head decked with earrings. Living currents swirled in the wide breeze-rocked arms of the white pines. Sunshine glinted like laughter through droplets on the tips of tree-needles. The air crackled.

Totality. Wholeness. Unity. Joy. The quality that made, not this trip, but me, worthwhile is larger and more loving than any name I might assign.

The irrefutable truth which I can choose to remember or forget: I shimmer.

SATURDAY, JANUARY 31, 1981

Look at me. I've frittered away the whole bloody day. Little to show, all alone. Scared someone is going to figure that out and decide how my Sundays (or Saturday nights, or afternoons, or free time in general) are waiting to be filled on a permanent and regular basis.

I don't want anyone knowing where and with whom I am all the time. Each person can have their slice. I belong to myself.

TUESDAY, FEBRUARY 10, 1981

I don't like the way the world is, and I wonder how anyone can remain a human being and participate in it. Yet, the world has probably changed little in all these years people have been in it. Human nature hasn't changed either. So what's in front of me is not so different from what has been in front of everyone else.

It's not the world that is gray and death-dealing, it's this machine that scoops everything in, manufacturing trash. A subroutine for every thrill. It's tight. It's net. There's less and less substance. Most people don't seem to mind.

SATURDAY, FEBRUARY 15, 1981

Once they've exterminated all of the old, stately living things from this earth—forests, whales, rivers, mountains, soil, thought. Once they've concreted everything that can be covered or channeled, boxed all that can move, industrialized every process, and computerized all insight, there will be nothing left to do but exterminate ourselves. Finally then, after who-cares-how-much time passes, living things will again shine with the undisturbed grace of old age.

The essence of what remains will permeate whatever is next. Will it be radioactivity or human love? Who chooses? How? What should I be doing?

TUESDAY, FEBRUARY 17, 1981

I don't want to be Cyclops railing at Noman for ruining my world. It's easy to blame "them," who is no one in particular, just the tendency we all have to do stupid things when we're out of touch and not paying attention.

MONDAY, APRIL 13, 1981

I have learned how to pay my bills, take the car in, spend time with myself. Maybe I'm not perfect about it. It's lonely a lot, but not nearly so empty.

WEDNESDAY, APRIL 15, 1981

"It would take a miracle," Dominic said. "The way you are living is ridiculous."

Actually, it would take two miracles, one for me and one for him. I wonder what happened to the marriage counselor idea. He was going to arrange it. I was afraid to ask. Afraid I'd have to go. Afraid they'd send me back.

"I'm going to draw up an agreement," he said.

So that's that.

Flashbacks. The first time I saw him at the softball game at the Chippewa Falls School. Catching him felt magical, but once I did…

Skiing at Sugarloaf and Boyne, watching *The Way We Were* at Studio M on a subzero night. LSU and Notre Dame in the Sugar Bowl. *Gesu Joy of Man's Desiring.*

Ann Arbor. A summer. A wedding. Newlyweds. Walking into our very own house. Paint, wallpaper and furniture. Trips to Sturbridge Village, Kentucky, Stratford, Toronto and France.

The cabin. I won't be able to go there anymore.

SUNDAY, MAY 10, 1981

Now that it's over, truly over, done, finished, divorced, I'm lost. I'm best at planning, not so hot on execution. What a way to have a late-twenties crisis. Should I have bit the bullet like everyone else?

FRIDAY, MAY 22, 1981
IBM MEETING, ATLANTA

There is no place to sit and think in the Atlanta Airport. They do have chairs where you pay a quarter for 20 minutes of TV. Then you don't have to think. Look at the vidiots all in a row. Going to the places that vidiots go. Overhead, the sign says "Terminal."

We reduce the death rate from cancer. We do bypass surgery to cut the fatality rate from heart disease. Smallpox is eradicated. Polio, diphtheria, and whooping cough are all but done. What are they going to leave for us to die of? Car accidents and industrial pollutants—or just the usual walking suicide.

Somehow, living longer got confused with staying around longer.

At IBM we do things "for business reasons" and pretend like we work for the earth's highest good. *Don't take things so personally*, they say. What am I besides a person? If I influence the world, it's by making my tiny corner of it safe, or comfortable, or unfit for the development of persons.

What does it all mean? It doesn't mean a thing. And I can't work on it anymore.

Now upon this course, I'd be a fool not to leave IBM by the fall, be gone from here. They'll say—*Poor thing. She's reacting to her divorce.*

THURSDAY, JUNE 4, 1981

They can't see. They believe in the safety of their sterile, narrow slots. All I can do is write it down and show them, turn it into a book. Write a book that lasts until it ends. Having started out all broad, the truth will find itself, which is really myself, with a pen and a notebook. The past will touch the door to the future. An infinite present will gush out faster than the big-bang speed of light in a new universe.

If that happens, you can coast.

FRIDAY, JUNE 12, 1981

Why is it OK to try to figure out what kind of career you want, but not okay to go out and practice knowing people and learning to live with them? When you fit your own life, a job doesn't get in the way.

THURSDAY, JULY 2, 1981

Like Anteus needs his dirt, this girl needs her solitude. Whole days when the mind can be active, yet undisturbed.

MONDAY, AUGUST 10, 1981

Maybe buy a piece of land and build the fireplace for a house. Maybe Utah or Wyoming. Maybe lots of things.

FRIDAY, AUGUST 21, 1981

I haven't felt like a part of nature since January. Here, it's machines inside of machines.

So deft in the eddy, you forget the stream.

TUESDAY, AUGUST 25, 1981

Don't tell jokes to people who are not open to laughter. Don't waste insight on people who aren't confused. Don't sow seeds on rocks or amid thistles.

Just go. And write about it.

FRIDAY, SEPTEMBER 25, 1981
THE CABIN

You can always go to the woods and see what it has to say.

On the first day I ever stayed home from Mass, I saw a tiny yellow bird kick back and trill a song from the bellows of its striped chest. They don't sing like that in church.

The day I murdered a Goose Creek cattail. I thought it was dead and dry, and when I yanked, it screamed to keep its roots in the cold mud. To finish what I started, I had to suspend part of my awareness—observe without feeling and complete the violence.

Am I crying because the redwinged blackbirds have already left? The ferns are finished. No cedar waxwings, swallows, or unidentified tufted treetop tweeters.

In the times I spent here I was tamed by ducks and blackbirds, crows, the pines, wind, beavers and a river. (Not bad!) Are they going to be responsible for what they have done to me?

Funny, I don't want to leave here without a deep change happening to me, but I am so curious to see what it will be this last time I can't see it. It's happening. I just don't know what it is.

It's the cabin.

And it's a closed chapter of my life.

FRIDAY, OCTOBER 2, 1981

Three more nights to sleep here, then it's an empty apartment again. I was small and scared coming in. I'm large coming out. Smiling. Singing into my notebooks.

I sat and thought and learned in here. Funny melancholy—like I am going to miss all those old friends, my problems. That's not an invite for them to come back. I've had a lot of fun in here—amusing myself.

Why this physical move? Why not? Am I running to or from?

I want to see the West. So I should do that—as opposed to not. A family, or the promise of one, could draw me to one spot or another. I have neither. On the outside I'm looking for fun. On the inside I'm looking for a husband. Except you're not supposed to admit that. Are husbands made for you in heaven? Or can it be just anyone who is willing to try? What's in between?

Timing.

It *could* be anyone, but you're a fool to sign up to work on all the differences between you and someone at the opposite pole. I couldn't handle a businessman. A corporate clone, a 40-hour-a-week ladder-climber. I need someone who doesn't share my background. How else can I escape it?

My goal is to find someone with similar expectations for life who is roughly at the same spot as I am in realizing them. Then we do it.

Evaluation items: is this person dedicated to understanding himself and the world about him? Can this person adapt? What will make this person give up? Does this person think his world is a good place? Does he think he matters?

I want so much for someone to see these things I see. To help with the focus.

Someone who would want to make a baby for the right reasons.

Instead of a husband, I could find the reasons why I don't need one.

SATURDAY, OCTOBER 3, 1981

I had such a nice lunch with my nice sister. We wore our nice clothes. She stuck me for the check.

"What time do you have to be back?" I ask.

"Oh, I don't know. Maybe I'll give them a thrill and go back early. That'll shock 'em."

We were in and out of the restaurant in less than an hour. It gave us plenty of time to talk about how to arrange things in her new purse. She advised me to put my money into a condo. She explained the critical experience I lack—once you get a bunch of expensive furniture, things start falling into place. In time, you get to do what she does—earn enough money at the job to pay someone to clean the expensive furniture. Two lives in one—the one you lead and the one you hire out.

MONDAY, OCTOBER 5, 1981
GRAND RAPIDS

Lunch. Relief from the rain.

Driving out of Detroit, I tried to be conscious of what I was thinking, but each time I looked it was nothing at all. I wanted to remember my mood, but there was no mood there to remember. I tried to make a mood with music, but couldn't decide which tape to play. I put on the radio and forgot to push buttons to avoid advertising. I noted the irony of *Another One Bites the Dust* and *You Can't Always Get What You Want*, but I didn't really think they were being sung for or about me. I tried to remind myself to note every detail so I could tell what had changed when I returned. Ten Mile and Telegraph, National Bank of Detroit, 10:48. If I didn't have plans, I wouldn't be able to move.

There is nothing to say. Everyone knows—or thinks they know—what I am about to do. There won't be any news until I do it.

I feel awful. No I don't, just numb. Drained. Empty.

The whole looming future is ready to be gobbled into a past. You don't have to chase it.

Let the system quiesce.

WEDNESDAY, OCTOBER 7, 1981
KADOKA. BREAKFAST

What makes this truck stop delightful is the non-uniformity of it all. The lumpy seats, rattling fan, souvenir junk. There are probably a thousand other crummy places just like this out here, but it still isn't Denny's. Out this drafty window it's flat, windscoured. Billboards plead for travelers to stop. Can't imagine it's easy to escape from here if this is where you were born. I wonder where the hell I really am.

I've done a lot in two days. Left Michigan, saw the Badlands, the Little Bighorn, Mt. Rushmore, the Black Hills. It's hard to believe the first dramatic step is about over. I'm not sure what I learned from this drive other than that I could do it.

I can't find a map anywhere that shows where I've been. One with two sunsets and a sunrise. Council Bluffs, Rapid City, and Casey, Iowa. A nap in Plankinton, South Dakota. You don't see places so much as signs, and you pronounce their names silently, absently, while thinking about something else. Omaha. Fine food. Escape. Two cats dreaming in the back. A fishwich. At the Days Inn in Lusk, thirteen white paper coffee cups to clean out of the car, a shower, a nap, a bath, clean sheets, and crying because there was no one to tell.

FRIDAY, OCTOBER 9, 1981
RED CLIFF INN. LYONS, CO.

Well here I am. That's something Dominic would say.

Is it bad to sit here scribbling drivel when I have so much to do? Find a place to live. Find myself. Folks back home are waiting for news. I could get a paper, make some phone calls, get out my typewriter, fix my brown pants, write a letter to someone, go to the john, or just keep sitting here listening to this cat purr and waiting for the waters to stir.

How do you learn to be self-starting?

I'm having trouble with the easy stuff. I only seem willing to undertake endeavors that will shock people. As though I am trying to teach the world a lesson. So as not to learn a few myself?

How late is it? How should I mark the intervals? Odometers don't tick. I should take a class, acquire a fine art. My guitar is all the way out of the case, but I'm afraid to pick it up and find out I have forgotten how to play it.

I am tired of being responsible for myself all day long.

Wine with dinner. Deserve a treat. I might relax. Can I work this corkscrew? Am I strong enough, can I get it, will I spill it, should I drink it? OK, wine is poured, now what? Oh, yes, scramble the eggs. Then eat them, slowly, filling each minute while you think up what to do next.

Repeat slowly after me: Interesting people attract other interesting people. What you're doing could turn out to be interesting. So could you. Don't stop believing. These are little setbacks. Don't take them too hard. Even if you die, it was coming sooner or later.

Who are these two people that live inside me? The calm, detached observer and the excitable, frenetic doer? Why can't I balance or better homogenize them?

THURSDAY, OCTOBER 29, 1981
BOULDER, COLORADO

Dear Everyone,

A lot has happened since I last saw you!

After spending last summer plotting a new future, my go-west fantasy turned real. On a day when it rained so hard the Detroit expressways flooded, I loaded a desk, its chair, my sewing machine, typewriter, cooler, guitar, rug, kitties, bookcase, and a bottle of Cognac into my Omni and drove. 2,000 miles in 3 days.

My destination was Boulder, but I wanted to get there by way of the true mountains and not the highway from Denver, so I descended from the north into Estes Park first. I had been watching the line of peaks for miles and miles, but I still wasn't ready for what I saw when I got right up next to them. If I hadn't known better, I'd have thought I was on the moon. I pulled over at every opportunity so I could gape, which I hoped would lessen my chance of driving off the road in amazement.

There is a big wide world out west of Chicago and now I've seen some of it.

Arriving was a jolt of consciousness. Boulder seemed too complicated, so I took a room for a while in the town of Lyons, a little ways up in the mountains, to get myself oriented in a less hectic setting.

For months I had been revving up to get the energy to leap, purging everything holding me back. By the time I jumped, I was weightless and just had to believe I wasn't empty. If it takes might to jump, it takes calm to land. You have to start planting little seeds you hope will grow, and you can't do that with your wheels straining to spin harder.

At first all I had were pep talks: You'll figure out what you want by getting involved somewhere. Interesting people attract other interesting people. Do at least one thing on the list every day. Stuff like that.

Now I have moved into Boulder and have two rooms in a house I share with Andrew, a psychology grad student and Shelly, who is also a student, though it seems she is majoring in fun. The house is big. I have my own bathroom and we're strict about the kitchen, so it's almost like having my own place.

It was easy to find a job. I answered some ads and the first offer was my first choice. I'm in training at a place called Fine Design that does all sorts of graphics and artistic design work—informational flyers for a natural food store, posters and programs for concerts and conferences, a catalog for a community education program. At least that's what I've seen so far.

In my old job at IBM I had been trained to look down on a place like this, where everyone works long hours at tasks a computer could take on in a nanosecond. Being terminally efficient isn't the essence of this job. My co-workers fire their efforts with their drive to be dancers, sculptors, painters, and poets. With all of that artistic synergy, the place buzzes with the excitement of making things that are beautiful.

Not that I've "made" much. I'm kind of a gopher, running to the typesetter's a lot. People have noticed how I'm good at editing copy, and I've gotten to paste up a few simple flyers—a process just like the newspaper in high school, but with equipment that allows you to be precise. I've been told I have a "natural sense of composition."

So I guess the pep talks paid off. Even though the skeptics will say I still don't have much to show for myself, I feel solid. When I wake up in the morning, I look forward to the hours ahead.

I'm planning a trip to Dallas at Thanksgiving to partake in the family turkey at Mom and Dad's. We'll be at the tail end of the pre-Christmas rush as work, and things are "flexible." That means Thanksgiving week isn't all that busy, but once I get back, I have to jump in and be ready to work hard to the end of the holiday jam. In January, they promise a lull. I hope I can do some skiing.

TUESDAY, NOVEMBER 10, 1981

A jowly man with tailored slacks and a silk scarf at his neck picks up Shelley for "lunch" in a Lincoln Continental. He would be a perfect sugar daddy, she says. Except that she's scared to be alone with him after dark.

I see how easy it would have been to come to this town and get addicted to cocaine. Instead, I'm growing entangled in the idea of being in love.

Robb. I should be writing down words about this, but I don't know what they are. I have so much to say about the frustration of shining my light on blind people, yet cannot describe how it feels to be seen and cherished. To match wits with someone smarter than me. To speculate together on the beautiful treachery of the invisible. To make love.

At Fine Design, reciting the pep talk about interesting people, typing the hand-scrawled bios of a series of dance instructors. ("Don't worry. I can read just about anything. I used to teach high school.") They were only the small-talk questions anyone would put to a stranger parked at the typewriter in his cubicle. The more he seemed interested, the more the tale poured out. The tears surprised me—nothing he saw. It was the first time I told the whole story like that. Curl-framed face—the kindness it it when he asked me to have dinner. The way he said, "I want to know all about you."

This doesn't mean that *click!* I've found my direction. I am still stumbling along a drunkard's path, but it seems headed the same way as his calliope-wagoned traveling circus. If I stash my baggage and hop on, I'll be thrown off at the first bump.

If he can slow down enough, we will travel.

TUESDAY, NOVEMBER 17, 1981

Even though (because?) I conceive of the invisible world as such a beautiful place, it has aspects that are dark and frightening. Something in me wants a piece of that fear.

In some circles, it is called evil, or the devil. The dark side of the moon. It is the dimension behind not-fitting-in. If you don't investigate, your life will be a shallow, monochrome thing, founded on platitudes.

If I try to explore that darkness before anyone understands where I am going, I could die—in the deepest and most frightening sense of the word. It's hard enough to find someone who understands my direction and dangers, but even more difficult to trust someone to pull me through and not back.

You can go forward. You can go farther and farther. But you're a fool to go over the edge when the odds aren't in your favor.

WEDNESDAY, NOVEMBER 25, 1981
BOUND FOR DALLAS

My stomach hasn't hurt like this in two months. The last time I tore the cellophane from the Maalox—the fumbling desperation of an antiacid addict—it was in the gray bathroom of Galpin Street.

You can say *The Plains* quietly, inside, and hear the windswept Conestoga west. The music swells and the magic with it. You think it's eternal until you spot Denver's chemical silo sprawl, or look down on the road-and-farmland grid superimposed on the parched drainage paths of the fabled Platte.

It's tricky with airplane food. A challenge. You have to employ all your senses, intellect, and expectations in order to recognize it as food. Three silver-dollar sized objects under a congealed puddle of sauce. A ring of tomato residue. Ravioli, they say. I wonder if I'll eat it.

THURSDAY, NOVEMBER 26, 1981
THANKSGIVING

This is the same bed and even the same sheets where I used to sit, door closed at night, penning the frustration and confusion.

I can feel the rainsoaked breeze.

Thank goodness I was ahead at Scrabble. If I hadn't been, I'd have been accused of poor sportsmanship for throwing my letters in. I was sick of the bickering. Everyone has a role they try to play, and funny, only Joann gets to pull hers off. She used to be blocked by my relentless perfection, but now, by virtue of the loudest voice, she is boss. Dad wants to be the prankster, but because everyone refuses to laugh, he has to keep trying harder, making Joann yell all the more, while he gets stuck in the asshole role again.

Quitting the game gave me a chance to get myself to bed before anyone isolated me to a corner for a nightcap and interrogation.

"Wonderful dinner," says Joann, and Mom responds "Humph. Not really."

How can I tell her I know? I see. I felt the strained hollowness, too. How can I tell my poor mother, who has been working and shining for days, the problem with her holiday bash is that it's too clean?

If she was so bent on being efficient that she got up a 4:30 to make the dressing, why didn't she say so? If it had to be all done before 7 a.m., at least we could have done it together. She made twice as much as she needed and froze the other half for Christmas.

Can't we have one day's freedom from the scourge of cholesterol? It should be butter and not margarine, cream and not skimmed milk or Cool Whip. The mushrooms and onions for the peas should be sautéed, not microwaved—for the kitchen aroma, for the pleasure of watching them turn color. Rolls should present more interesting challenges than how to get the plastic off the package. Sweet potatoes taste better when you open skins, not cans, to taste them. Carving the bird was private. No cluster of observers hoping for a juicy slice of skin. No carcass to pick after dinner. No chance to say "Let's make soup!" The bones were already in the trash compactor.

In record time, the kitchen and the dining room were folded and shined back into what they looked like yesterday, or last summer. Why not order up the whole thing on a computer shopping terminal? Maybe there's a movie you could show yourself and be done with it.

How can I look Joann in the eye and say anything, when I all that's on my mind is how much I've learned in the past year, and by acting on what I've learned, I'm thrilled and relieved to be free of everything she is choosing: a BMW, a house in their hundred-thousand dollar price range, a class in how to wear makeup, and two new dresses so she's "all set for the holidays."

She makes a sad, thoughtful commentary on the direction of American life. It's "getting to where" people put their jobs ahead of their families. She whines about how bad she wants to quit her job and be a "full-time happy homemaker." The requirement to buy a certain house in which to do that chains her to the job.

FRIDAY, NOVEMBER 27, 1981

First we drive out to see JR's house. Then we come home and watch *Dallas*. People clamoring to climb into the TV screen.

We meet Roger and Donna, Sandy and John. We cluck and goo over the $250,000 dream house Sandy is convincing John they can afford. Then they will all be neighbors. Sandy is sunny and cute with perfect hair. They deride nerdy "friends" who talk tacky and don't know how to dress. My dad gets to say the n-word because Dominic isn't here to mind and nobody else seems to. When everyone left we had a sarcastic chuckle at how "that Roger sure is a live wire"—meaning he didn't say a word. His wife Donna is fat. Peter never says anything either, but he's handsome and makes money out of money, so he's covered.

An honest or sincere sentence—or even one worth remembering—would have been so out of place in the day, I didn't dare utter one.

No luck escaping to bed unscathed. It started in the kitchen when I said the wrong thing. Hands full of empty glasses from the living room, I asked Mom, "Anything else I can do?"

"Yes! You can explain a few things, starting with a year ago... All you do is hurt people—your father, your sister... You've lied since you could talk... Why are you so *hard?*" My dad and Peter instantly made themselves scarce. (Tomorrow Dad will yell at me for upsetting his wife.) Joann joined in, but her act blew completely out of control. She was hysterical, screamed "You ungrateful bitch!" not because it made sense, but because it seemed like a good idea. Poor thing. She deserves some kind of credit, although for meanness or idiocy, I'm not sure.

I was agog at the show. If you stop the tapes and read the script, it's pitiful. Usually I am the hysterical one in the holiday scenes. Screaming at my dad. Because I can't take a joke—about bed wetting, about the flaws of every boyfriend I ever had (except Dominic!), about how you have to be as smart as Nancy to be so dumb. There had to be screaming, so Joann took it on.

Was there something I could have said that wouldn't have sucked me into the drama? My silence gave Mom a chance to try out "Why are you so *hard?*" in all imaginable intonations.

If I beat my words against their brick wall, my head is sure to follow.

I am tempted to start striking prisoner's ticky marks on the wall. Three days down. Three to go. How will I ever make it? Never again? I wonder. Stay in neutral, don't think too much, and the days will slip by

If the world really works as they say, no place in it will be safe for me.

SATURDAY, NOVEMBER 28, 1981

I had hoped to tell them I am "dating someone." How can I tell them the truth about blue-eyed Robb, when I am sufficiently unsure about the whole thing that if I had to stand around and defend it besides, I wouldn't know what the hell to think. I look at a life with Robb and it's better than anything I see around me. It would be honest.

I blew a marriage once already. I'm nearly 30 years old. I want to establish a home and a family with rituals and traditions. I don't want to be professionally and perennially on the move. I hate the dating game. Must you really endure many moons of loneliness and/or social guerrilla warfare before you can settle down?

Settling down. It sounds so much like turning into a statue. I look at it as breaking out. I want the freedom to do yoga and meditate in the mornings before breakfast. I want roadtrips with blues guitar and funky harmonies. I want to inspire someone the way he can inspire me—by simply being there. I want someone who will receive my slow meal rituals, someone who can absorb the magic I can radiate. I want mysticism and laughter, work and solitude.

Robb.

Am I in love with him or the idea of him?

SUNDAY, NOVEMBER 29, 1981

Things I learned on television today. Phillips Petroleum is going to show us how to make our children "wonder about wonder" by opening up a world of curiosity for them. They will give children computers at home so they can learn without even knowing they are learning.

A bleep-bleep blinky-light noise comes from a 64K chip that adds two plus two while the voiceover that used to counsel against ring-around-the-collar tells us we're about to learn how a child's mind works. We will, too. If we reduce it to that.

They're crowing about the jazzy way a computer is a View-Master and a box of flash cards all in one. So you have 10 minutes worth of circular logic dealing itself out by the picosecond. Why do you want your children drilled and shaped by something which, at its foundation, is finite and predictable? It doesn't matter. By Thanksgiving the American public has been fully motivated to buy whatever is stacked up in the warehouses, all ready to ship. The featured item in this year's annual consumption spree? Computers.

In Dallas, they're selling houses. Houses thrown all over the rolling plain and threaded together with concrete. The house I like is the one that sits unpainted between the fenced herd of diseased cattle Diamond Shamrock purchased for study, and the Texas Instruments communication towers. That clapboard house is graceful and balanced, built by the hands of people. It's waiting to be torn down. As soon as the land transaction beneath it clears.

Las Colinas is made of mirrors. You don't look at the shiny exterior of an office building and say—*Ah, if only these cold, deaf windows could talk.* Add a dome and you have the setting for one of those man (handsome!) vs. electric-eye-army adventures where identically clad soldiers wield death and communications equipment.

This is progress. We have bought it and we call it good.

I don't want to be inside when the gate clangs down.

A new dark age is upon us. We are already overrun with barbarians

MONDAY, NOVEMBER 30, 1981
AIRPORT

Crossed the finish line. Relief.

My mother is so irrational because she doesn't listen to what she thinks. She alternates between wanting Dominic and I back together and conniving to get my food processor out of his house. She wants to be told this is all a terrible nightmare, but no matter how hard she cries or tries, that just ain't forthcoming. The little girl she knew, the one whose every move she could puppeteer *is* dead. She's gotta pick up the pieces and get moving. Even if she kills the woman who has emerged, she'll never get her little girl back.

If she heard me say that, she'd say, "Nancy, how did you get so *hard?*"

Other trips I've taken have given me perspective and insight that helped me reject what does not belong in my life. To follow that pattern now, I'd have to reject my family.

Not the people, but the example, the lifelong roles. They taught me there is but one way to live. It's the only one they know. I prefer another—any other. I'm torn apart, trying to reject their choices without rejecting the people. These are my parents.

It makes me want to cry to see them so tired and small in simpleminded contentment in their niche. This is their crumb, the toss from the magnates of the publicly held corporation for whom they are the minions. How could they complain, secure within so much that shines?

Even if it's clear to me they're not as happy as they could be, they might be as happy as they expect to be. That should be enough.

I don't want to pity them or look at them and feel sad or think them fools. I just want to love them.

TUESDAY, DECEMBER 1, 1981

A year ago, a soul squeaked into a rented haven on Galpin Street, one as good or as bad as any other. Mine. With two army blankets, a foam pad, and a little bit of cottage cheese to stick in the fridge. Sat in the overhead-bulb-lit hallway, ate Doritos with hot sauce and drank beer. Wrote about falling over the edge of the abyss.

Tonight, bread bakes. With Robb in my bedroom, I pen, in the kitchen, sentences on the wisdom of this adventure. I try to be careful and smart, despite the weightlessness of the downdrop roller coaster. After the chain-chugging ascent, is this relief, or reward?

Things that could be amiss in this union:

- You're exploiting him. You see him as a free ticket to writer stardom and Boulder introductions, LSD and guitar lessons.
- He spends money on you and you know you are a tightwad.

- You're goon-struck by his humble beginnings, hippie youth, tragi-dramas and subsequent reform.
- You always want to save the soul of the boy with the broken heart.
- You like what people who can't possibly know you say about you two as a couple.
- You just want to play house.
- You didn't really know what to do next when you got to Boulder.

Reasons to take hands with this person and slip into the deep currents of living:

- He has stumbled on the edge of the abyss and chosen life.
- He has the same kinds of questions I do.
- He wants to hear what I have to talk about.
- He is ahead of me in exploring the miraculous territories most others fear or ignore. I contribute the connections that develop in the quiet.
- This is fertile ground in which to plant my dreams. Suppressing them is a mistake I will never make again.

Monday, August 9, 1982

I never thought I'd come to call the problem too damn many bodies in too little space. It feels more acute in Boulder than in Manhattan where people don't assume that a garden, a fireplace, and a view are rights. Planned Unit Developments will have it all. They will stack PUDs in all the currently unused spaces—alleys, garage roofs, canyon walls. Then they will fight over the water and fog up the air so bad the solar panels will only be for show.

Tuesday, August 17, 1982

Dear Iris,

As welcome surprises go, hearing from you was one of the year's best. I have thought a lot about writing you, but so much has happened, it's hard to know where to begin. And I wasn't sure you even wanted to know.

Mostly I have given up on my friends from Detroit. Yours is the first genuine letter I have received since I left. I guess I made everyone so uncomfortable that in their eyes I was best forgotten.

Preparing to go was like attending my own funeral. I was the only one who was excited. All my well-meaning and overly-concerned friends predicted futures for me ranging from lonely, depressed poverty (at best) to suicide (because I was too proud to ask for help). No one approved of my taking my happiness in my own hands, which is what I have done.

I am pregnant. And thrilled. Due in November.

OK, the details…. Robb and I met at Fine Design, the graphics design studio where we both work. I was assigned to help him get a big catalog out, and by the time it was finished we had explored how fully physically compatible and spiritually simpatico we are. We quite literally make beautiful music together. Funky gospel harmonies that get at the truth of a Jesus story better than a priestly drone ever could.

I am stalled on telling your more about Robb. I'm timid with people from my old life, too used to having my happy details twisted and flung back at me to prove me wrong.

In January we moved in together and bargained projects and deadlines with our co-workers to take the month of February off and go to Central America. Somewhere in there we decided to get on with things and quit using birth control. The first half of the trip was pure frolic. In the tiny country of Belize is an isle called Placentia, reachable only by boat and bisected by an 18-inch concrete sidewalk people call "the street." (Understand its purpose by imagining pushing a wheelbarrow through the sand.) We slept in hammocks in the yard of a kindly grandmother who summoned us from the supper table on the first night so we wouldn't miss the sight of a huge moon rising out of the sea.

The second half of the trip—for me—was a bladder-yeast-morning sickness-diarrhea miasma. We came home early.

From that, I remember a ride in a beer truck from Punta Gorda to Belize City, a hotel room in Chetumal, a life-saving glass of fresh squeezed orange juice in Tulum and a constant search for clean drinking water. Turns out I had a nasty kidney infection. So this little goober has gotten himself an exciting start.

I am recovered and strong now. Back to work. Swimming every day. Soon we will take off for a month to go look for land in Idaho. Yes,

Idaho! Because we don't want to raise a child here—or anywhere close to the cancer of the techno-machine. We hope to find some acreage with a fixable shack, a place we can build a life with the work of our own hands. We'll grow the veggies and kill the meat we eat, and overall try not to consume more than our own share of the planet's resources. I have long known I don't want to live in a glass and concrete hamster cage saturated with electrical impulses. With my help, Robb sees this. With the help of stories of his upbringing in the hills of Kentucky, I understand the practicalities and possibilities of living closer to the land. Belize inspired us. Simplicity.

We're looking to establish a "new ancestral home," as Robb calls it. If all goes well, we'll buy land on this trip, return to Boulder to have the baby, and move to Idaho when winter ends.

I am in limbo with my parents. I wrote them in April about the baby and haven't heard a word from them since. People in my childbirth class, people at work—everybody—says I have to make contact with them, that I can't "hold all this inside." Whatever I'm holding inside might be nothing compared to what they'll unleash. Maybe later I'll get a big surge of blossoming motherhood and want to share every juicy joy. But for now, I really don't care.

About telling any of this to Dominic. I don't want to put a burden on you either way. Whatever you say or don't say is up to you.

Thank you again for getting in touch. I thought everyone east of the Rockies had written me off.

FRIDAY, SEPTEMBER 3, 1982

What did I ever *do* all day at IBM? Hide. At first I got away with holing up in the library and figuring out what operating systems and data base managers did. Later, when I was "supporting customers" there were a variety of offices to go to. All suitable, as long as people didn't quite know how to find me and drag me into the rat's nest of accusations over machines and software that didn't work.

I wandered around looking for something interesting to do and got pissed when anyone asked me to do anything—copy some specs, order a manual, or (horrors!) try to get someone from a development team on the phone. Eventually I did so little that people realized there was no sense asking me to do anything.

Yet nobody could criticize me because I was their genius. It was their fault for not properly challenging me. Nobody knew how the empress got her clothes…

Back when I wanted to quit being a language teacher and find a job working with computers, Iris was the guidance counselor and math teacher at the same school, and we both liked fooling around with puzzles. We'd comb through her files of sample questions for psychological tests and offbeat math stuff and work the fun ones together. One day we came upon a blotchy over-photocopied multiple-choice test where each question gave you a sequence and you had to identify the next item. It started with numbers—easy enough, 2-4-6, stuff like that. It got harder, went on to letters and ultimately, complex geometric shapes. It took us a whole afternoon, but we got them all.

Shortly after I had an interview at IBM. The first person I talked to was discouraging—Latin and French are not computer languages. They put me in a quiet room to take the secret aptitude test that would rate my ability to work in the field. They handed me a crisp copy of the sequence puzzles Iris and I had just worked out. I took my time, filled in all the answers, checked them over, and handed it back long before the time was up. Then I had another interview—interrupted by a phone call—and they hired me.

Later I found out that prior to the test they were politely shuffling me and my liberal arts resume out the door. They thought I gave up on the test and quit early, thus demonstrating that I was not data processing material. The phone call during the interview was to say "Don't let her get away! She aced the aptitude test in 20 minutes!"

Even so, they never paid me as much as the guys they hired at the same time.

MONDAY, SEPTEMBER 20, 1982

My parents called. At least the suspense is done with. Salient points:

- My letter from April got lost. It just arrived. With postmarks all over it.
- They talked to Catholic Charities and have all the information

about adoption.

• Nobody knows. Especially not Dominic. We could still get back together.

Whew. I forget what an iron grid their system is until I run squarely into it.

What makes me so hurt and angry by their rejection? That I've worked so hard—lied so much?—to avoid it. I'm frightened to be cut away at last. To be my own big girl. It's more scary than dumping the husband they so approved of. This gets right down to the core.

I had hoped they could feel some inkling of anticipatory happiness for a grandchild. Instead, I get questions about why I think "a child out of wedlock" could be God's will.

SATURDAY, SEPTEMBER 25, 1982

I don't suppose anything remains novel, a lark, or even a good idea after some interval. A job, a relationship, a farm in Idaho. The rationale for commitment: it gets you over the humps.

Some nights when Robb crawls in bed with me, something rankles. I get flashbacks. Been in this movie before, competing for space against the spread-eagled limbs that will share the bed henceforth.

The person who is the person flashing from Robb's eyes. The way he burned himself out at work yesterday to take the stress off of me. These are the first things to escape my brain when the slightest thing goes wrong. I forget how he has always come through—in his particular way. He stands by me.

TUESDAY, NOVEMBER 2, 1982

Reading *The Grapes of Wrath* wiped me out because I'm afraid the same thing will happen to me. I can espouse all the principles I believe are important—live close to the land, trust in the family you bear and the community you serve. Own your own ground. Don't go to bed with a banker. Avoid the path of the techno-bulldozer. Don't own anything you can't fix.

It doesn't matter. Nobody is safe. The bombs they drop and shoot will kill every living thing. Me, my children, my future. So why bother?

You have to do something, so why not get ideas about eternity from trees and rocks and rivers, understand purpose from birds? So much more comforting, their message, than that of a skyline or the words of a gifted management consultant.

SATURDAY, NOVEMBER 13, 1982

The news is all about "the talks" but not about what they are really saying. They quibble over whether "defensive missile systems" in outer space violate any treaties. They admit the possibility of "accidental nuclear war." The arms race seems to be a race to see who can be first with a good reason to try out their arms. A reason that can leave them not-responsible for what they destroy.

Poor little political system. It doesn't work anymore. So what do you do? Can't just throw it out. Have to pretend it does work until it's impossible even to do that. When you say it's broken, too many people too afraid to admit it are too willing to fight you—to the death.

It's like the war in Vietnam. Or cleaning your plate in a restaurant and eating the jello and then the lettuce underneath it. Plodding forward. Ignoring alternatives.

No wonder this baby doesn't want to come out.

The Valley – I

THURSDAY, JANUARY 27, 1983
KOOTENAI INN, ST. MARIES, ID

Dear Iris,

I'm sitting cross-legged on the floor in a 16 x16 room I share with two guitars and a mandolin. A typewriter, three gallons of paint. A basket of dirty clothes. Two cats, 25 pounds of cat food. A windowsill full of non-perishables from the Safeway across the street, a coffee maker, my yoga book, coats and gloves. Daniel asleep on the floor, Robb in the bed. On the dresser is a little pad where we write down every penny we spend.

We've installed ourselves in this partially restored inn, built in the days of riverboats. We'll be here a month. While we get the house in shape.

It's 2 a.m. Daniel stiffens, wags his head, grunts a little and spastically finds his thumb. That's his life. I stiffen, too, wondering if he'll wake up. That's my life.

He woke up. Nursed. Burp. Diaper change… And three days have gone by. Yup, this is my life all right.

So far, in his nine weeks on the world stage, Daniel has found his feet, slept twice through the night, become adept at getting his thumb into his mouth, gotten a chapped chin, and fallen in love with a plant. Right now, he's crying, angry. Because I'm not paying attention to him. I look up and make eye contact, say a few words—and he brightens like a firefly.

What a trip here! Four days. Daniel and I in the car, Robb in the truck. Once we got ourselves on the road, we did one brave thing after another: accelerate to 45, shift into fourth gear, feel the wind catch the load.

We drove 90 miles north, made a left, and stopped in Cheyenne. ("Don't open the door yet. First let me hold back the cats.") A cup of coffee, feeding Daniel, peeing, diapering and getting gas took about two hours. At this rate, we definitely didn't have enough road money. At sunset, just outside of Green River, the lights quit on the truck.

You simply can't keep up the pace on the anxiety, and sooner or later it just goes away. The weather stayed good, and it didn't matter that all the plastic had blown off the load four miles north of Boulder. Robb's steering arm stopped being sore. We bought a bottle of Bushmills and began having wonderful evenings in dive motels—late movies, carryout food. Three bags always lined up against the wall—Daniel's bright red diaper satchel, my ex-business-trip Samsonite tote, and Robb's stained canvas pouch, pinned closed across the broken zipper.

What scenery. No question this is The West. "Can you imagine stopping here, staying here, living here?" we'd say. Wind, relentless wind, whipping at these ramshackle towns. Inner landscapes match outer ones, Robb would say. As the miles passed, it seemed as if we were swimming up the good side of a wave.

Our first day in Idaho was sunny, and there hasn't been much snow this year. We struck out for the house right after breakfast, winding up the lakeshore bluffs until, just past the town of Frederick, we turned off the highway onto the gravel road leading into our valley. We jounced through the undulating hillocks, mud squishing under the tires. Some of the patchworked fields were bare chocolate-colored furrows, others, dry-grass yellow, and some had needles of iridescent green sprouting along contour lines in the brown loam. *This is our valley.* One of us, probably Robb, said that. It's what we were both thinking. I wonder how the transformation will take place, the one that will make this fresh, breathtaking scenery feel familiar and ordinary. *The road home.* It strikes up the theme from Bonanza in my head. That, and *The Mother Earth News* are still about all I have to go on. I am eager for the time and the lessons that will make this into a life.

As we climbed, the wet road became muddy, then icy, and finally snowcovered. There were no other tire tracks. Robb's Kentucky-bred driving skills weren't adequate for fishtailing up the steep curves and soon we spun out, sliding gently backwards until we landed softly, but permanently, in the ditch.

I jumped out and sized up the situation: noonish, winter, sunshine, and the closest house two miles away. A pickle, for sure, but not dire. Before the cold descended, we could easily reach Delbert Johnson's, the ranch that takes up the other 3,000 or so acres in the valley. My sense of adventure returned. I dug for my camera, took a picture, and started to laugh. Robb was annoyed. It reminded me of my honeymoon with Dominic and his annoyance when I took a picture of him from behind, peeing into the shrubbery behind Louisa May Alcott's house.

Robb had already taken off running down the hill. I rescued Daniel from his carseat. Robb's panic made me disgruntled, but in the rhythm of walking down the road, I gradually grew content. Things don't happen as planned—that's part of the plan.

Delbert Johnson has a hay barn that sits on a rise back near the turn-off. I climbed up and settled into a sunny, sheltered spot in view of the road. I nursed Daniel, changed his diaper, and smoked a joint. Before long, a pickup appeared and an elfin man, white hair at the temples beneath his cap, scrambled up the rise and introduced himself. Delbert Johnson. His son Rick would be coming along pretty quick to pull out the truck. He asked about our plans, and when I told him, he said, "Pioneers." I shrugged. So did he.

These days, Robb disappears every morning before the sun is up and comes home after dark with a black face. When I hear his footsteps creak in the evening hallway, I run to the bathroom down the hall and start the bath. That guy can sure work! Myself, I wander around with my eyes lowered and my mouth shut, watching the ladies and trying to figure out which role is mine. (Daniel has slept, dined and overloaded a diaper since this paragraph began.) For instance…

Tonight we went down to the bar for a shot and beer and ran into

Glenn Westover, Robb's most recent best friend. He owns the small mill in the next valley where Robb bought 2,000 board feet of lumber. He made Robb help load it and loved working him into the ground. Said he'd give us manure for our garden and sell us beef for a dollar pound. They talk about how smart we are to be doing what we are doing, how most young people with new families expect so much more. I am leery of all this praise before we have actually done very much. So I don't say anything and nobody asks me questions. They can have their conversation just fine without me. I wonder what the ladies are supposed to do besides sit and listen or nurse their babies and wait on dinner while the men stop for "just one" on the way home.

Restless. That's what I am. I've been a barreling freight train these last years, moving, moving, and changing. As the engine slows, all that boxcar momentum pushes behind it and says "Go. Go." For a while, it's been okay to cope with my discontent by making dramatic life changes, but it's time now to stop that. I have taken that option away from myself. If I am unhappy, the thing to change is me. So I call this endeavor The House at the End of the Road. Right now Robb is the only person I know here, so he catches the brunt of the crabbiness and lethargy that ensue from this confusion. He's already working so hard, pulled in a thousand directions at once, while I can't seem to find the direction I'm supposed to be leaning my shoulder into.

I am learning things. How to chain up the car and truck. Chopping firewood. The difference between hay and straw.

There's nothing here I can criticize. We are doing what we wanted to do with the resources we had. We started with the $28K I saved from IBM and my divorce, paid $20K for the house and the land, and portioned out the rest of everything we'd need to get the place rolling: the year's supply of food, building materials, tools, animals, feed, etc. There'll be no rent or utilities. In a year or more, we'll need some source of income, but it will be small. And we have a year to figure that out.

Robb just laughed at me because this letter is still going on. Sez it ought to be bound.

Life goes on here. It's fun. Do come and see.

MONDAY, JANUARY 31, 1983
KOOTENAI INN

Dear Everyone,

This is an attempt to use up all the postage stamps I have received in the mail over the last six months. My days are rich and busy, to say the least—so much to tell about and not much time. So I've cranked this sheet of paper into the typewriter in hopes it turns into a letter before Daniel is in college.

I've received almost as many questions about Robb as postage stamps, so here's a mini-biography. He grew up with his whole extended family on a farm in Kentucky, with home-made toys and gospel music. When he started school it was the first time in his life he was around kids who weren't cousins. By the time he was 16 or 17, he hated everything about school except art and drawing. He joined the Navy, finished high school, caught airplanes on an aircraft carrier for a few years, and was discharged just as Viet Nam was heating up. He got married, worked construction, and went to Art School for a while. There, he took the classes he wanted to without paying attention to requirements, and moved to Boulder before graduating. There, in the late 60s, he became one of the founding flower children who transformed that cow-college town into a hippie paradise and became part of the literary circle associated with Naropa Institute and Alan Ginsburg. He lived in a remodeled school bus for a couple of years, then in mountain cabins and attic apartments for perhaps ten more. He began writing for magazines and newspapers, but his wife sought the full trappings of the yuppie life. While he was working the crazy hours it took to pay their bills and a mortgage, she took up with someone else and that was the end of that. He went through a period of recklessness and grief, but by the time we met, three years had gone by and his broken pieces were pretty well reassembled. He had his self-respect back and a less glamorous, less adventurous, less bone-chilling life going on around him.

We get along really well. I think it's because we want the same things in the broad sense—to do simple things and do them well. Which is why we have moved to this remote parcel of land in Idaho. It's paid for and we have enough money to buy a year's supply of bulk food, building materials, tools, a woodstove, a chainsaw, a rototiller, baby chicks, a pair of rabbits, a goat (maybe), feed, canning supplies. Our neighbor calls us "pioneers," but we looked more like Okies getting here.

There are lots of reasons why we picked this. Robb grew up in the country and the cabin was a big influence on me, and we're both trying to reclaim something special we found in those settings. I'm excited about making a house gracious and "convenient" without plugging into any public utilities. It will be sturdy and honest and good to have a little hand pump over the kitchen sink to draw hot water from the basement—water that comes from a spring on your own hillside. It's good to eat food from plants you have tended yourself and to kill the meat you eat. Instead of having jobs that allow us to pay a mortgage, we'll invest our labor in our home.

That home—what a sight when we first arrived! Mud everywhere. Water from springs saturated the hillside and ran into the basement. So much for our plan to make that our bedroom. Upstairs it was breezy—because windows had been broken. Someone had gutted out a deer in the kitchen. The colors of the living area hadn't changed since we bought it last October—sea green, lemon yellow, pumpkin orange, and robin's egg blue. With one hand, Robb yanked a piece of plywood down from the ceiling—definitely space for a loft up there. Daniel never made it out of the truck.

Last summer, I made fun of all the lists and files Robb spent so much time compiling, but I sure can't laugh now. When we rolled into town, he knew what order he was going to attempt things in, what tools and materials he needed, and exactly how much he could spend in every category.

As he gathers various supplies, he makes friends with all the people he meets—loggers, tradesmen, politicians. He asks them all the same questions: Who settled this county originally? What are the winters like? Who lives over there? From the collected responses he has begun to put together a picture of life around here.

I was with him when he stopped at Reid's Chainsaws for the first time. Reid's place is mostly empty—the firewood takes up as much room as the saws. A few of them are stacked on metal shelving, but most are lined up on the floor—boxes of saw pieces waiting to be rebuilt. Reid has just opened this shop after working on chainsaws for seventeen years in other people's shops. He laid out all the pieces and parts of a saw, explained what needed to be done, put them back in the cardboard box and said, "Come back in a week."

I'm making my first inspection tour of the house on Friday. Over the past five days, Robb has gutted the inside, built the loft, had 2,000 board feet of rough-sawn lumber delivered, torn off the rotting back porch, insulated, and ripped down a bunch of old animal pens sagging into the creek, salvaging the lumber. He's reassembled the wood cookstove, replaced broken window glass, and got the drain draining again. He still keeps cautioning me not to expect anything great when I see it on Friday. I think he's afraid that if it doesn't look like *Better Homes and Gardens,* I'll think he's been wasting time or something.

Now it's Monday... I sure have a lot more to say about my house now that I've seen it! For the past three days, I have been parked in my kitchen watching Robb build it while I nurse, burp and waltz Daniel. Occasionally I even help. What a lot of work! He took the rough-sawn lumber and the soggy gray boards salvaged from the creek, along with hammer, nails, handsaw and plane, and with them, he is creating a kitchen that meets my exact specifications.

I have come to appreciate in the last three days what it is that carpenters do. Carpentry is not unlike sewing. Much of the art seems to be in knowing where to put the first nail. It's one thing to watch and admire, and another to be the one who has to remember to leave and inch here for the trim, put a notch there for a shelf that will come later, and in general make it all come out even. And sawing wet boards by hand! Also carrying around 16-footers, stamping out ceilings, ripping down plywood, dismantling mistakes.

The result? My kitchen! You should see it. It has an eating area looking east to where the animal pens will be. Shelves for dishes in an alcove. Pots and pans will hang from a frame in the center over the cookstove. The sink is in front of a south-facing window that looks uphill across a clearing and into the trees. We'll plant the garden there.

The bread counter is perfect. It faces downhill, north, overlooking the road and a meadow where the creek meanders into to a cedar grove. I made the motions of kneading bread and Robb measured the exact height of the heels of my hands to know where to place the countertop. I have sanded, sanded, sanded, and oiled it. Now it's covered with a red-checked oilcloth, waiting for me to make bread. Underneath are shelves with room for storing 5-gallon buckets of flour, oats, raisins, nuts, and other baking stuff. Above it, a shelf for the smaller things—baking powder, vanilla, sesame seeds, bread pans…

In the center of the kitchen (three whole steps away from either the bread counter or the sink) is the main counter opposite the cookstove. Again, built to the exact height of my hands, this time chopping vegetables. It's made of rough boards that won't cringe at the whack of a cleaver or cower at the approach of a kettle of hot jam.

With the rest of the wood pulled from the creek, Robb paneled the lower half of the living room walls. Fifty-three soggy boards he sawed by hand to do that. Wow. He built a wide bench into the wall that, with some padding, will be like a couch where you can recline against the woodbox that divides the kitchen from the living room. There are countless other things to make—a table, bookcases, cushions, quilts… The touches will come once we can live here.

Daniel has just finished nursing, choking, sputtering, sneezing and burping, so now he sits, all toothless and cheerful talking to me from his plastic seat.

I like the idea of my baby boy growing up here. He'll know the forest, farmers' fields, baby chicks. He can gather eggs, watch the neighbor's calves being born. When he's big enough to sleep in the loft Robb is building, he can spy through a knothole on what's happening by lantern light in the living room. These pretty little dreams come from a lady who can't tell half the time if he's crying from hunger, pain, boredom, gas, or fatigue. We are constantly telling him what he will be able to do here. He is unimpressed.

I need a rocking chair.

Monday, February 7, 1983

Dear Iris,

It has happened! We are here! Tomorrow morning I will open my eyes and know how it feels to wake up in this, my new, real, and permanent house. The house at the end of the road.

I am sitting at the bread counter. The yellow light of the kerosene lamp falls on the page as I write. Hanging from the wall at my left: measuring spoons and cups, the pastry cutter, spatula, whisk. My chair is a five-gallon bucket of flour.

On Thursday, my order comes in at the food co-op in St. Maries. A hundred pounds of potatoes and fifty pounds each of onions and carrots. Three hundred pounds of flour and fifty of pintos, soybeans, black turtles, garbanzos, peanuts, sunflower seeds and dry milk. A lot of food, huh? Also spices and rice, bulgur, millet, cornmeal, peanut butter, tahini, cooking oil, coffee, miso, honey, molasses, raisins, tomato sauce. I spent the entire bulk food budget. Once we plant a garden and get chickens and a milk goat, I think I can cook *Recipes for a Small Planet* from cover to cover.

The food trip—my department—includes garden and livestock as well. I got two doe rabbits from a sign I saw at the co-op and Robb landed a buck bunny from a neighbor in the valley who works on the road crew. We feed them little rabbit pellets and a bit of alfalfa hay. "Mating" takes about seven seconds. At least I think that's what they did. I'll have to check the *Mother Earth News* article Robb clipped for the files to figure out where and what to palpitate to see if the does are pregnant.

I'm feeling better about myself and other people, after having discovered the food co-op. Mostly it's a food-buying club with an address in town. They have a pretty wide range of stock of all the basic natural foods, bulk spices and treats like carob brownies and soy ice cream bars. Also a woodstove with a sign above it that says, "This co-op needs firewood." You can take a shower there for fifty cents (a dollar for non-members). It was easy enough to make friends. I put in the biggest bulk food order in their history.

At the co-op, it's other people like us—babies and limping trucks. Although these women have their babies at home, not in hospitals, and certainly not by Caesarean. I wish I could tell stories like they do—laughing about how mad they got before feeling like they were going to shit out a watermelon. Their faces wrinkle, their bodies scrunch and hands clench, but it's all fun. Nobody wants to hear the story of your operation.

Most of the co-op folks live over on the other side of St. Maries, so after we move out to the house, I won't get to see everyone so much, just whoever happens to come into town on my once-a-month volunteer days in the store. That's when I'll put a pot of beans on that stove, wash my hair, hang with Daniel, do store chores and get to visit when someone comes in to buy six oranges or a pound of granola.

Robb is snuggled into the bed in the loft with Daniel. From down here at the bread counter, I can see the flickers of their lantern. I should go to bed, too. But this evening is so exciting, so perfect, so magically good, I don't want to blow out the light and make it end.

THURSDAY, FEBRUARY 10, 1983

Dear Iris,

Today was, I suppose, a fairly typical day on our little farmstead. It began a little prematurely at 2:30 a.m. when Daniel learned a locomotion trick and scrunched forward to wedge his head into the front of his crib. We soon had the family back under control, and then sometime after 3 o'clock, Robb woke up yelling—dreaming he was plotting to stab an heiress named Sybil with the hunting knife in his tuxedo, interrupting me who, in my dream world, was living in the loft above a school where a crippled guy in a plaid shirt practicing his country swing was always in the way when I went downstairs to pee. Daniel repeated his head-wedging trick at 5:20. I got up.

Ordinarily I don't pay so much attention to time in the morning, but we wanted to be in St. Maries to meet the truck at 7:30 when it arrived with our year's-supply-of-food order.

Morning progressed at a typical pace. It took about an hour's worth of fiddling with the cookstove fire to make coffee and heat up the potato soup to heat. (Good Idaho food, huh? Without refrigeration, you eat some unusual breakfasts.) While we waited, the snowplow came by and the driver, our neighbor Kelvin, came in to chat. The three members of the road crew are good acquaintances—they either own or have access to back hoes, graders, loaders, caterpillars and the like. Not to mention plenty of experience. Best of all, you can hire them out. The backhoe has already dug the trench that drained the water from our basement and made a couple of little ponds uphill hear the creek.

We made it to town about 9 o'clock. The food truck was long gone, but someone had sorted and stacked my order. It weighed about 900 pounds all together. I could start my own store.

After the food was loaded, we did our town errands in what we figure was the habitual northwestern rain in Ken Kesey's books. We discovered a second-hand store, but its proprietors, Stan and Marsha Gerhardt, were the best discovery of all. We made a date to visit their home and buy some chickens. We found all sorts of things we needed there: chicken wire to keep the deer out of the garden, some metal cabinets to keep the mice out of the food, a 3-foot piece of culvert to put in the spring, two grocery bags full of back issues of *Organic Gardening*, and every kitchen utensil I need but don't have yet, including a complete set of silverware. At the Safeway, a splurge—some Pampers. Then we rummaged around in some trash cans and dumpsters in search of containers for all these sacks of food. Heading home with our loot, Robb got stopped by a cop for driving too slow.

Once home, we drank some shots of another "treat" we bought ourselves in town and unloaded the truck. Then Robb cut firewood while I tried to convince Daniel a nap would be fun so I could start washing all the jars and bottles I'd scrounged.

Later… I'm sitting at the kitchen table Robb made yesterday, surrounded by all my sacks of food. I did get the jars washed. The cats are trying to catch the moths playing *kamikaze* with the lantern.

Daniel is getting to be a little more fun, although he still doesn't do much. Push a button—sometimes he laughs and sometimes he cries. He's sure seen more and put up with more than most fellas his age. He'll spend his first years with no electronic noises in the background, developing his awareness of sounds by hearing pens scratching, the fire crackling, the creek that burbles past the house. And the smells! Coffee in the morning, bread baking, wood smoke, pine needles. Even the water seems alive. How could a light bulb ever captivate him the way a lantern flame does? It's as good for me as it is for him.

I am really happy. Not delirious—steady and mellow. It surprises me how much gentle pleasure I can get out of doing the dishes while out the window I can see the water source in the hillside. The water pours in and splashes over my hands like liquid diamonds. Food tastes so good eaten by the lantern light after a hard day of real work as Daniel sucks his thumb and drifts off in his crib.

Next day… I was ready to mail this, but…

I am in the loft surrounded by cats and sleeping Daniel. Robb is in the basement making himself a shop—tools, chainsaw, workbench. He calls it his office. My office, then, is right beside it: washtubs, and the metal cabinets we got yesterday for storing the reserves of food that don't fit in the kitchen.

Those very reserves of food remain a small mountain occupying most of the kitchen floor. I would be putting it all away if I were not nursing a pulled "lifter" muscle.

Yesterday when we were loading up the food order, I decided it was about time I made an effort to get stronger, and wrestled the five-gallon bucket of molasses into the truck myself. I was dismayed at how, even with a full-body heft, I could barely get it up on the tailgate. But I did it, and got it off the truck, too, and up the porch steps and into the kitchen. After it was in the kitchen, I read the whole label and saw that five gallons of molasses weighs seventy-nine pounds. Is that really so much? I guess so. When I woke up today, my neck was so stiff I could barely put my sweater on.

Whiskey before breakfast. I thought that was the name of a fiddle tune, not a form of treatment, but I guess Robb's right when he says it's not gonna feel better until it all relaxes.

And so this is short. Off I drift…

MONDAY, FEBRUARY 14, 1983
EVENING, AT THE BREAD COUNTER

Dear Everyone,

Robb is one determined man, going up and down the stairs, bent on getting the hot water project finished. We are almost home free. Because I designed it, Robb talks about the system like it's some kind of engineering marvel, but all it's based on is what we learned in the fourth grade— hot stuff goes up and cold stuff goes down.

We had the guy who made the basement stove put coiled copper tubing in it with plumbing fittings on the ends leading in and out. Robb added pipe to connect them to the top and bottom of an old hot water tank. When the tank is filled and the stove is roaring hot, the water starts exchanging like crazy, and in less than 20 minutes all the water is boiling. The tank is situated directly under the kitchen sink, so we can draw the hot water straight up with a hand pump. This is several feet away from the stove, which is necessarily next to the chimney, so there's more pipe going between the stove and the tank than you might think, and it elbows around at interesting angles. Robb painted the tank red. The pipes are gleaming copper. He has named the contraption The Mantis.

For the most part this evening, I am not-writing this because of trying to waltz the-burp-that-will-not-come out of Daniel. He falls asleep on my shoulder, then wakes up and cries 5 or 10 minutes after I lay him down. I am one with his digestion.

Getting the hole in the floor for the pump is what's making Robb tear his hair out. Two-inch floorboards with three-quarter inch plywood on top, and the pipe needing a hole that's a lot bigger than what the brace-and-bit drill will make. So he's drilled, and sawed, and still the pipe doesn't quite go through. Now he's sawing some more. He's soaking wet from the leaky pipes, and muddy from where he's been crawling. He's been wearing the same long-johns for days. He gets first bath.

Back at the bread counter. How long was that interlude? Daniel asleep. Black bean and barley pie cooling on the counter. Downstairs, the hot water is zinging through its exchange and the big red pump beside the kitchen sink is hooked up and steaming. Time to start pumping hot water into the big kettle and pouring it into the bathtub.

Robb just popped open a can of beer, singing, "It's going to be an Aviance night."

TUESDAY, FEBRUARY 22, 1983

Dear Iris,

Things I have done so far today:

- Went out for breakfast alone in town. A frivolous expenditure, perhaps, but deemed necessary after yesterday when it rained and Daniel cried all day. We feared Mommy would run screaming into the woods in her longjohns, hair a-flying.
- Made oatmeal rye bread. It's rising.
- Took a bath

You can give a pyromaniac no finer toy than a wood cookstove. *Living on the Earth* says the kitchen is the center of the home and the fire is the center of the kitchen. As keeper of the cookstove fire, I *do* feel like I am guardian of something important. When the last coal disintegrates to ash, it *does* feel as though something vital has departed from the house.

In the morning when I come down and strike a match to the day's fire, a doorway opens and our lives emerge from wherever it is they go while we sleep.

I am loving this cooking. Without eggs, butter, meat, cheese or refrigeration, it's fun trying to come up with things that are both nutritious and edible. Vegetarian biscuits and gravy, anyone? Thank god for powered milk.

My relationship with Daniel is based essentially on crying and what will keep him from crying. He's crying now, but I have put him in his bed to cry himself to sleep. I don't think you're supposed to admit you do that. I sure read a lot of things when I was pregnant that said to never let your baby cry—because an infant doesn't have enough wiring to cry for no reason. He cries because he needs you and if you don't come, his psyche is tinged with hopelessness.

I believed that stuff with all my heart when I was pregnant. I still mostly believe it. But it doesn't place any value on all the times I do show up. I tell ya, the guy is loved. And he's growing up with parents who understand what it means to want to be happy. Which, I think, is already more than we got.

I don't know what the truth is, only that if sometimes I don't just put him down and go away when he's screaming, I'd be screaming, too. As it is, every muscle in my body stays rigid until he stops, and, as maybe you can tell from the last few paragraphs, when he's screaming, his screaming is all I am thinking about.

But wait. He's catching his breath. That's the first step. It'll taper off. Now, if he can just find his thumb…

Oh why isn't there a way to hold them and show them how much we love them and make the screaming stop?

Also this week, Daniel has read and reread the entire cover of *The Thorn Birds*. My son. The mouse in my pocket. Parents are strange and I've become one.

Robb is cutting up firewood outside in the rain. Just heard him say, "Cock-sucking sonofabitch." But he's still sawing. So how bad can it be?

My temper is short. It's getting dark. I should go be a mom or a housewife or something.

THURSDAY, MARCH 10, 1983

Organized food storage and laundry better. Split kindling and stove wood, set it to dry. Walked Delbert's logging roads to the top of the ridge. Robb got firewood. Life is easier when the drain drains reliably.

FRIDAY, MARCH 11, 1983

Daniel went outside, tasted pine needles, sat in the basement and tried out the Johnny Jump Up, wearing a blue visor. *I hear the marlin are biting,* sez Robb on his behalf.

Robb began a table, then cleared brush, collected dog-pen poles and made walkways up near the creek.

I cleaned house and unpacked boxes, looking for film. Then wrote letters, did wash, and organized the canned goods in the basement.

In the evening we picked guitar, ate butter beans and popcorn. Talked about what we *could* do.

Saw a deer out the window at breakfast.

SATURDAY, MARCH 12, 1983

Robb roughs in the first log-end wall and window of the wood room beneath the kitchen. We shovel on a load of manure from Delbert's barn. Daniel supervises from his plastic chair.

SUNDAY, MARCH 13, 1983

Dear Iris,

At the Quick Stop, Robb ran into some guys we met when we came through here last fall looking for land. They live in a commune on Ridley Peak, about 40 miles away. Robb brought them home, and they spent the night.

We started to chat about what we're doing, tell how great it was to get a load of manure from Delbert's barn yesterday, and the one guy asks, "Cow manure?" We say yes, and he says, "Horse is better."

That's something I keep noticing when the men get together and talk. Why do they do that? Be competitive, or act like your very best isn't already good enough. I'm thrilled with that truckload of manure. It's going to grow food we will to eat. In my mind, the trip isn't so much about doing everything flawlessly as it is about becoming satisfied with what is already good.

It was great fun, though, to serve them hearty soup and crusty bread. Oh what talk! It was like a meeting of news-hungry people from far-flung planets. Robb told the tale of Tim Leary's visit to Boulder last year. They explained about forest issues—pesticide spraying and clearcutting, how the timber on National Forest land is practically given away to the logging companies.

What did I say in that conversation? Nothing. I guess I don't have much to contribute, really. None of them needed to have me explain how working at IBM isn't where it's at. Still, they worshipped the food as well as ate it. The work I did around them—providing their nourishment as well as Daniel's and all the rest of Daniel's evening care—all this demonstrates security and warmth. That matters, too, even if it isn't at the level of the words.

I am more than a seven-dimensional waitress, though, aren't I?

New day.

Daniel is fat and beautiful. He sucks his fist, drools, smiles, and giggles a lot. He woke me up screaming last night. He'd rolled over. I rolled him back. It was like rescuing a capsized turtle.

The bottom line: we're doing well. Working awful hard physically, but it feels good. We've escaped the mental wear and tear of working in Boulder. It's a nice switch to have real tangible things to show for your efforts.

The pace is erratic. Robb works a lot harder than I do, so I try to be cheerful. Sometimes I'm not. There's so much to learn.

Will mail this in St. Maries today. It's my day at the food co-op. Write. Visit.

MONDAY, MARCH 14, 1983

Returned from St. Maries with fabric for diapers, mortar for the log wall, a wheelbarrow, chicken feed, dog food and dog, Jake. Jar lids, corks, chainsaw bolts, embroidery thread.

No mail.

TUESDAY, MARCH 15, 1983

Frost overnight.

I took pictures, made bread, put away canning supplies, cut out sample diaper. Sent in two-year subscription to *Parabola*.

Robb cut firewood, tried to pen Jake, and improved the log walk in front of the house that keeps us above the mud.

WEDNESDAY, MARCH 16, 1983

Nuclear war is inevitable. Committed ourselves to making further construction underground.

Started cabbage, broccoli, tomato, pepper and cauliflower seeds on the windowsill.

THURSDAY, MARCH 17, 1983

Dear Everyone,

Tonight we're celebrating the stairway to the basement and the door from the loft. Now—ta-da!—instead of going outside, down the porch steps and back in the basement door to stoke the downstairs fire, you need only climb down the ladder in the corner by the bookcase.

The basement hole was a breakthrough in more ways than one. Robb cut it with the chainsaw. Doing it by hand seemed so daunting after the struggle for the hot water pipe. Robb wished aloud that he had thought to cut the hole with the chainsaw before we moved in, and I said, "Why not use the saw anyway?"

We opened the doors wide, and yes, it was pretty stinky when the opaque gray smoke filled the living room, and true, there were wood-chips to be swept up from just about everywhere, but it was a two-minute job, as opposed to one that would have taken all afternoon—or more.

That hole was so easy, we made another! The second one is an opening out of the loft where we sleep. It's just big enough to squeeze through and onto the porch roof for easy access to clean the chimney. We fashioned a door with a little window in it and painted it red. Because the road rises steeply past the house, when you walk up a little way and turn around, the door is at eye level. Makes the place look like a family of hobbits lives here.

Friday, March 18, 1983

Still frosty. Pipes frozen in the morning if we don't leave the water running.

Robb helps scrub diapers.

Truck stuck getting a load of manure from Delbert's. Only got half of it thrown off.

Cleaned up the house—put a thousand little pieces of paper in their proper places.

Robb stayed up half the night reading *The Complete Book of Composting.*

Saturday, March 19, 1983.

Injuries and sore muscles make us decide to take it easy.

Visitors from Ridley Creek. Conversation is of the future. Looks grim for those who trust the system.

Monday, March 21, 1983

Trip to Spokane. Graffiti in Rockford: *Jodi gave me herpes.*

Our treat—a John Prine songbook, a welcome switch from meat or booze. On the way home, met Delbert on the road massaging a newborn hip-locked calf. Did dishes, talked about UFOs and played "Sam Stone."

Baby bunnies. Dead. All of them. Ugh.

Daniel is so sweet.

Wednesday, March 23, 1983

For me, a day in the kitchen: Peanut butter oatmeal cookies, gingerbread, barley rye bread, a tomato-garbanzo loaf. Only made it outside to feed the bunnies and split a little wood.

Robb cut up the largest mistletoe tree and started on the beds and terraces behind the house.

Thursday, March 24, 1983

Cabbage sprouted. So did a few peppers and cauliflower.

Garden day. Hard work! Shoveled wet clay, carried manure by the bucketful. Just to make a little bed to plant some peas and lettuce.

Daniel jumps in the Jump-Up almost every waking hour.

Sweep the basement. Do the dishes. Sick and tired of dirt. Where do the days go?

Great soup: Sauté onion and sunflower seeds in oil, thicken with flour. Add milk powder, tahini, miso, cumin, horseradish, water. With rye bread.

Sunday, March 27, 1983

Tom from the Ridley Peak settlement has been here for three days. In addition to the pleasure of having help, his presence has provided a much-needed break in our rhythm. He split wood and stacked it both in the basement and in my woodbox. He and Robb double-dug beds in the garden. I washed bottles and jars. Daniel smiled a lot.

Delbert visits. Talks about how the tractor companies beat out the horses. Could trade in your horse—that was the bait. Then came the endless stream of indispensable add-on gizmos. No switching back. The horses were gone.

Monday, March 28, 1983

"Remember the day you hand-sawed 53 boards to build the bench?" I ask Robb. That was the day we stayed after dark for the first time. The first meal here and the last of the road food: cowboy coffee with cremora, avocado, cream cheese, jelly, peanut butter, a banana, and bread baked in Boulder.

I wonder how old a child is before being able to understand the notion of feeling better after the nap.

Wednesday, March 30, 1983

Chickens! Six little Clarabelles settled into their straw-lined doll house.

Stan and Marsha. Lessons on life. It's hard to remember to do what's best for yourself. They are in their 60s. Getting rid of all but three chickens and hoping someone will buy the store. Stan has hardly any breath—emphysema—but still, he always has a project going. He pauses every few steps, every few sentences—life in slow motion. Marsha says every day together is precious, so it's good to take them slow.

I don't relate to all the born-again talk, though.

THURSDAY, MARCH 31, 1983

5 eggs!

SATURDAY, APRIL 2, 1983

Clarabelles provide the breakfast eggs sturdy enough in flavor to hang in over black beans.

Slow Saturday morning. Daniel cries, eats, laughs, snuggles, jumps up, cries, snoozles, eats, cries, rolls over and finally sleeps. Robb reads Alan Ginsburg and Gary Snyder aloud while I cook. We drink coffee. Beans simmer. He plays. I sing. Forty degrees. Rain and flurries. We plan our immediate future—chores upon chores.

SUNDAY, APRIL 3, 1983

Monster omelet for breakfast. Robb cooked, did the dishes, kept the fires going, took care of Daniel, cleaned up, bathed, shaved, read all about potatoes in *Organic Gardening*, took a nap and woke up frustrated because he hadn't done anything all day. So he ran up the hill at dusk with the chainsaw, cut the wrong tree in the dark, but brought in a load of wood all the same.

I got up early and appreciated a nap in the late morning. Garden plan—how much of what to plant where. An overwhelming task.

Make a coldframe tomorrow. Can't wait!

MONDAY, APRIL 4, 1983

Another good night's sleep! Spuds and nutritional yeast for breakfast. Daniel asleep, beans on the stove. Sunshine—no fire in the basement. Feed the bunnies and the 'Belles. Get cracking on the seedling house.

A coldframe: measuring, deciding how high, how wide, leveling, hammering, listening for Daniel. Stretching and nailing chicken wire and plastic. Ripping boards with a chainsaw. Rice cereal for Daniel—he wears it from his knees to his eyebrows. Putting the tools away, reading aloud. It all adds up to a day. Always best when we do it together.

MONDAY, APRIL 11, 1983

What a pleasant, soft evening. Golden lights. Daniel asleep. Fire crackles. Popcorn oil heating. *King Rat* and Faulkner.

Carrots, beets, radishes, mustard, lettuce, endive—a little salad garden started in the coldframe. Two new beds up on the hill freshly mounded with hoed-in manure and covered with mulch.

At Christmas we'll complete one full cycle. There will be a tree tall to the peak of the roof. Daniel will probably be walking, saying some words. Maybe we'll eat a goose, or venison, or elk.

Thursday, April 14, 1983

Laundry out the wazoo.

Many advances. Wood room grows. The yard is raked. Scored a big box of lettuce and celery trimmings from the Grocery City dumpster to feed the bunnies and the 'Belles. Daniel's lightning pincer fingers. Snatch and swallow. Grains of rice. Beans. Carpenter ants.

Sunday, April 17, 1983

Tomorrow I need to rake up the bunny and chicken shit, layer it with dirt and straw for compost. Get the slivers out of my fingers. Start some sprouts, figure out a way to use the failed bread, make a poultice for my sore shoulder. Also plant beets and chard.

Are we making progress? We must be.

Monday, April 18, 1983

Finished the chicken yard.

Daniel sucks his thumb, his little wind-up tune plays. Robb makes kindling by moonlight. Kitties, dog, chickens, bunnies all sleeping.

I change a diaper, then scoop up a swaddled Daniel and carry him up the hill to say goodnight to the world. Golden windows glow below. A few of the things on the clothesline are dry. Leave it all there, hope it doesn't rain. What a mystical sense of the universe you'll have, I tell him. Go ahead, cackle at the moon. This is where we've arrived. And this is where he begins. He will *not* grow up afraid of the dark.

Just working on my karma. Trying to be good for a while. To my body, my boys, my animals, my comfrey.

TUESDAY, APRIL 19, 1983

Daniel will fall asleep, the fire will burn, the water will boil and the eggs will cook.

The bunnies are fed. The chickens. Jake. The floor is swept. The diaper is changed. The clothes are soaking.

Change the crib sheet. Water the coldframe. Fix the chicken yard. Pet the cat. Subscribe to *Atlantic Monthly*.

The guest will leave. The clothes will dry. The window will heal.

APRIL 20, 1983

Dear Iris,

Well, the whole thing was silly. Most importantly, we learned something.

It all started the day before yesterday, I guess, when we were getting the wire on the chicken yard. Only it's hard to say "we" were working on it, because my part of the job was to hang out on a blanket with Daniel and try to convince him not to eat dirt.

Robb was having a rough time of it. I'm not sure why. Something about it was frustrating. I couldn't get him to take a break, let the tension pass, do the task without self-made obstacles. Or he could have waited until Daniel was napping so we could do it together.

His heads-down, all-out, do-it-if-it-kills-you way of plowing through tough jobs can be his best friend and worst enemy. I know it's not my job, nor even my right, to lecture him to make him see that. We learn what we learn when we're ready. I kept my mouth shut, but it bugged me. He knew it. We tried to play music together after dinner, but even though we weren't fighting, it felt like we were.

As I lay the morning fire, the tension was still in the air. He was awake in the loft just overhead, so I started talking about it. How it's stupid to do a job when you hate it, how the bad vibes get all over everyone and that's not fair. Besides, we came here to escape schedules and expectations, to give ourselves the freedom of having the slack to do a job in its own time, so it feels right.

Thinking about it now, I can't say I blame him for getting mad. Who wants to hear all that, first thing in the morning, before coffee, even? He barreled down the ladder from the loft, furious. That was too much. I was right, even if he didn't want to hear it. So my brilliant response was to pour out the just-made coffee right in front of his eyes. I must have put down the coffee pot, because next thing it flew past me—a line drive through the kitchen window.

That was yesterday. The start of a really full day. The day our new closest neighbor, Charlie Hart came to dinner. The morning before that, before we ever started with the chicken yard, a ramshackle-loaded pickup topped with a mattress had spun around the curve and down the mountain past the house. (First rig that's gone by in that direction. Meant the shortcut over the pass to St. Maries had opened.) Robb went investigating in the afternoon, saw the truck and found the driver settling into the formerly abandoned cabin near the cutoff to the highway, and invited him up for spaghetti. He came the next day, yesterday, the coffeepot day.

It didn't take more than a few minutes past the introductions for us to all agree that this life we're choosing is pretty tough. "Yeah," said Robb, in a tone of honest regret, "I threw the coffeepot through the window this morning." With those words, I got the acknowledgement I needed that the whole goofy argument was regrettable on both sides. Sometimes that's the most difficult thought for couples to find together.

But Charlie! What a picture! I'll bet he weighs 300 pounds. A glorious salt-and-pepper beard, gimp leg from a motorcycle crash, and a disability check that's always late. His wife, Poli, who is Korean, will join him in a few days. They are going to get some baby pigs from the pig farm in Frederick and start a little operation.

He said no-thanks when I passed the salad. "Not a tooth in my head, little lady. I can eat *steak* but I'll choke on a piece of lettuce." We brought up the idea of trading labor over the summer, helping each other out, but no, he doesn't work, only watches. "Oh, I love to be around work, I just can't do it."

So all in all, life stays rich. And calling to me from every quarter. Daniel is waking up. The fire might be out. Chickens need water.

I wonder how you are. Please write. Come visit.

FRIDAY APRIL 20, 1983

Robb stood back over near the trash pile and looked at the first shakes he split, fastened to the wall. And called it good. "Look at it with a bit of a squint and you get a twinkle of how it will be when it's all done." I guess.

We both slept badly last night. First a yowling Daniel, then a yowling cat in heat. Still, we got up this morning without being irritable and angry with one another.

We're getting used to it. Accepting it all. At least that's what we say. I think we might be right.

SATURDAY, APRIL 21, 1983

Charlie's out in the yard. Is he helping Robb with the saw? A spectator/commentator when I am trying to figure out something I don't understand would drive me out of my ever-loving gourd. Especially if he talked all the time—and talked loud to boot.

TUESDAY, MAY 3, 1983

Keeping track of the days. Which is this one? The feelings go up and down. We think we are getting happier. Are we working as hard as we were? Seems a frequent question. Should we be? Are we working hard enough? That's the worry.

FRIDAY, MAY 6, 1983

Ah, little bunny, what kind of mama are you? Living on gleanings from the Grocery City dumpster. Not enough sense to cover your babies or keep them in out of the rain.

But if ignorance disqualified us for motherhood, the earth would be empty.

SATURDAY, MAY 5, 1983

Rain again. Splitting firewood in the spattering damp by lantern light.

I'm determined to make the coldframe perfect. Sometimes I wonder if I can pull this garden thing off at all. Still other times, I doubt if we'll ever stop competing with everyone, real and imaginary—the richest compost, deepest garden beds, the best produce, tastiest food.

We're just trying to satisfy ourselves, right?

Sunday, May 8, 1983

Hanging clothes on the line on Mother's Day. So this is it. My thumbs red, stiff, and cold, can barely turn the little feet of Daniel's jumpsuits right-side-out. The baby bunnies were all dead this morning. Jake ate the eggs and ruined the basket. Daniel won't nap or stop crying. I want to be coddled and felt sorry for. Cat scratched in the coldframe this morning.

Much worse things have happened to other people.

Thursday, May 12, 1983

Even the rocks are alive. It's all connected. There is so much to learn. Take care of my earth, my plants, my body whose left side has been numb and out of sorts for days. Has my right brain shriveled up completely? Am I ascending in a spiral or riding a slinky down the stairway to heaven?

Jump. Jump. Ker-plunk. Thunk. How did the Johnny Jump-Up come unfastened from the ceiling?

Sunday, May 15, 1983

Re-enter the rotten part of the cycle. Arguments over sleeping bags, ruined socks, papers, junk—who trashes the most of whose stuff. "It's all gone sour," sez he. "We never should have tried it with a baby," sez she.

No planting done. Got sick and puked in the mulch instead. Fever, chills. Did I eat something spoiled in the kitchen? Robb bleached the whole joint, making me feel (again) like an incompetent slob. "I knew it! We should have been doing this all along!" he declares. I've never bleached my dishes in my life, and I don't intend to start now. Bleach stinks and makes my hands dry and cracked.

Now he's sick. Does Daniel have it too? Or is he crying because it's all out of whack?

Let me out. No that's not what I want. This is the house at the end of the road. Teach me what I have to learn. Now.

Maybe tomorrow I can get something planted.

Wednesday, May 18, 1983

The basement is full of food. We aren't going to starve. The garden is not critical to survival. This is the first year. We are learning how.

Today we visited Nate and Jackie (Jackie's birthday) on the other side of St. Maries. Other people, other women. The co-op people. Someone told me all her first bunnies died, too. You learn what to do. Most of the men are gone, working, planting trees.

Nate gave me cuttings of willows and cottonwood. In the damp spring air, he cut switches with his pocketknife and handed them to me one by one. Tree planting time for me, too.

Maybe I can be one of the ones who planted trees before the deluge. Roots are stronger than seeds. Propagate roots. Everything that lives could be underground someday.

My work makes this whole draw rich, whether it's seeds or trees or the best intentions of my living. All we ever are, all we ever make—ultimately it composts and nourishes what follows. It is the spirit, not the detail that is preserved.

I want to hear red-winged blackbirds again.

WEDNESDAY, MAY 25, 1983

Only here…

- …does a baby goose pace its cage, searching, searching for the mother it never knew in the hatchery.
- …does the Pentecostal preacher from Spokane stop for coffee while bear hunting.
- …does the yipping of coyotes pour down over the hill while you set out seedlings in the moonlight and you are suddenly afraid of being alone with—with—with what?
- …do you spend two days chasing escaped bunnies and argue about whether your curried lentils should have rice under them or not.
- …do the log trucks leave three inches of dust in the road where a caterpillar has traced a curly pattern trying to find its way out of the alien stuff. You think I would have rescued it, put it back into the moist grass. But I didn't. We all spend out lives somehow.

MONDAY, MAY 30, 1983

Dear Iris,

Today I'm in kind of a daze, thinking hard, resonating, with an essay by Wendell Berry I read last night in an old copy of *CoEvolution Quarterly* Robb and I found in the second-hand store in St. Maries. The ideas in the essay aren't exactly new to me, but they are the very ones I need to be reminded of.

The essay is about the idea of commitment. "Commitment to forms," Berry calls it. A "form" is a set of rules that restrict and offer possibilities at the same time. If you choose to write in a poetic form, like a ballad or a sonnet, the restrictions on meter and rhyme can send you in directions you might have never found. Marriage is a form.

A certain amount of rational analysis, he explains, is involved in the choice of a form, but ultimately the commitment is made on faith—faith that the form will deliver on its promises. When you make a commitment, you live the form from the present forward. Regardless of what you and your rational mind anticipated while evaluating the commitment, there is always a point—or many—in the living out of the commitment when it turns out to be harder than you thought, and you want to abandon the form. Only by continuing—on the faith built into the commitment—do you attain the goals your faith says the form contains. You will not blossom inside the form if you do not stay within its constraints.

Wendell Berry takes several lyrical pages to say all this. It's like the foundation of my life has been articulated for me.

Our form, here, is the family we have founded upon this piece of land. We've committed to live simply and in tune with the natural rhythms of the earth and to engage with whatever lessons present themselves. We knew it would be hard, but saying that ahead of time is much simpler than living the experience of it being hard. It is a comfort to me to know it's normal for it to feel hard, and I can warn myself that it can even get harder. Commitments that are difficult to keep aren't bad commitments. They are commitments that are playing themselves out like all commitments do.

I am so happy to have made this commitment. So ready, so willing to keep working through to what it can bring.

Leaping from the level of commitment to the experience of living on this land and in this house, my typical routine goes something like this: get up early, build a fire and put the coffee on, milk the goat, rescue Daniel from his crib. Then breakfast. Feed the animals. Do the dishes. Play with Daniel until he takes a nap. That's the way it's supposed to go anyway. Most days it's two in the afternoon before all that happens and I've usually managed to half-complete some kind of project which layers a mess all over everything in the meantime.

Three days just passed. This letter has become one of the unfinished projects. I'll just mail it, or you may not get it until Daniel can read.

THURSDAY, JUNE 3, 1983

Dear Everyone,

We got a goat. A little nanny we've named Gardenia. She's a dainty lady, about three feet tall, and she gives us a half gallon of milk, morning and evening. I milk at 5 a.m. and Robb milks at 5 p.m. We tether her various places in the brush during the day so she can munch. We had planned to let her run loose after about a week, once she was used to where she lived and wouldn't wander off. We let her free yesterday and she "roamed" all the way to the back door and waited patiently to get in, dropping special raisins all over the porch. I kept leading her back out to the brush where there were all those tender munchies to eat, and she kept coming right back to the kitchen door. Finally she left and went up to the garden.

The books say that goats don't *graze,* they *browse.* That is, they'd rather eat leaves at the level of their face, and don't eat from the ground. It's evolutionary—there are microbes in the ground which can make them sick. Apparently Gardenia hasn't read the books yet, because she was ready to graze away the entire garden. She's tied up again.

Daniel sure laps up the goat's milk. It comes out at the very temperature he thinks milk is supposed to be. All you have to do is walk into the kitchen with the pan full of frothy white stuff and he goes wild.

I have so enjoyed the bevy of Clarabelles clucking and scratching a swath across the hillside. They have no question or care about their purpose in life. They do their work when they take three vigorous scratches in the ground with their rough and pointy feet, then step back and peck at whatever specks have been uncovered, whether they are food or not.

They nap in the late morning, take dust-baths in the heat of the day, and go to bed without a fuss at the same time every night. Each morning they lay an egg, shrieking with such surprise you'd think it had never happened to them before. Once there were the beginnings of a garden, however, they demonstrated how they know a lot about probability. Scratching there reliably yields seeds, sprouts and earthworms. Now they are penned up.

No freedom for the geese. A garden wouldn't last ten minutes under their care.

OK, two days went by. I better find an envelope.

MONDAY, JUNE 6, 1983

See the baby.
See the chickens.
See the gooses.
See the boy.
See the summer.
See the milk. Mommy will make the milk into cheese.

THURSDAY, JUNE 9, 1983

A prisoner of Daniel and Robb. Of shit and slop. Dust. Dirty dishes and laundry. Dirty bodies. Dirty bed. Where is the plenty? I don't feel like unbraiding the shoots of weeds from the carrot sprouts. But I do. Leaf by leaf. The woodbox is never full. No help or hope.

There never is when you let stuff aggravate you.

WEDNESDAY, JUNE 22, 1983

Reasons we have come up with for feeling so low:

• Getting older, being in transition from younger to older and facing that.
• Being lonely. I got married because I was lonely and for the same reason got divorced, left Detroit, started this whole trip. It was much easier to forget you were lonely in crowded Boulder. Being human is lonely.
• The House at the End of the Road. All the problems we

have always run from have arrived to catch up with us.
- Sources of anger: global destruction, international banking system, pollution cartels, and every other destructive thing we are powerless against. We have only ourselves and each other to take the anger out on.
- Global destruction. Today could be the day. Why get up? Why plant vegetables, split shakes, build a root cellar? Why talk about Daniel's future?
- Each of us is in control. Things feel the way we want them to.
- And the facts, ma'am? Charlie comes by regularly, especially for morning coffee. It's hard to talk with Poli. Her English isn't so good and she shouts, though I don't think she means to be shouting. She berates Charlie in front of everyone for not working. The garden is growing but frost the last two nights nipped, maybe killed, beans, corn, squash and tomatoes. Six baby bunnies—out of 15—alive and healthy. Lasagna for dinner.

MONDAY, JUNE 27, 1983

When I sort the laundry, I bring in two piles: Robb's clothes and "my" pile—clothes for me and Daniel, diapers, sheets, towels.

I get all hurt because no one understands my work. I get angry with Robb for not hearing when I try to explain—if you put junk on top of the woodbox, I can't put wood in the cookstove when I'm holding Daniel. If you don't rinse the turds off the diapers, the water in the wash boiler is raw sewage. When you say you'll do the dishes and then you don't, there's nothing to cook the next meal in. It's about helping each other. It's not a power trip.

I push hard every day on Sisyphus's stone. Each day more clothes and dishes get dirty, all the people and animals are hungry again, books and papers get laid and left everywhere. Yet, if I give up and quit for a day—or let it go just once to get outside and work in the garden—"we" have a discussion about how the "gradual deterioration" of the house is getting "us" down. The truth of the matter is, I have already been gotten down by the constant cleaning up after the others. We then fight, fling accusations, keep score. I decide to be a better sport, cheerfully see myself as Woman, my chores important, vow to do them even better so he will be pleased and proud. And the cycle begins again.

My new refrain: this is hard.

I want to raise a flag that says, "I am intelligent. I have read. I have insights." The angry response would be that I am so self-centered I think my every passing thought is of interest to the entire world.

It's lonely. In the Idaho boonies. A woman with a man and a child. A soul in the world.

Charlie reports that he's gone ahead and let the chickens move into their loft. Oh, it could be so much worse!

WEDNESDAY, JUNE 29, 1983

A man's home is his castle. God save the queen.

WEDNESDAY, JULY 6, 1983

Another disjointed day. You'd think I'd catch on to how such days are pretty much a function of my role—along with cold food, bathing in the dishwater and drying with a wet towel.

TUESDAY JULY 18, 1983

Things Robb has said to me in anger over the past few weeks:

- All of the joy has gone out of what we're doing.
- We don't like each other anymore. The time we spend together is pure hell.
- You don't like yourself. I watch you clinging to one straw after another.
- Building the wood room has been no fun at all. Even if I begin to enjoy myself, I know it's fleeting. You might come down and wreck the good feelings at any moment.
- I have a lot of repressed anger towards you.
- Everyone is depressed.
- Nobody is happy.
- I like to have Charlie around so I don't have to deal with you.
- The other women are getting more and more attractive to me.
- No matter what you do, no matter what the other people

say, once people think you've fucked up, they'll never really
forgive you.

• I don't like you.

• I don't trust you or any woman. I learned that in therapy.

• I'll bet that book is full of venom.

I try to be fair. For my sanity, I'm going to work on my quilt squares
and spend as much time as I can in the garden. There is a row of canned
cherries on the shelf downstairs. Soon I'll be canning rabbit. The broccoli is delicious. I planted marigolds last night.

Thursday, August 4, 1983

Wendell Berry says you don't remake the land so much as you remake yourself. How true. The land—the garden, the animal pens, the
pasture—is a picture of the people who have made them. We do essentially what we want. We make what we are.

Daniel grows—crawls, bites, cries and fails to entertain himself. It is
beyond my imaginative power to believe that for the greatest portion of
the time we will know each other on this planet, we will be able to talk
to each other.

No question the other mothers seem infinitely more accomplished
in their roles than I am. They don't say, "Oh, I did that," or "I made that
mistake, too." They say, "Oh no, that's not the way." Their babies don't cry
to be held, can entertain themselves, and will go to strangers. I wonder
where I failed. Need to remind myself that we are *all* doing our best with
the equipment we have.

In general, things are better. Not ecstatic, but better than just livable.
The lesson about controlling our own happiness comes hard—but we *do*
decide if we're going to be nice to each other or not, and in what spirit
we will take one another's every word. It is our choice to either plod back
up when we are down, or to try and drag the other one down with us.

Monday, August, 22, 1983

Daniel's and my days have a pattern? That of my praying he'll do
the same thing today as he did yesterday. If each day would be the same,
I'd know what was coming next, and maybe I could brace myself and
cope. Keeping Daniel fed, clothed and relatively happy all day is an end

in itself, an accomplishment. Isn't it?

I'm tired every day. Not getting enough sleep? What difference does it make? There doesn't seem to be room for more sleep on either end of the day.

The day took its maudlin self-pitying turn when I went up to the garden and all the marigolds I'd planted around the edges of the beds to deter bugs were gone. In their place were little trenches Robb dug around each bed to keep the weeds from encroaching.

Big deal. The marigolds weren't going to be all that spectacular. I don't think he cares very much for or about me. I don't think he wants to get any closer to me. I don't think he sees a real value in the things I do beyond the fact that someone has to do them.

WEDNESDAY, AUGUST 24, 1983

Daniel asleep. Robb suffering loudly from a runny nose and chest cold, me wallowing in the ultimate indulgence: I get to drink all the coffee and at my own pace.

I've been reading *The Egg and I*. This book was recommended to me by the librarian. A woman goes off to live in the boonies with her husband, but she doesn't want to. She drinks coffee and smokes cigarettes in her bathrobe all day, can't light a fire and complains all the time. My first reaction is that she's nothing but a narrow-minded whining old hen. Thinking harder, the main difference between her and me is that at least she's funny.

What I really want to know is—why this incredible feeling of futility?

Does this cool wet weather with its familiar mists signify that autumn in upon is? If so, the summer's work was badly done. Where is the bounty? We'll have to eat more than a few jars of jam in the coming year.

Just look forward to next year. We apply what we learn from our mistakes and do better.

It's not the end of the world if I fill my canning jars with produce that I buy.

I'm still looking for someone who'll tell me what to do. Who'll tell me when I am done that I have done well.

Reminds you of first grade, doesn't it?

Robb, who has been very kind all day, despite feeling rotten, reminds me that we always learn what we need to learn.

Even if we don't want to?

Tuesday, August 30, 1983

Sunday afternoon Delbert pulled up. "You said you wanted the hide if I shot a bear?" he asks. Nervous. Turns out he mentioned to a buddy of his from Coeur d'Alene that a family of bears had moved into his oat field. The guy drove down, shot them, and then went and got Delbert. A mother and two yearling cubs.

Three dead bears in the back of a pickup at dusk. I offer them coffee. Delbert brags to his friend about everything I do. Both of their mothers cooked on stoves like mine. "Look at that rig she's using there," says Delbert, indicating my coffee-filter drip system. "Wait'll you taste this coffee." I was proud.

We butcher the bears in the wood room all night. We hang them in a line, two cubs and a mother. We follow a guide for butchering wild game and do each step three times. Bloodbath. The insides of a bear look just like the insides of people.

Without sleep, the next day, we make hams, render fat for soap, put up 49 quarts of stew meat, start scraping the big hide.

We've hosed and hosed the wood room. The boards are still bloody. The smell is faint, but it carries me instantly to all that carnage. Every time I walk through there I could puke.

When something has to be done, I can roll up my sleeves and do it.

Monday, September 5, 1983

A day spent alone trying to get to the root of this darkness haunting me.

It began Thursday as I kicked myself for being only partially ready for winter. No root cellar. Planted too few of too many things in the garden.

And today, coffee grounds everywhere. I threw them across the kitchen after I came in from the coldframe that had been mulched with cucumber peelings and old bread.

Then, I looked for the sponge to start to clean the coffee grounds up, and found all my sponges disintegrating in bleach-water. I lifted the burner and hissed them into the stove.

A few days ago, when I came in from the garden and found the dishwater reeking with bleach, I upended the whole dishpan, making a horrid mess. That made Daniel cry. Which made me squelch the anger to cuddle and comfort him. What am I creating that he absorbs?

When Daniel's washcloth disappeared from its hook last week, I wiped his face with the shirt Robb had left on the chair.

My, my. Aren't we grown up?

Rage. How do I keep from passing it on?

Robb asked what was the last thing that passed through my mind before the coffee grounds flew.

Can't we run the kitchen and garden my way?

List of things pushing me around without my control—

- The prospect of living in a lightless hole with Charlie and Poli for a year because somebody pushed the button.
- The backache that feels like an aching kidney.
- The idea of shooting stranger on sight after a nuclear war. I don't want it to be that way.
- Being pregnant? Didn't I choose that?
- Having another C-section. I don't want to. The whole thing scares me.

Thursday, September 8, 1983

What I'd like to fling back in his face is that lyrical little speech he used to give in Boulder about whether or not I could hold up to this work, how I'll have to work harder than I've ever imagined and that he doubted I had the will to do it.

Well, the laundry is done, isn't it? I split my own stove wood, get up every morning and start a fire. Get the meals. Feed the animals. Milk. Make cheese.

Now it's later. I want to be calm and keep a grip. Why? Am I losing a grip? What is it that needs to have a grip kept on it? Why must I hold it together? If it won't stay intact of its own accord, is it worth maintaining? What does it look like when it falls apart? Why do I only lose it when I'm alone?

I don't know what help I need, so I don't know how to cry out for it.

My throat is sore from screaming. It made Daniel cry and set off a whole chorus of nervous clucking in the hen house. But, with my arm drawn back, I stopped, closed the window and didn't fire the lantern chimney outside. I wanted to see it shatter on some rocks. Not really. What I wanted to see was everything exploding and breaking, shattering—windows, canned goods. Cartoon sparkle of smashed glass. The explosion is inside me. It went off with the screams. It's over now. For good?

I don't know if I should discuss this with Robb or not. Or if I shouldn't maybe stop by the mental health center in town when I go to the co-op next week. It's like the aching kidney. Who am I getting even with by not taking the obvious steps to deal with problems?

SUNDAY, SEPTEMBER 11, 1983

It is probably safe to conclude that the idea of having another baby is not sitting well.

More coming at me than I can cope with? I don't know. I put myself here, didn't I?

Canning…cherry sauce, raspberry jam, cherry ginger jam, beans, zucchini, bread and butter pickles, green tomato chutney.

It's a wonderful day to be a chicken. Food in every color coming through the slop hole.

WEDNESDAY, OCTOBER 5, 1983

I thought it might be instructive to keep track of the things I am learning—or think I am learning—by going to the counselor.

Session one (the day I walked in the door): There is a name for the way I have been feeling and behaving: depression. Consider paint. If you store all your colors in a single pot, everything you paint will be gray. No matter how pretty the colors were that you began with. No matter what colors you add, the pot of color is gray.

Feelings arrive one by one and in all colors. The ones you examine come and go. The ones you ignore are tossed inside and their colors mix to a single muddled gray. No matter what colors come in, it all feels gray. Whenever the cauldron of gray goo boils over, undifferentiated gray feelings leak all over you—in ways that makes no sense, in ways nobody appreciates.

Session two (under hypnosis? I didn't really feel hypnotized): "Think back to when you were a little girl…" A wave of non-specific sadness engulfed me. Startled me. I had a happy childhood, didn't I? What was wrong? I couldn't talk, only cry. I don't much remember my childhood. Made my mother mad once when I said that. She began an indignant list of all the places we'd gone on vacation. Mostly I remember myself pirouetting for other people's pleasure. And I never had any friends, real friends. It was weird, though, how much I cried. It's not like I suffered as a kid.

Session three: As children we have problems, both real and imagined. We develop the very best tools we can to deal with them. Little people invent little tools, even for big problems, and stick with those tools, even if they don't work, because those are the best tools they can come up with. By the time we become adults, using those tools without expecting them to be effective is a habit. To grapple with inner discomforts, people often have a tendency to use their familiar—and inadequate—tools more, harder, faster. It's like taking a bigger hammer to a screw that won't go in.

My problem: feeling inadequate and bad. My tools? Be different. Overachieve. Don't notice what you can't change.

When other people (Robb, the mothers of other babies) look at me cross-eyed, I take it a thousand times more seriously than they do. The gray glob—everything I've trained myself not to notice—starts its ooze. I cringe and cower inside, resolve now and forever to do only the most wonderful and perfect things so maybe I can win back a portion of all that lost admiration and respect. Except that nobody but me is keeping score.

Session four (yesterday): My mother has small tools, too. She has used them for many years trying to solve her own problems, whatever they are, problems which are hers and not mine. The tool she uses most is to behave like a chicken. Scratching because she scratches. Some of the rottenest things she has ever said to me, she insists later she never said at all. Like a chicken, scratch-and-peck, she has a topic in mind, but doesn't pay much attention to the things she says. Even if she does happen to hear herself, she forgets. She will strut-walk through here when the next baby is born and say things that are just as upsetting as when she came after Daniel's birth. I'll hear a whole concatenation of criticisms stretching back into the can't-remember. For her, it will just be more scratching. That's what she *does*.

The scorched-earth chicken yard didn't get to be that way because chickens have a grudge against all living things.

THURSDAY, OCTOBER 6, 1983

There is a good part to every day.

WEDNESDAY, OCTOBER 10, 1983

I have been reading *Women's Diaries of the Westward Journey*. So much that's familiar. The never-ending struggle to stay clean, to keep things on an even keel with children, to put together a meal against exhaustion. The triumph of maintaining. The joy of morning quiet and putting your hands into clean water. In the minutes I spend with those pages, I feel a kinship, company. I'm not so alone. It is not easy to be among the first who are doing something new. I can choose to conduct my life with dignity as these women did, or I can whine and carry on like the spoiled self-appointed heroine of *the Egg and I*.

MONDAY, OCTOBER 15, 1983

I'd swim to shore if I could. But I don't know what direction that is. Or if there is a shore at all. Am I drowning in two inches of water?

You are a life. You are living your life.

THURSDAY, OCTOBER 25, 1983

Radiant Indian summer. Bunnies in the yard. Daniel and Robb cuddling.

FRIDAY, NOVEMBER 4, 1983

Dear Iris,

The weather is gray and I am lost in a nuclear funk. Nuclear madness. Nuclear angst. It's killing me. This week, anyway. There was a demonstration about it in Coeur d'Alene. The picture in the paper showed a counter-demonstrator with a sign that said, "Kooks Against Nukes."

Nuclear reality is a dense gray mass that hangs out where my guardian angel used to be. Sometimes it incapacitates me. Sometimes I probably forget it entirely. But not today.

All these nuclear weapons lying around like windfall apples in the Garden of Eden. The magic word is still "yet." Sooner or later somebody will decide it's "worth it" to use one. Or that they had to "make that regrettable choice" for some good reason.

I have started working on a quilt for Daniel's first birthday. A dozen squares with numbers and appliqué figures on them. One moon, two chickens, three stars, four tulips, and so on. The proportions are rotten, the numbers crooked, the curves angular and the points round. I was thinking about how it might not hold up under more than a couple launderings, since it's all sewn by hand. Wondered what to do to make it survive into "something Grandma made" that he can show his kids. Then I remembered—relief-like—that I was off the hook on the preservation thing because the world wasn't going to last long enough for him to have kids.

The thought slid through so effortlessly.

I remember the awful fight I had with my parents when Daniel was born, when they came to make me try to give him up for adoption. They said it was a sin to raise a child away from the concrete and electronics necessary for him to function in "today's society" when he is older. I tried to explain how "today's society," at the rate it is rolling, might not even allow him to get older. My dad exploded at my stupidity. Bad-wrong-stupid—or a grasp of the obvious?

Is there a way out? Does anything really change if we go out and catch cold demonstrating in the rain?

Refusing to participate in the madness is something we can do every day. In theory. I think we have to go beyond that and strive to participate in something else. Live our lives as though the changes have been made. Learn what the changes need to be by living them, not arguing for them. Demonstrate the possibility of a new way. Doing that—or trying to—is so un-glamorous, such a small part of a huge change, that it's difficult to see such slow, earthbound work as changing anything at all.

I've met so many hippies who migrated north and inland from the California summers of love. (I was 13 years old in 1965, and none of it registered.) In Boulder, the hippies blended into their niches and founded new institutions that grew up to be just like the old ones—clothing maker, organic grocery store, herbal tea man. They went on to do what good businesses do—drive the more humble operations out of business.

Here, hippie ambition has a different feel for an organic gardener, a beekeeper, a rare book collector. Gentle people, not without faults, although their faults seem connected to an inability to function in (you got it) today's society.

Does the world need a new Movement? The leftovers from the sixties are tired. They have families and have discovered responsibility. The coming generation scares me. The brightest of my younger cousins wants to be a stockbroker because it's the most straightforward way to get rich. A friend's teenage son, a video game freak, talks about "our soldiers" and comments on the news in a tone that belongs in a sportscast. Makes you wonder if this global consciousness we've evolved deserves to make it.

I used to think I'd be far away from it, whatever "it" might be, because I moved to the boonies. But "far" is relative. Nuclear waste is splashed and sunk all over the "empty" West. Nuclear winter would be for everyone. I try to imagine living underground for a while—we've got a basement with a water source and all of this food. But it doesn't take very much imagining to see the Harts at the door. I don't want to imagine anything further than that.

It would never happen that way. Us up here with all this food. Someone would come in the first week to take it away. Robb says that's why it's important to be defensible, to have weapons. I don't believe that. It's better to die in the first week than to pivot your survival on acts of violence.

Yuck. Enough gloom and doom. My bread is mushrooming out of the pan, and I have vowed to cut out and sew down six carrots before dark.

THURSDAY, NOVEMBER 17, 1983

What if today was the day and as I sat on the bench sewing wings on bumblebees, there came the flash, the beacon of the end?

You wouldn't see it here. The flash would be somewhere else. Death would arrive more slowly to this place.

FRIDAY, NOVEMBER 18, 1983

All I want is to be safe. There is none of that. The reasons make me wonder why the human race is worth saving.

It's *me* I want to save. My life, and the lives of the people I love.

TUESDAY, DECEMBER 20, 1983

Dear Everyone,

Robb and I were splitting firewood yesterday towards dusk (which is to say, probably 3:00) and the cloud-cover started to pull off. "Ooh," I said. "You thought it was cold last night. It's going to be really cold tonight." He laughs at my attempts to squint at the sky and predict the weather, but this time I was right.

In the morning it was 40 degrees in the house and the fire hadn't gone out. Delbert came up to visit and he said it was -10 in Spokane. We usually figure it to be about 10 degrees colder here. The tap is open and the water is running.

We parked a 12-foot Christmas tree in the living room last week and wired it to the high peak of the ceiling. We hung our 6-foot popcorn garland and all 9 of our ornaments on it. Pretty sparse. We added some of Daniel's toys to fill in the holes. We did all that while he was asleep, and when he woke up, the tree scared him.

Slowly he's discovered its uses and amusements—eating the popcorn, yanking on the feet of his clown and making the whole thing dance.

A few nights ago, as Daniel was in the final stages of being waltzed to bed, the UPS man delivered a package from Mom and Dad that was twice as tall as Daniel. After about a half hour, when the packing material started to bore him, Robb helped him pull out the two-foot-tall plastic puppy on wheels which has changed our lives. He can't sit on the thing and locomote as designed because his legs are too short. Instead, he grasps the wooden handles sticking out of its ears and waddles it backwards all over the house, looking like a fat guy in the suburbs behind a lawnmower. Suddenly he can "walk." For whole-family entertainment, we set him up in the saddle and roll him back and forth across the living room, playing catch.

We haven't decided when to eat our Christmas goose. We've been invited to other houses for Christmas dinner and Christmas Eve, so maybe it will be a New Year's goose. We butchered one goose for the retired logger who helps Robb tune up his chainsaw. It took all day to pluck it. The final stage required tweezes. We set all the feathers in a box behind the stove to dry. Later Robb touched the box and floating feathers filled the room. Quite a bit of down in a single goose in mid-winter. I'm working toward a featherbed.

Well, I've covered all of the animals, indoors and out. There probably won't be any other news until May. That's when we're going to have a baby. But then, so will the goat and the chickens and the geese. If it arrives late enough, maybe I'll have time to get the garden in. What a summer ahead! It will make 20-below seem like a real snap.

TUESDAY, DECEMBER 27, 1983
LAUNDROMAT

New notebook. New era?

Christmas was a bummer. It always is, isn't it? All the ghosts of Christmas past reminding you it will never be so golden warm as the Christmas when you were four.

The socks got burned up. Score another one for my favorite irritators: drunken inattentiveness and violations of my personal world. I think I'm getting over it. It nagged at me all day. I still keep remembering them—the two black stripes, one fat, one thin, the perfect woolen sock yarn, seized the instant I scored all three balls of it at 42 cents each in the Spokane Goodwill store. Tiny needles. Nice weave.

Glenn could have apologized. Even if it was hard for him to do so. Pouring a round of drinks was certainly no solution. I've heard Robb expound on the pathos of the Glenn character—full of unearned pride, can't stand to be wrong, hides behind gruffness and bravado. No surprise that all Glenn could say was something stupid: "That's what you get for leaving your junk so close to my chair."

Robb was so proud of me for "having class" and not lashing out at Glenn. Being bigger than the situation and blah blah blah. Like he gave me a whole lot of choice, backing me into a corner and kissing me every time I opened my mouth. I wasn't allowed out of the vice until I agreed to pretend like it didn't matter. He'll watch Daniel on Thursday and I can make another pair. Does he think this was one day's work? I raged inside.

Time. That's what hurt. Seeing all that time go up in smoke. Daniel asleep, the house quiet. Those are the most valuable moments in my life these days. The guilt for unswept floors, unwritten thank-yous for Daniel's birthday, all that, on and on, would be assuaged in the Triumph of the Socks. In how little the stitches were, how warm they would be, how well they'd hold up, how I'd wash them, and eventually darn them. Just figuring out how to *do* it had made me so proud. No one could possibly understand what I was whining about if I tried to tell them.

When we resumed the flow of dessert and drinks in the living room, Robb started talking about what a great short story this would make—if you accentuated some details and eliminated others, of course. Virginia's eyes sparkled with the thrill of such literary brilliance under her roof, and together they made it fill the room.

It was like being encased in plastic that absorbed everything I wanted to scream at Glenn. Nothing came out of my mouth for the rest of the evening.

So what goes in the story? Cold mornings, slow stitches, picking up speed. Dreading how crabby Daniel gets when we have dinner there? Everything late, late, waiting for Glenn and Robb to come in from milking and drinking whiskey in the barn. How about Virginia's dinnertable story of her irreplaceable pet chicken, killed by an unforgiveable dog? Glenn, drunken and mumbling, always the pyromaniac, stuffing the wrappings from our gift exchange into the fireplace. "Has anyone seen my knitting?" Innocent question. The fire goes *woosh!* Stink of burning hair. Glenn says, "Might as well just leave it now." Robb's hand on my arm.

It would be easier to forget if it didn't fall into the general class of faux pas my father needs forgiving for.

Life.

Other people.

Sometimes I get so sick of it all. I want to laugh and have fun and quit making such an effort to be bigger than everyone else's shortcomings. Wouldn't need such an effort if I wasn't so efficient at ferreting them out and lining them up, neat and precise, under my skin.

TUESDAY, JANUARY 24, 1984

Every time I hear the speech about how well we are doing, how the weirdness between us is past for good, it means the weirdness is back. The speech usually comes from under alcohol, alcohol that was first applied to soothe something.

I hate the speech because in it I'm reduced to a figure for the writer's backdrop. The woman who has understood great mysteries by having children. Or who cries a lot and grows anyhow. I am simply an object in the panorama of the life he wants to see go past him.

The feeling that I am getting no respect. Derision for me in the form of derision for the things I touch, keep, am in charge of, or proud of. Variations on a theme I would call "Jokes that Hurt."

Oh, I don't know. Caught in this trap. It's no different, really, than any of the others.

Still, he can go to the woodpile, to the clean outdoors, and blow frustration—me—out of his head. I'm left inside to clean up after him. Not fair.

WEDNESDAY, JANUARY 25, 1984

The Secretary of Defense has something to say about the most recently dead Marine in Lebanon. Someone wants to sue General Motors to prevent them from teaming up with Toyota to build a car. It's noon in Washington and Detroit, where well-pressed people have been bustling about under fluorescent lights all morning. Far away on a snowy hill, Robb and Daniel are asleep upstairs. I made a potholder yesterday. I'm getting fat.

SATURDAY, JANUARY 28, 1984

There is a little pep talk delivered in infinite variations by everyone from Erma Bombeck and Phyllis Diller to Ann Landers and Dr. Joyce Brothers. It goes something like this: If no one has managed by now to teach him to empty his ashtrays, pick up his underwear, clear his dishes, hang up his clothes—you won't be able to teach him either. Don't even bother to try.

Ugh. It's true. He's never going to realize what a rotten housekeeper he is. The clothes are different, but it's still Ozzie and Harriet. In this day and age, it should be more metaphysical than that. But it ain't.

Children are trainable. Your man isn't. The mutual overlooking of the peccadilloes leaves time and energy for other things. If you can't find an effortless way to do the overlooking, you are wasting a lot of effort. Because either you are going to leave him because he won't put his damn clothes away, or you are going to get into a never-ending war over it, or you are going to forget it.

Learning to forget it is the hardest.

Sunday, January 29, 1984

Nancy was taught that most people are uninteresting, and that she is better than most of them anyway. She grew up and rebelled a little. Now she seeks out the drama of others' lives and the rivers of their emotions. Her fascination with people is in theory. In person, she does not enjoy them.

We have to make allowances for Nancy. Give her some slack. She is a fried mother. Soon she'll have another. She'll be out for several years. After that we can decide if what is left of her is worth dealing with.

In universally appealing tales, the protagonist-as-victim works well, sez Robb.

Tuesday, January 31, 1984

Everything is wrong and I don't know how to make it right.

Why can't he stay out of the kitchen? Why does he feel so compelled to "clean up" and move my things around so I can't find them? Why doesn't he move his own trash instead? From the basement, from the wood room, from the kitchen, from the loft. But dare I open my mouth?

He never listens. He never has. It's a little late to be angry about that. I remember back in Boulder, before we had even moved in together, thinking that if I was patient, maintained my own space and kept thinking for myself, one day he would listen to me and be astounded. He has never listened to anyone, probably. Whatever the case, I was really dumb to think he would change.

Saturday, February 18, 1984

Dear Everyone,

On New Year's Eve I was coming down with a case of the sniffles. I intended to cure myself by burrowing into a quilt with Vitamin C, soothing tea, and a book. We were all but buried in snow, the road impassable. The basement bulged with food—sacks of beans and grains, seeds for sprouts, the fruits and vegetables I had canned, bear hams, potatoes, onions, carrots. A mountain of firewood outside, split and dry under tarps. In the year that was ending, we had been challenged beyond our expectations. Our successes fell short of what we hoped, but also landed solidly enough in the direction we want to be going.

The sounds that night were house-sounds: my boots on the linoleum, water curling into a teacup, the clunk of the kettle set back on the cookstove. The pages of Robb's book made a rich, hollow crinkle as he turned them, and the kerosene light beside him hissed. Daniel, asleep, breathed long and slow. I cradled my cup and invited the hot tea to wash over the roughness in my throat and soothe it away.

A loud thumping on the steps made us jump. Have the goats escaped and run onto the porch? Knuckles rapped sharply on the glass. Our eyes darted together for a frightened instant. Even if a rig could have navigated the road, we would have heard the ringing of tire chains and an engine. Headlights should have glinted in the window. It was not possible for someone to be at the door. Next, a male voice. "Hey! Robb!"

Robb pushed himself up from the chair, strode deliberately past the cookstove and undid the latch. I followed with a lantern. A shivering, snow-coated figure in sneakers and a denim jacket stamped once, twice, on the landing and then stepped inside.

"Hey there, Robb," he grinned, pulling off a glove and reaching for a handshake. "You said to come and visit sometime. Remember?"

No, we didn't remember. Apparently he was one of the guys who helped out Stan and Marsha at the secondhand store in St. Maries.

"Well, come in," Robb said. "I'm sorry. I forget your name..."

"Clayton."

"Yeah. Sure, well, come on in, Clayton. Let's get you thawed out."

Robb pulled a chair up to the stove for him. I added wood and set the leftovers back on to warm, handed him a cup of tea. A puddle spread out from his feet as he sipped, ate, and chatted. He accepted our invitation to spend the night.

Clayton, it turned out, had spent the day walking over the mountain from St. Maries on an unplowed road where snowdrifts can be waist-high. He arrived empty-handed because the strap on his backpack broke at the base of the hill. In the ensuing weeks, that missing gear would frustrate him enormously. *I'll be able to help out with the food when I get my pack. It's got lots of groceries... You got a nail clippers I can borrow?*

*Mine's in my pack… After I get my pack, I'll have my driver's license and I can get a library card…*It's no wonder the strap broke, what with the weight of all that pack eventually contained: art supplies, woodworking tools, chainsaw, axe, maul, wedges and the very alternator we needed to repair the truck. He had even more treasures stored at Rhonda's house. Rhonda's unfeeling mother had kicked him out.

The first morning, under direct questioning from Robb, he unfolded his plan: walk 13 miles to Frederick, find the owner of one of the abandoned cabins buried in the snow on the mountaintop he had just floundered over, and strike a deal to caretake it for the winter. These cabins all list and sag. They are in advanced stages of dilapidation and don't have any sources of heat. If this didn't bother Clayton, it bothered me plenty. Whatever lunatic things he wanted to attempt were his business, but I didn't see how his plans were going to land him anyplace but in a bedroll on my living room floor.

Thus began my winter's battle: kindness and charity against "Look Bud, I didn't ask for you." I'm still not sure which side is winning.

To my surprise and his credit, Clayton did manage to move into a cabin three miles uphill from ours. He dragged a Franklin stove up there on a sled and got firewood with a hatchet. Each day before dawn, he trudged down to our house, shivering and talkative, to shatter what used to be my sanity-saving morning quiet. I wanted to "get it," to figure out what you said to yourself so as not to mind him, or what you said to him to turn him into someone tolerable.

He is desperate for someone to like and accept him. There are things I certainly like: he shovels snow, built shelves in the basement, splits firewood. He curls up in the chair with Daniel and reads him Mother Goose. I give him food. Robb gives him cigarettes. I am disappointed by how much I hate the morning sound of his footsteps on the porch.

Over the winter we pieced together the details of Clayton's eventful life, though it's hard to pin down exactly how old he might be. He is either the eldest or the youngest of a dozen or so kids. He spent the first six months of his life in an incubator, was thirteen when he made his first guitar, fifteen when his stepdad threw him out of the house and nineteen when he delivered his wife's twins: a two-pounder and an eleven-pounder. The log house he built for "Ma" before leaving Wisconsin for good is state-of-the-art and self-sufficient—why I do believe there is even a perpetual motion dynamo in the basement. He's done stints in the Navy, in the Marines, in jail and in Hawaii, where he won something called the Hundred-Mile Marathon. Last week, someone asked Robb, "Was that guy *really* Elvis's hairdresser?"

One morning, as I remove the burners of the cookstove, preparing to build the fire, Clayton's feet predictably stomp onto the porch and my heart predictably sinks. Daniel is waking up and Robb is still asleep. I can't tell him to turn around and walk three miles back up the hill to his wet wood and Franklin stove, nor pretend that nobody's home, or that I don't get up early every day, build a fire, and make a pot of coffee and a pan of oatmeal.

I unlatch the door. He is just dropping by with Robb's rifle that he borrowed yesterday so he could shoot one of the dozen or so deer he always sees once he gets uphill and around the bend. He's returning the rifle because it's just not worth it to go through another ordeal like the one he had yesterday...

I turn my back to him and scour the firebox with a wad of newspaper, sending yesterday's ash through the grate. I'm supposed to be curious, to ask questions. His eagerness is palpable. I peek at him. He twitches his head at a crick in his neck.

I lay a teepee of kindling over the newspaper. His story escapes in hopeful blurts. He separated three deer from the herd right away. I set the stove lids in place, open the firebox door and squat to peer inside. He trailed those deer through dense thickets. I put a match to the newspaper, adjust the draft, and the flames begin to lick and crackle. Clayton's hacking, clawing chase continued. On hands and knees. I wonder if he will quit if I act interested, or if that will encourage him even more.

I rescue Daniel from his crib, change his diaper, fill his cup, stir oatmeal into a pan of water and say *un-hunh* when I can't stand the anticipation in the pauses anymore. Twigs in his face, Clayton stealthily tracked the doe. I measure the coffee, add wood, and rearrange the blaze so the cone of rising flame is beneath the pot of water. The doe, exhausted, was hiding. Though he couldn't quite make out her form in the darkness, he could see the rising steam of her breath. I take down bowls, dig out spoons, refill Daniel's cup. The doe was inches away from his face. Too close to shoot. He could sense her sensing him. Coffee. There will be coffee. Then the doe bolted. She knocked him down.

"Clayton," I break in. "Do you want some oatmeal?" I had to save him, lest he drop the useless rifle, wrestle the doe to the ground, rip her apart with his bare hands and devour her raw, unborn fawn and all.

These days, Robb and Clayton have hatched a plan to earn money. Clayton is eager to prove he can outlift and outwork Robb, who has a saw and a truck. They painted "Firewood for Sale—Cheap" on the sideboards, drove into Frederick, parked outside the Senior Center and went across the street for a beer. When they came out of the bar, they stood around by the truck awhile and took orders for fourteen cords of wood. Robb saws and drives, Clayton loads, unloads, and splits. They take only cash and divide it equally: a third for Clayton, third for Robb, and a third for the saw and the truck

With his first influx of cash, Clayton went on a three-dollar shopping spree at the never-ending rummage sale in the basement of the Senior Center and emerged with a wardrobe that brimmed from two grocery sacks. Then he went across the street to Grocery City and got himself a slab of bacon, a can of tobacco, and a six-pack. He went home, boiled up a pot of snow, bathed, and brought his beers down to our house for a celebration.

Both Daniel and I wake up each morning a little bigger than we were yesterday. He's taller. I'm wider. Walking and speaking English don't interest him much. He gets what he wants without them.

The littlest one of all somersaults and dances.

That's the news from the woods!

THURSDAY, FEBRUARY 23, 1984

Last night, after all the guests were gone, Robb was still nervous and off-the-wall, being that strange guy he turns into whenever we have company. Daniel was asleep, and out of the quiet of the first moments of relaxation, Robb accuses, "You just want to pick a fight, don't you?"

"Huh? I'm tired, used up, my body hurts," I say, "That's all."

We go through the usual. "Let me rub your legs." But it's my back that hurts. His hands get tired rubbing my back, so he rubs my legs.

"Everyone had a good day here except you," he tells me, "and that's your problem and not mine anymore. I've been polite as long as I can and you're not getting around it anymore, you're just gonna get stuck. I love you and I'm getting some."

Here I am. Who's next?

Is anyone ever going to do something just for me?

FRIDAY, FEBRUARY 24, 1984

This one really hurt. But it made him feel better, he said, not backed against the wall with no alternatives.

We're driving into St. Maries, cruising the centrifugal hills and curves near the lake and he tells me he's decided to leave me, and is getting a room in town.

He can't walk out and leave me all gimped up and pregnant after he just sold the woodpile. I sob and plead. He drops me off at the co-op. Nobody there. I let myself in the back door and cry all the way through starting a fire and taking a shower. He shows up later. He's changed his mind.

Now I'm afraid. Afraid to be less than wonderfully happy. Afraid to talk about the things that are bothering me. Afraid I won't want to screw enough in the coming weeks. Afraid I'm doing the wrong thing in the arena where no lies are told. Afraid he'll find out there's no feeling inside of me, no love, no nothing.

I'm afraid I will never be the person I am trying to become.

MONDAY, FEBRUARY 27, 1984

My new game, I guess, is survival. The key is to pretend everything is just fine. Fine, fine, fine. I feel like I am on probation.

I lay in bed last night unable to sleep, thinking "How am I ever going to get through this night?" I wanted to scream, "Lemme outa here!" and at the same time had no idea what the "here" was that I wanted to be let out of. No, I can't leave. The one who is pregnant absolutely cannot leave. But that doesn't matter. I don't want to leave. I will not solve my problems by running. I will stay and learn what is to be learned.

For a while, anyway, I'm going it alone. Put up with his crap. Spread my legs as required. He says he wants me to beg. I don't know how to beg for respect and tenderness. I hate it, but I don't have any alternatives.

And certain moments are jewels I would never trade. Like sitting on the floor this morning, streak of sunlight on the carpet, Daniel's uncertain fat-legged steps turning him into an upright being.

WEDNESDAY, FEBRUARY 29, 1984

Someday we'll laugh about how we couldn't tell green wood from dry and got the woodpiles all mixed up.

And we'll chuckle over the weird panic we felt when we thought that somehow $1200 had disappeared from under our noses.

I'll look back on those early winters spent cooped up with kids.

I'll wonder aloud how I ever made it, but I already know the answer. Just like you always do—because you have no other choice.

TUESDAY, MARCH 6, 1984

Raspberry tea on a spring-like day. Feeling better. Feeling normal. Daniel asleep. Robb cutting wood. Clayton down the hill hammering.

Stuff's getting done. A few seedlings started on the windowsill. Pickled eggs. Canned meat. The loft cleared out, painted and carpeted. Goat barn shoveled out. Everything mulched.

The truck still needs a new front end. The kitchen floor is doomed to look ugly forever. The basement is clogged with stuff Harold delivered after Robb and Clayton sold him some wood—carpet, linoleum, plastic buckets, a wheelbarrow, a crib, tires, skis. I don't think we agree on what to do with the garden. I don't think we have enough penned space for the birds. Given a choice I'd still rather not look at Clayton. Robb came home plastered the other night. I was furious, but I didn't let on. We've all had sinus infections for nearly two weeks now. The legs are shot—jangled nerve endings sending messages that my thighs are on fire. I'm still drowning in a sea of vulnerability.

A baby steals your freedom, pregnancy cuts off all escape. We all know what screwing makes, and until I can find another flowchart to follow, our sex life barely exists. My enjoyment of it is certainly nil.

But the sky is blue today and we limp along. We're working together again.

TUESDAY, MARCH 13, 1984

At the bread counter. Writing things down. But I can't think of much to put. I guess I write more when things are out of balance, when everything is incongruent.

When I visited Virginia on Thursday, she used the words "alcoholic" and "Glenn" in the same sentence, tentatively, like she was trying out the sound of it. She is always clucking about his emphysema, hoping he can get in at the VA hospital and get "cleaned out." As if it's his lungs that most need cleaning.

Two things aggravate me about Glenn. One is the way he reminds me so much of all the ways my father makes me uncomfortable. A man, still groping, after 60 years, to relate on the level of feeling without ever respecting anyone else's.

Robb says Glenn is just struggling to be somebody. That's why he bullies and lectures the listeners he entraps. He fixes it so you must either listen or violate the rules of politeness. How can you insult a lonely, friendless old man?

The other grudge I harbor against Glenn is that he gets Robb drunk, and when Robb gets drunk with Glenn, he is not nice to me. Glenn sure hates women. It's hard to come home and be nice to your old lady when that's what you've been soaking all afternoon.

Glenn joke: the crummy thing about sex after 60 is the view. Laughing at that touches a really sad place in my heart for Virginia.

THURSDAY, MARCH 22, 1984

Dear Everyone,

Enter Harold.

His life story came pouring out with the first cup of coffee he drank at my kitchen table—along with all of the details of his medical problems.

"They did surgery on all of the glands under my face," he mumbles. "I can't hear out of my left ear."

He tells you stories that plead for you to see past his stumble and his droopy face to a younger man, robust, hard-working and lucky.

"I get so dry. They took out my saliva glands. I keep a squeeze bottle in the truck. But it's messy."

He apologizes for the numbness that prevents him from knowing whether the cookie he is chewing is dribbling down his chin or not.

He talks about living all over the drylands of Idaho and Washington, remodeling the dirtscape with heavy equipment. It started when he made a killing on a semi-load of scrap metal. It was enough to buy some land, which he irrigated, and sold. He bought more land, kept irrigating, eventually finding himself rich and getting richer, accumulating, improving, and leasing land on which asparagus is grown. He is proud of how he has always provided his Rita with every material comfort he can imagine.

He talks matter-of-factly about getting ready to die. Any possessions that Rita doesn't want, he is bent on giving away, and he perceives that we, who are "just getting started" need everything: rugs, linoleum, insulation, tools, windows. He has a pickup bed he plans to make over into a trailer for us and wants to give us his kitchen cabinets as soon as he tears them out and builds new ones for Rita. The most pressing matter at hand, however, is to cut down several trees towering over his house, and that's what he has enlisted Robb and Clayton to help with.

Robb regales me every evening with accounts of the day's work. The trees have interlocking branches and are pitched at dangerous angles. Robb's job is to make all the decisions about where and what to cut, ensuring that no limbs or sections of trunks land on power lines or rooftops, all the while making it seem like Harold is in charge. Clayton does everything involving climbing, lifting, or danger. Rita bustles out now and again to scold Harold for exerting himself, or to call them all inside for snacks.

"At the end of every day, Harold asks me back," Clayton brags. Rita has offered to wash his clothes.

I have met Rita only once. She came with Harold when he brought Clayton home late one afternoon. The fire had been out since morning and we sat in the deep chill of the living room.

"Oh, I collect antiques, too! You have some lovely pieces." I wondered which of our *objets de furniture* had caught her eye: the green naugahyde recliner a firewood customer had paid Robb to haul to the dump? The table Clayton built out of sticks?

She gushed about the paneling. I explained that the reason why you could see insulation between each board was because when we nailed it up, we didn't know the wet, salvaged wood was going to shrink so much after it dried out. By the time I got to the part about our plans to cover the gaps with batting strips one of these days, she was off and commenting on Daniel's charm. I wiped his nose and she chittered away, delighted to have come.

So…that's what it's like at our house.

I'm puffing out, beginning to huff.

Tuesday, March 27, 1984

"If you've ever had any rape fantasies, now is the time to get them out and enjoy them."

Fantasies? Well, the what-would-it-be-like thought has run through my head, like any woman's, I would think. Swift on its heels, the how-would-I-stand-it thought arrives. No part of you says—*Why not? Let's give it a try.*

So he came home drunk at 2:00 in the afternoon and I wasn't angry. His usual drunk, blustering inconsiderate self, but no, I really wasn't angry. It helps when it's not late at night and I'm not fried and lonely. But I didn't know there was more on the program than his mere drunken arrival.

The conversation in the bar must have been about how to handle women. *Throw 'em down. Take what you want. Show 'em you own it. Makes it kinda fun when they fight back and cry a little…*

And afterward, I was able to say some words about how, if one approach didn't work, I suppose it was OK to try another. And he did bring me a hot towel when I asked for it.

"Revolting" was the word I managed to say. "Degrading" was the real word in my head, but I still can't get it to come out of my mouth.

I hung around the rest of the afternoon unable to do anything. The dishes are still there in the sink this morning. I never made any dinner. I just couldn't. I stared at my quilt without touching it for half an hour, turned every page of the new *CoEvolution Quarterly*, let the fire go out. I wanted to go somewhere alone and safe, curl up, be warm, go to sleep and forget. I was afraid of him—afraid to talk to him touch him, go near him. He might find me appealing again. I wanted to hide.

And I was disgusted with myself for wallowing in all this self-pity and hurt. So you got fucked when you weren't in the mood. You're never in the mood. You've been reluctant for months. Don't go around with a long face trying to punish him for the part of the blame which is your own.

So I tried a nap on the floor. Maybe I'd do the housework if I just didn't feel so tired. I rolled in a ball. It was cold. Nothing secure here. He was asleep on the bench, four feet away. I wanted him to be nice to me, to be sorry. I toyed with the idea of taking a walk. Mostly for the pleasure of him waking up and finding me gone. That would be punishment, bringing more resentment, passing the anger back around like a fireball. I worked harder on the notion, tried to turn away the vindictiveness until I was sure the motivation for going up to sit by the creek was that it would be good for my head to get outdoors. Whether he woke up and missed me or not.

But before I got out the door, he jumped up and grabbed me. "Something terrible is going to happen to Pinkus again," he laughed. "You better get ready to cry some more."

Oh no you don't. That's when I got out the word "revolting." I was too sore, still, from an hour ago. There was only a half hour of daylight left and my head had been promised a spin outdoors. I got away. Later he told me he had to beat off in a towel and it was humiliating. Poor baby.

I sat around reading about Gadhafi while he read about Lebanon until it got late enough to curl up in bed. It was cold. I kept to my side, but was careful not to turn my back on him. I can't talk about this until I can get out from under the self-pity. I was also afraid of more anger crystallizing inside him, anger he would send my way.

During the night I was stroked and cuddled and murmured to. Once I woke up and he was sitting up, smoking, thinking about "nothing, just trying to get to sleep." This morning he was kind, grateful for coffee, grateful for breakfast. He snuggled up for a long time with Daniel, and then went out to find Clayton.

The question I don't know the answer to: where do I put these feelings so they don't hurt someone else later? Anger just moves around, from father to son, and now to me. I want to cry. No I don't. I refuse. I want to smash something. Not that either. I need to have this house clean and the rug shampooed before he gets back, lest I leave myself open for accusations of being unbalanced, pregnant, and depressed.

SUNDAY, APRIL 1, 1984

The Feast of All Fools

Who says I am right, that my way of doing things is the only—or the best—way for them to be? I do know that you do have to finish what you start straight through to the cleanup, or else we will be inundated with garbage.

I tell him I'm exhausted, he asks, "Why? What did you do all day?" Split wood, made soap, made bread, weeded the coldframe, kept Daniel, got two bales of hay from Delbert, went the rest of the way to town to get compost from Grocery City. The surge of anger that went through me when I passed the Silver Buckle and saw his and Glenn's trucks parked outside.

It would be odd to have an honest, un-fearful conversation about all this with my mother. Or his.

THURSDAY, APRIL 5, 1984

I get so disgusted with the part of me that can't hear the wind blow in the chimney without straining to hear if it's an approaching vehicle. The part of me that watches the clock and paces. That takes him so seriously when he says he is coming right home. The part that counts on him being here because I am lonely and want company. That runs tests on him like not telling him a single thing about my day, just to see if he asks. And then gets all mournful when he doesn't.

Give him a break. Brand new job. It's no picnic all day at that pig farm. Pressure, fear of failure—he's probably not thinking straight at all. So I should just expect him to be stupid for the next several weeks. And inconsiderate. Thoughtless. Irritable. I should pass out sympathy and understanding. But I don't know where I am going to dredge up as much as he seems to need these days.

It's not hard to make a strong argument that the asshole is me. It's so hard for me to be calm. To act like I don't care. To make the things I don't like not matter so much.

WEDNESDAY, APRIL 11, 1984

Dear Everyone,

The snow line is creeping up the hill, the creeks rage with snowmelt, and I don't know what to do about the geese. Last summer when I got them, I imagined down comforters, naturally trimmed grass, and triumphant Christmas dinners—all of which hinge on spring goslings. With the change of season, the geese have fallen into a wild reveling over the experience of being alive. They rove in a pack, strutting, flapping, bugling, and preening. Eating hail. Drinking rain. Diving into the culvert to swim under the road over and over again, like it's a playground slide. It *is* a playground slide. Daniel slaps his rubber pants in the open doorway and shouts, "Dusses! Dusses!"

Amidst all these antics, I don't see any behaviors I would call "mating." I consulted my livestock books, and although they promise it will happen, none of them are explicit about what the geese will actually do. Robb and I followed the books' recommendations and dragged a few empty 55-gallon barrels down the bank, stuffed them with straw, and hoped the wild honkers would find them inviting and safe places to nest.

To distract Clayton from expounding on what it might take to induce geese to do the wild thing, I commissioned him to repair the gaps winter has made in the chicken fence. It's time for the chickens to give up sovereignty over the garden. I can't find where they are laying their eggs, either. My satisfaction with a tight chicken yard will help me endure Clayton's bragging about it, and he can probably use some eggs, too.

So far, his chicken-penning efforts have netted mostly talk. Whenever he has a chance, he reports that he's been "watching them chickens mighty close" and was getting "more and more sure" about the escape routes they were using. He taps a pensive finger on his temple and assures me that success in the endeavor depends on "being crafty" and "learning to think like a chicken."

Last Tuesday, when tall, black-billowed clouds scuttled overhead, unloading hail, sleet, and rain between bursts of sunshine, I peeked hopefully into one of the geese's honeymoon barrels and saw a clutch of chicken eggs nestled in the straw.

I reached in to get them out, but of course these crafty chickens would think to lay their eggs in the very back of the barrel, hopelessly out of my reach, and they would think to choose a barrel whose lid was only partially cut away. I shed my raincoat and stretched out as prone as the basketball-like protrusion under my longjohns would allow. With my feet in the creek and my knees in the mud, my shoulders jockeyed back and forth, worked their way into the half-moon opening. The straw poked at my cheeks and I closed my eyes, continuing forward. When I opened my eyes again, there was nothing to see. It was pitch dark. A very large Something was blocking the hole.

I managed to feel about and roll all the eggs towards me until they touched the obstruction in the barrel's opening. Happily, I didn't squish them as I wriggled back out of the hole. Thirteen eggs.

I may not be able to maneuver like a chicken, but I could out-think one if need be, and it was time to fix that fence.

It was beginning to hail as I huffed up to the chicken yard to inspect. The last die-hard snap on my raincoat popped. I crawled into the pen for a chicken's eye view of the fence, and squat-waddled along every inch of it. The wind blew. Then a blizzard of hail, the ground suddenly white. I lowered my head and inched along the fence, arriving at a six-foot gap where the wire didn't reach the ground. I crawled through with ease, musing craftily, "I think I know how they are escaping."

Down in the wood room, peering into the contents of tin cans on a high shelf, searching for suitable nails, some cold, turpentine-smelling liquid had just poured out of a can and down my sleeve to the armpit, when a cheery voice burst into the air, "Yoo-hoo!" Shaking the stinky wetness back down to my wrist, and rubbing my arm so my sweater would absorb the chill liquid, I turned to face Rita—blue curls, polyester pants, white lace cardigan—teetering in her pumps on the uneven floor boards.

I refused to be derailed from my immanent victory over Clayton and the chickens. I suppressed my obligation to wash my hands and come up with crumpets and tea. I held up the hammer and nails and announced cheerily that I was "just getting ready to fix a little hole in the fence" and I would be right back.

I started up the hill, and she was on my heels, assuring me she would be careful on the frozen, hail-coated mud. Only this morning she went to therapy for the wrist she broke the last time she fell.

I strode alongside the chicken fence and rehearsed the process in my head: stake the pole at the base of the fence so it won't roll anywhere, then drive a row of roofing nails half-way in, all along its length. Use the claw end of the hammer to stretch the chicken wire over the nail heads, then mash them over to secure the wire. Easy enough. I said something aloud about the weather to Rita.

"When is your baby due?" she asked, as I maneuvered into a squat and jostled my belly into a position where it blocked neither my view nor my backswing.

"Next month," I mumbled, a half-dozen nails fanning from my lips. "But I'm staying active. Keeps me from getting too uncomfortable."

"I took Harold to the doctor yesterday."

"Yes. Clayton mentioned you were doing that. How is he feeling?" I froggie-hopped uphill to the other end of the pole.

"Well, the one spot in his ear isn't healing at all. He has to go back Monday. So they can biopsy it."

Pound. Pound. Two strokes on each nail drive it halfway in. "Poor Harold. This is hard for him." Daniel was awake. I could hear him beginning to wail.

"Yoo-hoo! Harold! We're up here. Don't come. It's too dangerous." Harold's deaf ear must have been facing uphill. I could hear clunking and hinge creaks in the wood room where he was looking for us.

Rita resumed our conversation. "Harold thinks it's the cancer again. I think it's the cancer. I was up until two o'clock this morning thinking about all of it."

Good god, I thought. Should I drop everything and go for the crumpets? The situation Rita is facing is not in the same category of experience as my unmated geese and escaping chickens, or Clayton's relentlessly irritating ways. I glanced up at her black patent leather pocketbook and smacked the cuticle of my thumbnail square with the hammer.

"But I have decided I must go ahead with all of the work we have started. It is the best thing to do. I know that's what Harold wants." My thumb felt drilled. It throbbed and was already turning purple. "After all, I need to live."

I fought the urge to stick my thumb in my armpit, roll on the ground and yell. Daniel's wails were giving way to screaming. "Clayton says he will keep helping me no matter what happens," Rita assured me.

Forget your thumb. It still works. Pay attention and don't hit it again. Only two more nails. Now stretch the chicken wire over the row of nails. Bend the nails over the wire. One—after—the other. Down the line. You're done. There's water on the stove. Go down, rescue Daniel and make tea.

"Oh my!" beamed Rita. "You are quite handy. You've fixed that thing all by yourself. Yoo-hoo! Harold! We're coming down now!"

Rita led the way down the hill and when we reached the gate, Harold was behind the wheel of his truck with the passenger door flung open.

"We have to run along now," she sang out as she tiptoed across the muddy road. She climbed up, slammed the door and she twiddled her fingers towards me. I raised a toast with the can of nails. Harold raced the engine and peeled down the hill, spitting mud and gravel.

The next sky explosion was sunshine. Clayton sauntered towards me. Once he figured out what I had done, he would begin expounding on the fine points of finessing chickens back into the yard, so I preempted him.

"Chicken rodeo," I snapped. "See if you can get them into the yard before they roost somewhere else."

Inside, Daniel's face was red and streaked with tears, sweat, and baby rage. His hot arms slithered around my neck and I cradled his soggy behind, lifting him over the crib railing and into my arms.

MONDAY, APRIL 16, 1984

An afternoon of sad thoughts, angry thoughts. Is it the eighth month of pregnancy that does this?

I am bracing for another down period between us. What is on his mind? I surely don't know, but when he hasn't shaved for a week, wears his coveralls to bed, and is tired, tired, tired, it's time to look cheery and have a mile-long list of things I did all day when he gets home. That's stupid, though, because one slip, and out comes the accusation that I am depressed and unhappy, resentful about the coming baby and the guy who got me pregnant, how he feels fine all day until he pulls up to the house and finds the lady who drags everyone around her down.

He said last night that he knows I find him repulsive, but he's resigned to it, that's okay, doesn't mean he's not gonna get him some of what's his…

WEDNESDAY, APRIL 18, 1984

Yesterday at dusk, Harold drove out on Hayward Pass Road, parked his truck, and shot himself.

SUNDAY, APRIL 21, 1984

We now live in separate-but-overlapping universes. He comes home from work, talking just a little bit too loud, to announce, first that he's starved and secondly, so very, very tired. "Don't know why I'm so tired." I'll bet I could find a clue behind the seat of the truck. He crams some food into his mouth and goes to bed.

In the morning, "You stay here and get some rest." He doesn't build a fire. No coffee. I am just supposed to stay in bed until he's gone. Our paths have crossed twice—yesterday morning, and last night during one of the long sleepless periods we shared. "No, I don't want to talk, dammit. I am trying to go back to sleep."

Our single daylight encounter—yesterday morning—began with an argument. He says he comes home day after day, and nothing is done and all I do is lie around and be depressed. I blew my stack. Shrieked. Any point I had to make was invalidated by my delivery. Melodrama, he called it. Hardly inaccurate.

We made an uneasy truce. Let's not be fighting, we're supposed to love each other.

After that, I went out to split wood for the kitchen, feeling uncared for, lonely, wanting only to go somewhere and hide, but willing to build the fire and cook breakfast anyway.

My back and legs hurt, my belly is stretched so taut it shines, my kidneys ache. He's made it clear that my problems are my own, that's he's taking care of himself, and that's all. I wish I could just do nothing, but I don't, and in defense of myself, as I slivered off kindling, I thought over my week.

Saturday. Helped build fence, then burned brush. Came in at dark and fixed dinner.

Sunday. Got up at 5 a.m., so sore from the day before I couldn't sleep. Made bread and cookies, piled slash in the woods, and helped drag down poles for the rest of the fence. Helped string chicken wire and set the poles, started dinner. Went over to Glenn and Virginia's to pick up chickens and more chicken wire as promised, but Glenn was too drunk to cooperate. When I came home, Robb had eaten and was asleep.

Monday. Cut and burned brush all day.

Tuesday. Went to the doctor in Coeur d'Alene. Also the grocery store.

Came home, cleaned up, put away groceries, made dinner.

Wednesday. Cleaned the bathroom. Put up three canner-loads of pork—twenty-one quarts.

Thursday. Did laundry. Started to pickle eggs, but the chimney needs cleaning and it took four hours to boil them. Got busted for being so depressed I wouldn't even make it warm in here.

Friday. The day before. I couldn't remember the day before.

I sat right down there in the kindling, laid my head against the chopping block and cried. I hadn't felt like doing a single one of those things. But I did them anyway. Maybe I am depressed. I feel terrible. I'm not looking for medals. I just think it's unfair to get busted for not trying. So unfair and so unkind that I got semi-hysterical when he came out to see what was wrong. I spewed it all, gulps and stutters, incoherent, and once again, my delivery disqualifies my thoughts.

It seems I'll never get enough self-control.

Next time we talk about this, I'll be busted for blubbering like a baby during the night last night. But it felt better. A release, like squeezing a zit. Afterwards, I was finally able to sleep.

Pregnant women get laughed at for their behavior in the last month. But the ones who roll their eyes and make the jokes don't share the discomfort or wonder about going through labor. I don't think the last month of pregnancy is much fun for anyone. Lots of doubts and fears. Will the baby be OK? Will I be OK? How will Daniel do? Long or short labor? Can I do it? Another Caesarean? Can I take it?

MONDAY, APRIL 23, 1984

Today's theme was—don't hang around and pout because he doesn't seem to have confidence in you. Don't demand his approval for your plans. If you want to be somebody, do something. Today I made bread, scrubbed the kitchen floor, scoured the bathroom, packed the hospital suitcase and Daniel's things, split kitchen wood, got the baby clothes out. He came home. "It's cold in here. Isn't there a fire downstairs?"

I've given up on affection.

Don't try to convince him—or even suggest—that his behavior is strange. Guaranteed you'll end up crying.

I think about him all day long. Want it to be nice when he gets home. Hope maybe this will be the pleasant evening we spend together. There is never any evening together at all. Quite a trick to avoid someone in a house so small. In the first 30 seconds of being alone together he announces that he's going to bed.

When it's time for me to go to bed, the last thing I feel like doing is curling up and going to sleep with him. It's such a lie. The guy won't even eat a meal with me.

I wish he would be nice.

I should quit wishing for anything from him so I'll be pleased with whatever I get.

SUNDAY, JUNE 10, 1984

Dear Everyone,

Welcome to the summer of the Shocked Rat Syndrome. You know, those rats on the short end of some psychology experiment, who get shocks they have no control over. You've seen their pictures—wild eyes and tufts of hair pulled out. Tendency to be irritable with all the other rats… That's me!

Two babies in diapers, nursing Mary, bottle feeding baby goats, milking the Mama. Duck, duck goose. Baby chicks. Dzzzat! The buzzer just went off. Mary is waking up.

Robb is now a pig farmer. Or rather a pig farmer's assistant. The sign in front of the place says, "Swine Enterprises."

Pigs do not smell nice. Especially several hundred of them. He takes a shower before he comes home, but if he forgets even to wash behind his ears, he smells like pig shit.

There are parts of this that make it a great job. Lots of free things we can really use. He shovels up feed spilled from the auger system and brings it home for the chickens, the goats, and the geese. We can feed it to a pig, too, as soon as we build a pen to put one in.

This is a great big automated operation and they don't fool around with trying to save runts or what they call "cripples." Those are pigs with arthritis or who get injured somehow. If a pig can't compete, the others crowd it out and they don't get enough to eat. Rather than let them starve or be killed by the others, they sell them real cheap. Sometimes Robb will be able to bring some of them home. We can either butcher them real little like they are, or raise them up to get bigger. It's all ham, bacon, and pork chops to me!

Good lord, you gotta watch out for Robb when he gets a new thing to focus on. Pigs are all you hear about at home anymore. It wouldn't be so bad if he didn't do so many repulsive things during the day and then come home for dinner and tell you all about them. The first day, I put a gooey cheese omelet on the table while he was talking about the thirty or so abscesses he lanced. "You should see these things—big as a baseball, and just as hard. Stick a scalpel in it and puss squirts everywhere." That's nice, dear. Shut up, please.

The next day, he castrated sixty pigs. Without a knife. That sounded real pretty, too. Wednesday was breeding day. Then you get the details of what goes where, how to make sure it "took" and what not to touch, and if you do, what will get all over your hand. On Thursday, when a sick pig laid down and couldn't get up, the other pigs in the pen ripped her open and started to eat her before she even died. Friday he was chased by a 900 pound boar. He loves it. Brings his pig books to bed and stays up half the night reading them.

Actually, raising our own pigs won't be nearly so gross. These pigs act strange and get weird diseases because they are in such terrible conditions. They call the place a pig farm, but really it's a pig factory. I'm looking forward to having a chance to rescue a pig like the one that got devoured by its cellmates and raise it up here in relative peace and prosperity. Well, until the true purpose of its life is achieved, anyway.

Little helpless creatures calling me from every direction. Jump, Mommy! Jump! Dzzzat!

TUESDAY, JUNE 12, 1984

Coeur d'Alene. Parking lot. Mary's check-up in an hour. They're both asleep. Wake them up to eat? I'd be nuts. Wish I'd brought my sewing. I can see I am going to need a carefully packed sack. Organize for maximum flexibility. Take everything as slow as it needs to go.

Have to keep track of Daniel in all this car-leaving until he gets wise to streets, parking lots, and cars. The routine: unbuckle him from behind the driver's seat, help him down, help him organize his stuff. Hold his hand, slow steps, touch the car, around to the passenger side. Let go of his hand and tether him to me with a string of words. "OK, Daniel, that's right… You stay holding on tight to my skirt like that… I got the buckle open… now I am picking Mary up…"

It's a much better day than I thought, Daniel so focused on his most precious possessions—his traveling cup and the duck. His first experiment with responsibility. Do you want me to put your cup in the bag? Do you want me to carry your duck? No way.

Duk. Duk. Duk. Cuppeeeeee!

So much to do. I guess you just have to keep plugging and not get too insistent on finishing the big picture. Or the quilt.

There, across the street in the distance, the hospital. Funny nostalgia. Because I hardly remember. The biggest thing going on, I suppose, was being in pain. I spent a lot of time with a stiff shoulder or a numb foot, supposing I should roll over, knowing how much it would hurt if I did, putting it off as long as I could. Then I would have to pee. Or someone would say, "Roll over honey, and let me poke your incision." Or belly. Or whatever else needed poking on that shift.

Thursday, June 21, 1984

The shocked rat begins to understand something of her environment. She sits at a conveyor belt of ever-increasing speed. Trying to assemble peace of mind.

Sunday, July 1, 1984

It is important to me to be able to produce many things in my home. As we go through this period of relative prosperity, people who drop by go home with a loaf of bread, a quart of buttermilk or a couple of bars of soap.

Babies. Animals. Baby animals. Who takes care of me? I do, for Chrissake. If you can't manage even yourself…

He leaves his things all around and in general doesn't do what you would do if you were him because he is a different person than you. Yes, dear, they do make such critters.

MONDAY, JULY 9, 1984

I keep thinking all sorts of things about us, our relationship, the direction of our lives. But he's too tired, too spent at the end of every work day to discuss anything. He can rally for other people, but not for me. If he is alert enough to have a conversation with me, all he does is listen long enough to interrupt. I keep telling myself to hang in there, believe what I believe, live it, try to be real, don't complain, don't get bitchy, try not to be so angry all of the time, right will prevail, believe, believe, believe. Believe in what?

I know Rome wasn't built in a day and you can't change the world overnight and whatever I ever want, I always want it right now. While I am trying, often failing, to be large enough for everything, we drift apart. I do not understand what prevents us from getting close to each other.

When we aren't angry at each other, we are afraid.

FRIDAY, JULY 13, 1984

I should be nice, not angry. But when I sweep the anger away, try to be bigger than my pettiness, try to be nicer, try to come up with a charitable thought to cover whatever it is I'm mad about… I cry. Crying in front of him just causes more trouble. Crying on the living room floor with Daniel and Mary seems sort of contradictory. Crying alone just gives me all that much more to cry about.

There is a way I would like to live. A feeling I would like to have around my home. But I am outnumbered. If I had any character, any strength in my soul, I would live the way I thought was right. If I am so damn right, I should glow in the fucking dark.

The thought of the end of life on the planet is tearing me apart.

SUNDAY, JULY 15, 1984

In another week, my parents will be here. I'm giving myself the reward now. I started reading *The Milagro Beanfield War* this morning. When it's done, I have to spring into action and shine this place.

WEDNESDAY, JULY 18, 1984

"Please don't litter."

When I said that to my dad, he looked at me perplexed, startled. It's a perceptual thing. Woodchips, decomposing hay, and manure look much trashier to him than cigarette packs or empty film wrappers. It's funny that to them, lettuce trimmings and an empty matchbook are the same. If I throw my trash into the chicken yard, so can they.

"No character," says Robb.

What are your values? they ask. What made you do this? Don't you get discouraged being so behind all the time? Aren't you worried about your cholesterol? What on earth are you ever going to do with all this food? Aren't you worried Daniel will get typhus, fall out of the loft, burn up in a fire, get hauled away by an owl, freeze to death? Do you think you'll stay here? Won't you please just talk to the priest? Do you believe in god?

"This is no way to raise my grandchildren."

THURSDAY, JULY 19, 1984

I know they are uncomfortable. I'd be happy to make them more comfortable if we could be direct about it. I think they'd rather complain—in hopes of complaining me right off this hill.

They adjusted to water conservation and the dust (sort of). But I can't get them to try bear meat or help milk the goat.

"What makes them so sure they are right?" asks Robb.

Catholics are always right.

SUNDAY, JULY 22, 1984

"What do you think of our little milkmaid?" she asks Glenn and Virginia. She who refuses to set foot in the goat barn.

She "picked up some skim" at Grocery City, along with white bread, napkins, paper towels, and Doritos, and is so pleased about the antibiotics you can buy over the counter these days.

Authority and fear. It's as though they have come here to warn us of something. Yet they remain completely unwarned of the inevitable: a total credit collapse and a nuclear weapons dress rehearsal of some sort.

For my lifetime, I am protecting myself and my children from what

I feel are the greatest dangers to their happiness—television, the public school system, concrete. I want to give them skills they'll find useful when unpredictable things happen.

I wish I could tell them in a way they could understand.

Monday, July 23, 1984

You have to keep your mouth shut or you are going to lose your medicine. About quitting IBM and leaving Detroit, about being a writer, about applying for that teaching job in Frederick—which would have some advantages. Robb would be at home. It would give him time out of the rat race that he doesn't even know he needs. Maybe he would start to do some art again. It is easier when your few free moments come during the day without the other adult around. And me, getting away from the house would be a boon. But I don't know. Home is where the gravy is.

Tuesday, July 24, 1984

Toady-fry. Boordie. Zocks. The old Daniel-words evaporate as soon as he pronounces them right. No transition. The sound of them a memory. My memory.

I am content to just sit at times. Sit and look at the trees and daisies up the hill, listen to the flies, watch the laundry flap without thinking—*bring it in, fold it, put it away.* It is too hot to split wood. If I am sitting, shouldn't I at least be reading, knitting, sewing quilt squares? I used to sit and stare for hours on the Manistee riverbank. I watched birds and nurtured the seed that enabled me to fly. Long time ago.

With all of this doing, it is easy to get behind in your reflective thinking. If you don't keep in touch with what is really going on in your heart, your heart won't be in quite the same place you left it the last time you looked.

The heart improves itself regardless of the direction the mind wants to take the rest of the organism.

Lots of times the body just doesn't want to live up to the soul.

Wednesday, July 25, 1984

It takes a special kind of person to supervise the lives of row upon row of hogs in a sunless airtight barn. The kind of person who can castrate 60 pigs before lunch without flinching any more than he cringes at the prospect of taking a few losers out back and cutting their throats. He's got to be good with a cattle prod, too. Robb isn't really that kind of person, but anyone who does that job long enough, regardless of the reasons, becomes that kind of person. If I take the teaching job, he can get out of the pig farm. It has to do with values. Values we don't want to slip away from us.

SATURDAY, JULY 28, 1984

There is always a day on which summer ends. For me, for this summer, it's today. The flies are buzzing just as hard and the heat is just as oppressive as it has been for the last two weeks, but the season has flipped. No more greening or growing. We begin the slow shrivel towards autumn. My dream is shriveled, too. Okay, so maybe it's only tabled.

At first I want to be pissed off and resentful because of Robb's implication than he can manage the house and the babies with one hand behind his back—or holding a paint brush—while he accomplishes dozens of other things at the same time. I want to get even and come home and flop and read and ignore everyone and say "anh-hanh" when he tells me about his day. Soon he'll be telling me how to grow a garden, pot a plant, sweep the floor, or whatever it is he'll think he's discovered that day. As if I haven't learned a thing or two. What the hell does he think I do all day, anyway? Lie around, be depressed, read magazines, take naps, be a cunt.

It's stupid to be angry. Either he's right, or he has a few lessons to learn. Either way, no one needs a speech from me.

No one seems to need much of anything from me. At least not the things I want most to give. But that's beside the point.

No it isn't. That is the point.

Washtubs in the garden, doing laundry and crying. Why are you sad? I'm sad because nobody wants to share my life. I had a summertime dream movie in which I starred—vibrant. Washing, cooking, nursing, Daniel playing. Late summer twilights playing music with Robb, after he's rested up from work. Old time pioneer lady with new time religious overtones. It held for moments at a time. It didn't hold.

I was going to be super ready for my parents so maybe they could see. They showed up a week early, but a week's worth of preparation probably wouldn't have changed much, only heightened the disappointment.

In four weeks, I'll be teaching school. In those four weeks, the Vision That Nobody Wanted will disappear for good. Or for the winter. Or for the next few years.

Who cares? I care. Maybe I should stop caring, because it is making me so sad to care alone.

Wednesday, August 1, 1984

Baby girl…

Don't touch the hammer, Daniel. Don't touch the nails. Those are tools. Here is a domino. I am going to put it in this ashtray.

Jonathan Jo had a mouth like an O

Enjoy your children, they say. Take every moment. You will not believe how fast this passes.

Dust between Mary's toes. Time for baths.

Daddy got stuck. In the muck. With the truck. The ducks go swimming on the pond.

No luck said the duck when the truck took a duck for the muck. Shuck shuck said the goose. Bye, bye said the truck.

Daddy doesn't talk goose and he doesn't talk duck no luck suck a truck in the muck.

Duk. Duk.

Don't touch the hammer. Don't touch the nails. Don't touch the dishes or the things. Don't touch the goat turd, chicken turd, duck turd, dog turd.

You ken toucha stick!

When looking back, you'll wish you had cherished a little harder. Difficult to conceive, but it's what they all say.

Sunday, August 5, 1984

Driving to Latah. Wide world. Pink sky. The clouds in an even single-line inscription of Arabic calligraphy balanced atop Steptoe Butte.

It was mortality that was on my mind yesterday. My own, I guess.

Earlier this week, I was crippled with the number of things I wanted to do before winter that just aren't going to fit into the time allotted. Then yesterday, Robb was dragged down by the unfinished projects, too.

No fence, no goat barn door, not much firewood yet, no root cellar…

I remembered the same feeling from last summer. You can be despondent about the "unfinished work," but you must let go and accept the way spring's wishes are always for more than a person can do in a summer. And you grow a little. One day it begins to rain, and then snow. We will settle in for the winter and it will feel abundant.

Next summer will be the same. More projects unfinished. Because more were thought up.

It isn't a very big jump to see how the same thing can happen with a lifetime.

SUNDAY, AUGUST 12, 1984

It's hard to even justify writing about having a Caesarean, not to mention figuring out what to say. People who haven't had one don't care. Either it won't happen to them, or it didn't. Women who have had one don't want to talk about it.

Nobody wants to hear about the incision, the catheter, the nurses, the first bowel movement. You want to say it was horrible, but you can't even tell people it was bad. Your baby is healthy, right? Consider the alternatives. Caesarean babies have such round-and-perfect heads.

There is a corner of the experience that is very black.

When Mary was born, I lay there on that table waiting to feel the same delirious joy that took over while we were waiting for Daniel. Even though his "birth" was surgery, the people behaved like a baby was about to be born. But for the bunch who brought us Mary, it was routine and annoying. The banter about being called for midnight surgery when it could have been "scheduled" set the tone. They were pissed to be woken up and mocked me for my silly "trying." When I told them not to start because Robb wasn't in the room yet and the guy said, "I'm not starting, I'm just getting some of this scar tissue out of the way." What they said about Detroit…

I could feel my guts being wrenched about under the anesthesia. I was terrified the next tug would be too hard or too high and the wall of anesthesia would topple altogether. I wanted to cry and plead with them to stop, but that would have been stupid. On the other side of the sheet, my guts were laid out on the table. Strapped down and chemically paralyzed—this is no time to assert yourself. You may not like it, but they are going to do it anyway.

"I've never heard anyone moan like that," said the anesthesiologist. "All the way through."

SUNDAY, AUGUST 19, 1984

For over two years now, I have been either pregnant or nursing, and that will go on for another year or more. Then that's it. I want my body back. Being a fountain of life is an experience not to forego, but a truth at the bottom of the deal is that I am a being with a life of my own, one that's all but forgotten. I want it back.

The Valley — II

I became weak and strong at the same time… I am not asking you to admire me. This was not harmony with nature, no such thing. I am saying this only so you will know how it is to become like a chicken in a cage, mindless, never dreaming of freedom, but never worrying when your neck might be chopped off.

—Winnie Louie
   The Kitchen God's Wife by Amy Tan

SATURDAY, NOVEMBER 3, 1984

The kids are side by side in the double kitchen sinks, "sharing" a funnel, a wooden spoon and two small baskets. Daniel is showing Mary how to use a funnel to fill the baskets with water. Their laughter is the same color as the sun-splashed water.

Robb is riding his horse. It's Saturday. We both do what we always do on Saturday, which is flail for some moments of peace, enough of them to make up for…for…for what? You got me.

The first five or six Saturdays of the school year we got up and fought.

I don't know what we fight about. Yes, I do. We accuse each other of being less than perfect. I have never once won a fight with this man. If I cry hard enough he stops, but if I use that opening to say anything, the fight resumes and I have to cry all that much harder to make him stop again.

I never came out of an argument so shredded before. I'm as bewildered as a declawed tomcat on his first night back in the alley. You'd think I'd quit fighting. I'm trying to. But psychological and verbal aggression have worked so well for me in the past. I don't think I ever learned any other way to get what I want.

Just because Robb is the better fighter, we don't do everything his way. He listens to me, just never during a fight. Later, sometimes, he acknowledges the truth of some of the things I've said in fights. Hollow victory. Not worth having your psyche ripped to rags for you to bag up and take home.

Thursday morning, he told me in a genuine, happy way that he is a lucky guy to have a woman like me who makes so few demands on him. It's so wonderful for him to have the freedom to develop as he needs to. All of this is evidence of my intelligence, maturity and evolved consciousness, not to mention the harbinger of the success of this union. This would be what I need to hear, except—

Four weeks ago, October 5, to be exact, I declared the battle in which I had just been shredded the decisive one. I, the loser, negotiated a peace treaty—unilaterial and silent. It said—*OK, fine, all right, fuck you. You're a rotten housekeeper, even though you think you're so hot at it. Do whatever the hell you please. I'll be home from school every day within an hour after the bell rings without having expected you to have lifted a fucking finger all day long.* I resolved to act like it didn't matter one bit. No sense changing this guy, beating my head against a brick wall. If I'd have wanted a guy who wasn't like this one, I shouldn't have had babies with him.

I did it, too. I bit my tongue at the empty woodbox and the lousy food. I lost interest in seeing the bottom of the kitchen sink. It worked until he congratulated me for it. I came uncorked and let him have it.

He didn't take one bit of it. "I think I do just fine," he said. "The kids are clean. I sweep the floor. Say what you want, there's nothing wrong with me."

He doesn't have to meet the same standards I did because he's seen the light on how unfair they were. No human being should have to struggle under such expectations. Do I or do I not believe that?

Tears, frustration, hurt, and defeat. I didn't quite start to cry. I told him I didn't want to fight. It was the truth. I didn't want to fight because I always lose. I just wanted him to start doing a better job of being a housewife. He told me he didn't want to fight, either, it was too early, and he was having trouble getting up the energy for it anyway.

The kitchen was clean when I got home that night. It wasn't the next night, but it wasn't as bad as it has been.

Sunday, November 4, 1984

Dear Everyone,

Many changes here since I last wrote. Mary seems half grown up, Daniel isn't a baby anymore, and I'm a schoolteacher again. We bought an upright piano and have started a 16 x 16 addition on the house. Robb and Clayton finished work on a small tool shed/shop last month. Tomorrow we are going to butcher our two remaining geese.

The biggest change is in the rhythm of our days. Last summer I was holding down the fort, tackling projects 20 minutes at a time in between Mary and Daniel's alternating demands, while Robb wrestled pigs all day. Now I trot off to the Frederick School to teach Language Arts every afternoon while Robb stays home and tries to juggle the household in a way that creates space for him to paint and draw.

Lots of adjustment! Relinquishing the broom (and the mop and the dishrag and the diaper bucket…) was not so easy for me. Oh it wasn't hard to give up the chores, but things didn't begin to get smooth until I accepted the idea that there really is more than one way to fold a diaper, rinse a cup, sweep a floor, spend a day with Mary and Daniel.

The fact that life is settling into its new rhythm shows up most in our evenings. After dinner when the kids are asleep, it's calm and cozy in here. Robb draws and I play the piano.

Today, Sunday, is a turnabout day. Robb went to town for breakfast and I'm burrowed into the joys of my home. We have already covered the entire Mother Goose book twice (One, two, buckle!) and kissed all the kitties in it for good measure. Bread is rising.

Mary is busy with locomotion. Daniel was seven months old before it occurred to him that he didn't have to be a stationary object. Mary has been grunting and flopping her way around the room for at least two months already. Now she has figured out that if she climbs up on all fours and waits to keel over, she gets somewhere fast. She still can't seem to predict where, but that doesn't bother her much.

Daniel surprises us every day with all of the things he learns and invents. He is mastering his animal noises. No simple cock-a-doodle-do—he does impersonations. He brings his cup when we milk the goat and always helps carry in kitchen wood. When he's lugged a stick of wood up the porch steps and into the house, then teetered it over the edge of the woodbox, he announces, "Good boy!"

His very best trick so far was the day he sneaked up onto the bread counter and fixed himself a bowl of granola—milk and all. Robb was on his way over to find our why it was so quiet and met him on the way to his little table, where he planned to dine. He even put the lid back on the milk jar.

This letter has been going on all day. The bread is out of the oven. Time to wind up, check some fires, fix dinner, do a round of diapers.

Robb came home from breakfast hours ago. For much of this letter, he's been stretched out on the bench, reading aloud the interesting facts from a history of the Coeur d'Alene Indians. He just handed me a cup of hot spiced wine.

FRIDAY, NOVEMBER 9, 1984

Hoarfrost day. A straining raven flies out of the fog, beak open, throat pulsing.

A coyote yesterday morning running across the dawn valley, shrinking to a dot against the snow.

A log truck rattles empty around the curve and hits the open road. Eunice Taylor's sturdy black purse stakes out her place in the café. Icy rain. Jim Sullivan crosses the mechanic's parking lot, red earmuffs of his fur-lined cap pulled down. Toby Caldwell, hunch-shouldered, green coveralls, on the way to the Quick Stop. Marshall's welding shop. Always looks closed. You have to read the sign.

A whole world beyond the boundaries of my skull.

THURSDAY, NOVEMBER 15, 1984

Fear is the mind-killer.... It fills up the room like the sound of a train. Awash, I was. A hot tingling in my spine sits above the kidneys, an afterglow, for a long time. Wait 'till morning and see if it's better? Run away? Tell someone? Who?

It's the fear that's so horrid. Lights-out winter-dark fear. My hands shake, there's a stab in the stomach, even now, just remembering.

Smashed lanterns, spilled kerosene afire, splintered furniture. Crash and smash.

I want to strike back when he strikes out. It's easy to think of what to say once the venom starts pumping. Which makes me think there's a choice about it. You know where that channel is, and that you cannot swim against its current. You don't have to slip into it.

How do I get out of this river? I asked myself. Pleaded. Puzzled. Desperate. Unsure. *Afraid.* Scared to death. Not knowing how many cards I held, or how powerful I was—nor how detestable.

"I know you. I see you. I hate you." Smash, ker-plash, crash. Is he going to come up and prove it or just stay down there breaking things? " I am going to destroy everything before I go. I'll break every window. Water will never run into this house again. There won't be a single rig that runs." I wish he could hear how stupid he sounds.

An attempt to talk, the mere reminder that I exist, does that make it worse? Should I disappear? Is my silence arrogant? What happens next?

FRIDAY NOVEMBER 16, 1984

I felt so out-of-body all day at school that I talked to Mitchell, the counselor. It didn't help much. At least I know I tried. He said I can come back if I want to.

He kept wanting me to state my problems in terms of Robb, where it's only myself I can control

When I tried to explain how I've been telling myself that in the face of fear you have to muster courage, he sneered. Guffawed. Made the noise you make when you think something is really dumb. *Oh c'mon.*

The nagging doubt I can barely admit is real. *Have you chosen a bad mate?* A black-and-white question.

SUNDAY, NOVEMBER 18, 1984

Don't blame. Blame gets us all a big no place. Don't blame. Just work. Mitchell asks: *Do you ever picture yourself trusting him again?* I can't have what I can't picture?

MONDAY, NOVEMBER 19, 1984

You can never say to yourself, "There! Every disagreeable thing in my day is finished." Even at 9 p.m. Quiet. Babies sleeping. Stove done, dishes. Mary will interrupt my sleep.

When was the last uninterrupted sleep? One where I wasn't braced, wasn't guilty, didn't "ought" anything, woke up, rolled over slept some more, woke, again and again until refreshed. Detroit, I think.

TUESDAY, NOVEMBER 20, 1984

Mitchell says not to accept problems that are not my own. He also doesn't give me much hope while I am looking for it so hard.

My white knight has humpty-dumptied from his horse. Makes me sad. Makes me sick in the morning when I wake up. Makes me hurt. Makes me cry, but only a little.

Wanna trust him so bad. Wanna believe every word he says. Want everything to be OK.

I have to get cracking a bit here. I have to function more.

He has a sense of responsibility. He is a nice person. He doesn't want to inhabit an ugly movie either. He has never hurt me. He has never hurt the kids.

But he did pour kerosene on the kitchen floor—and lit it.

I don't fear for my safety so much as for my material goods. For these silly journals that are my hope of being someone someday. These nutty scribblings that will become so much dust, meaningless to insects and grass.

He wants to soothe my nerves this evening. He knows. Let him do it. Give him a chance. Give him some room.

Quit thinking about it.

THURSDAY, NOVEMBER 22, 1984

I wish I could travel backwards to the day when I was flopped, sweating and sticky on the green chair reading the *Milagro Beanfield War,* and my parents drove up. Red car in the yard. My dad stumbling out and shouting my name. Busting in, like always. Daniel just waking up. A goat to milk. My mother and her tut-tut smile because I was so silly as to not know when they were coming. They were a week early and I have the letters to prove it.

It wasn't as though that was such a great day. It's just the last day I can remember when I woke up in the morning feeling like my life was in my own hands.

Encouragement is what I want. Where can I get it?

SATURDAY, NOVEMBER 24, 1984

We met and fused in four glorious days in which neither of us had any faults. It was perfect.

Now we are rats whapping on a disconnected lever.

I am lonesome. So what? I have always been lonesome.

The trick is to quit feeling angry.

Truth is—Robb understands me better than anyone else ever has.

I sure can be unkind to him. When I fail to see the person inside.

Why is he not the guy I thought he was when I met him?

MONDAY, NOVEMBER 26, 1984

"Only two views?" I sputtered, muttered, fluttered. Go away? Unthinkable. Stay and wait for violence? Equally bad, especially because path #2 is a funny way of going down path #1.

"Only two views? There must be a third."

"Do you see a third?" asks Mitchell.

"No, you're supposed to tell me what it is."

Guffaw.

TUESDAY, NOVEMBER 27, 1984

I'm so discouraged.

I try and get myself some help only to be told, it seems, my problems are coming from places inside another person I can't reach.

MONDAY, DECEMBER 10, 1984

He needs to see a shrink or we can't stay together. He hit it off with that guy at the school party. Reardon. He has to go to somebody.

I don't trust the solutions he thinks up on his own any more. I've looked to him for so long, let him make the decisions, be the leader. He's done fine on a lot of stuff, but emotionally he doesn't have very good judgments, I'm afraid.

THURSDAY, DECEMBER 13, 1984

I want to know the story of my dad's "breakdown." Robb's mother just had one.

I remember precious little. A Hallmark Calendar, blue, by the windowsill at the telephone table in the kitchen. A word in the upper left corner in each square. His perfect, even, left-hand printing. Depressed. Depressed. Depressed. Underlined.

How old was I? What did they explain?

When Delbert came up and told Robb to call home, we figured his dad had the final heart attack. But his dad answered the phone. He said if he left her alone for 5 minutes, she'd be trying to kill herself. He had to take the doorknob off the bathroom door so she wouldn't lock herself in there.

Tuesday, December 18, 1984

I feel like I go back to Mitchell week after week only to have him shoot holes in whatever nice thing I may have to say about Robb in the past 7 days. I might go in there feeling good, but I leave with a cloud called "It's all fucked up" hanging over me.

Is he teaching me to state and view my problems strictly in terms of Robb? That's pretty stupid. It isn't that Robb doesn't want me to be anybody and purposely gets in my way. He just has this mind-set that makes him stand too close all the time so I can't keep him out of my shit.

Sunday, December 29, 1984

Who's boss. That's a big issue around here. It doesn't have to be, but it is. For reasons I'm not sure I understand. Being boss, king, top dog, order-giver—all that is very important to both of us. Who calls the shots, who gets the credit. Who says when we are satisfied. Whose description is most true.

Thursday, January 10, 1985

No elves come to my house at night.

Robb is in the kitchen right now being an elf. That is called support and encouragement.

Is this a tunnel? Do I see the endlight?

SATURDAY, JANUARY 12, 1985

I wish someone around here old enough to speak in sentences would take me seriously.

I wish I was a different person. Someone who could stand to live inside her own skin.

MONDAY, JANUARY 14, 1985

Driving into the neighborhood of the medical centers is science fiction. There is no life there, only suspension of death. Fluorescent quiet in the corridors of the South Med Center. Neonatal cardiology. Dead babies. Offices. Closed doors. Translucent glass. Yes, no, maybe. Pink warm slabs of human meat. Naked. Examined.

You go there when death is your alternative and submit yourself to disrespect and indignities. *You don't like it? It's your only hope. Shall I stop or continue?* The best you can hope for in there is to force death far enough back for you to scramble away undying, to seek health elsewhere.

This is only a hospital.

Who is sick?

Only one of you can be sick at a time. You must trim your situation to match the institutional interface. Swallow some vitamin C. Leave your coughing, sniffling kids with a neighbor. Drive your pain-crazed man to the hospital.

TUESDAY, JANUARY 15, 1985

A new view of the joint. I am in charge and we all know it. It reminds me of the alone days at the cabin.

WEDNESDAY, JANUARY 16, 1985

Chest pressure? A throat lump? Why do I do this to me?

Is it because I'm concerned—or not concerned enough—about Robb, whose face is black and blue and swollen? Whose head is packed with gauze. Whose eye they "went in through." Whose brain they don't think the infection reached.

Or is it because of feeling guilty for staying home from school and not going to the hospital.

Refilling the coffeepot in the kitchen sunlight. Reruns. Wash diapers. Talk with Daniel. I have one day, eight hours, to recapture every golden moment I found in two years as a homebody.

I think I remember a lot of not-so-golden moments, too.

Nice to be home, though.

It's good to want to do many things. Some people can't figure out what to do instead of sit. I need to remember not to feel bad about all the stuff I'm not doing if I pick one thing and do it.

FRIDAY, JANUARY 18, 1985

Moments of panic. Even though everything is okay. They come in the mornings. Do the diapers. Dress the kids. Feed the animals, give them water. Get ready to be gone all day. So much to do. So you do it. Do something. Now do the next thing. Keep moving and breathe. It helps the panic settle.

SATURDAY, JANUARY 19, 1985

We step out of the car and into the last of the day's light. Jake and Daniel exchange a wet and laughing greeting. I stand in the yard, cheek-to-cheek with Mary, inhaling the winter air.

If it's going to be this hard, this house is what I want to come home to. The yellow light on their perfect faces.

MONDAY, JANUARY 21, 1985

In the bed sat this fellow, this guy who hasn't been himself since, since…since whenever that point was I'm forever trying to name… He's back. Himself. I know that guy.

TUESDAY, JANUARY 22, 1985

If Robb comes home tomorrow, that will be a day sooner (maybe even two) than we had suspected. The house is a shambles. All the things I was going to do while he was gone are started. The car is full of laundry. The furniture is partially rearranged. Diapers are soaking. Need to put on a pot of beans for the Homecoming.

Mary and Daniel asleep. It's getting close to nine o'clock. Past my bedtime.

Daniel's goodnight ritual borders on the ceremonious. Mary's is still pretty undeveloped—tired face, droopy, droopy eyes. Legs can't hold her anymore. Little tired wail. Little bit of snuggle, then *splat!* Out cold on the crib sheet.

I carry Daniel out for a pre-sleep look at the stars. Goat tracks and goose tracks in the snow.

FRIDAY, JANUARY 25, 1986

Alone is not where it's at either.

It was lonesome here without him. Sometimes it is lonesome here with him. But it's good to have him home.

SATURDAY, JANUARY 26, 1985

Time chugs. So do I.

Four interruptions last night. Twice cough syrup for Daniel. Two generic wail sessions with Mary.

You forget how big Clayton's warts are until he returns to display them in all their splendor. You'd think he'd ease into it. Nice gifts from him. I gave him socks.

SUNDAY, JANUARY 27, 1985

Much of the strangeness comes from my own head. I was "in charge" for ten days. Ten days. And I'm right back to my old habit of wanting everything done my way.

SUNDAY, FEBRUARY 3, 1985

Dear Everyone

Coffee all around. We're well into the second pot. The sound of Mary's breathing upstairs. Ray Charles and Willie Nelson singing "Seven Spanish Angels" on the radio we bought ourselves for Christmas. Daniel and Clayton discussing Gustav the Giant and Arthur the Anteater. Robb in the corner in the good light, painting. It's the weekend! These are the moments that make it all worth it. We have been averaging 2.4 such moments a month this winter.

Which is more than some people get, I guess.

Well, that Perfect Moment went the way of a pair of diaper changes, several ample servings of cereal, peanut butter, and toast. A pile of dishes. But it's quiet in the house again and a cherry pie is cooling on the counter. All stoves are poked. Maybe if I make another pot of coffee I could finish this letter.

The problem with writing letters this winter has been in coming up with a chatty and potentially humorous perspective on infection. Sphenoid—now there's a funny word. It goes along with prescriptions, nose drops, CAT scans, spinal taps. Trips to the emergency room, quarantine… It hasn't been all that fun. Just ask Robb.

The current medical report is this: All the tributaries and canals connecting Robb's sinuses to his nose, and thus to the outside world silted up somehow, and the whole system turned into an infection. Surgery removed some infection and some sinus parts. I guess you can think of it as new drain tile for the brain. Looks like it's working.

Myself, I've been busy neglecting things. I made bread last week for the first time in months. There's one tiny loaf left. I wonder if I can stretch it seven more weeks. I could spend an entire day sewing on buttons if I felt like it. Then this morning the unthinkable happened—I ran out of soy grits.

The soap I was going to make is emblematic of how things have gone this winter. The butcher had agreed to save me all his fat for one week. I was to pick it up on a Monday. That turned out to be the same Monday I lost track of the number of vials of morphine the emergency room nurse injected into the IV tube before Robb quit thrashing, holding his head and swearing. I managed to pick up the fat on Tuesday. Eventually it made its way, rendered and filtered, to a bucket hanging in the wood room. While Robb was in surgery, an icicle was born. It grew down from the roof, past the kitchen and reached the ground by curling into a gap in the wood room wall, blooming onto the bucket of fat and cascading glacially to the floor. So far it's a good six inches at the base. I'll make soap in the spring.

Clayton wasn't around when Robb was in the hospital. He disappeared last fall with a hard-drinking carpenter named Mel who had a lot of work in his hometown of Weippe. He returned the very night I brought Robb home from the hospital. The kids were tucked in and Robb had just settled in bed when a rig pulled up. "Hello! Anybody home!"

I laughed aloud. I was glad to see him. At least I would get some help.

We began to swap stories of what we'd been doing, and soon it appeared that Clayton had just gotten over a life-threatening illness himself. One so rare it baffled the specialists, first that he'd contracted it, then ultimately that he threw it off, seeing as how it was incurable and all.

It's been a winter for snow. When you get out of the car in front of the house, you climb two steps carved out of ice, walk a trail whose sides reach your elbows, and down two more steps to the porch door. The wheelbarrow is sitting at the bottom of a hole next to a woodpile that has disappeared completely. The garden fence is 18 inches high.

First we had a blizzard, then the sun came out. Shimmering crystals of ice in the starlight, frozen nose hairs, and the only temperature readings with double digits were the ones with the minus signs in front. It was so cold Clayton moved in with us. Then the clouds came back, the chicken water thawed, Clayton went home and it's been snowing like crazy ever since. So crazy that we haven't had school since Wednesday. Now, out the window it is snowing hard—from left to right. Even if no new snow falls, if it's blowing like this when the sun comes up tomorrow, school bus drivers will be snowblind and I'll be stuck here yet another day playing the piano and doing needlepointe.

The only thing going on in my kitchen right now is boiling water. Not good. The light is starting to falter. It's still snowing, still blowing. Pretty soon we'll turn on the radio to see how everyone else's lives are doing in the weather.

Clayton has offered to do a little babysitting for us. We could go down to Delbert's on a Sunday night and watch television. We could go to the Sweetheart Banquet the senior citizens put on for Valentine's day, or to the Crab Feed at the American Legion. At last year's Sweetheart Banquet, doing the dishes afterward in the church basement, someone said there's so much going on in Frederick it's impossible to schedule anything.

I'm going out for a short walk to sample this weather.

SATURDAY, MARCH 9, 1985

I follow Daniel and we slither up the draw in our snowsuits. Pull icicles out of a waterfall, crawl inside an inverted truck body and spin the steering wheel.

At the stoved-in Ward cabin we see pots with potting soil in them. A wine glass. A speckled enamel pan lid. The archaeological record.

FRIDAY, MAY 10, 1985

The purpose of most of what Robb has to say is to shield himself from his feelings. Nervous chatter for filling the silence. It's getting to where I can't stand to hear him talk. Music history lectures instead of listening to the song. The principles of Soleri light wells instead of replacing the glass in the coldframe.

The hand-carved doors in the schoolbus and the beads and velvet of the Goss Street attic in Boulder are just different versions of the house Clayton built for Ma. You can watch them both groping to know everything. No matter what the subject, either one will cover a whole lot of ground unnecessarily.

When I bring up a topic Robb doesn't know much about, he slides into it by cautioning me on an obscure detail, as if to show he already understands the entire field at that level, rather than the sketchy outline I seem to have. He can twist any statement into an area he's explored so he can inform me. How 'bout I tell him what I think? We're not talking about that anymore. If I persist, he'll tell me who said that back in the dark ages.

Talk about computers makes him squirm. He has a question. Just one. He wants in answered in ten words. No more. Of all the relevant information about computers, this is the only piece he is missing.

How can you talk to a man with his dick in his ear?

Forget about making plans together. Talk about next year or next week, and he thinks you are making accusations about his inadequacies. Mention something you might like to have, and he can run from the loft to the basement in 12 seconds, ready to flee, ready to fight.

He steps on me and Clayton both to keep himself on the top of the pile. Knowing how much Clayton irritates me, he invites him to come early and stick around when he wants to shut me out. But he'll keep Clayton in his place by "privileging" him to hear something directed exclusively at me, "Remember last night when we were talking about blah, blah, blah," inviting Clayton to listen but not speak. Clayton does all the work around here, in exchange for the "rent" on the land under the cabin he's building. His work standard is "what Nancy wants," which allows him to act like he doesn't take orders from Robb. Robb makes sure I know about his every mistake.

Even though he pretends to be, Robb is not a planner. He's a worrier. So he reads libraries of information on every conceivable topic and repeats it all back to you in overlapping circles. He still does everything on the spur of the moment, though. That's why you can buy all the materials for a project and watch them be consumed one by one for something else.

Like Clayton, this man can be worked with. When I ask him to do something (clean the chimney, fix the drain) and he promises to do it later, tomorrow, whatever—really what he said was "no"—and put it out of his mind. Ask twice in the same year and you are a nag, but I'm getting better instincts for when to say, "Could you do this for me real quick?" Musing aloud about what I want Clayton to do can make Robb spring into action. He doesn't want Clayton scoring too many points with me. That's how I got the gate mended and the piano moved.

Now they're up hammering away at the summer kitchen because it's the thing I want the most. When I talk to either one about my satisfaction with it, he'll downplay the other's contribution. A small irritation compared to the pleasure it will be to spend the summer outdoors.

Why am I writing this stuff? Do I always take up the pen to rebel? If he saw this, the wrath would be horrid. Because it's all true. Why does the truth I see ignite the mighty ire? Now I'll have to try all that much harder to nonchalantly guard this silly notebook with my life.

MONDAY, MAY 20, 1985

Learning to navigate this. It helps to know the motivations. But observation can't be the only way you relate to the people around you.

MONDAY, AUGUST 5, 1985

Dear Everyone,

It's about 7 o'clock. I'm in the summer kitchen. Both kids are asleep—Daniel still taking his afternoon nap and Mary is down for the count. Robb is off playing music with some fellas in town, and I have just finished slicing up four big heads of cabbage, "as thin as a dime" like the recipe says, and sprinkled a heaping teaspoon of salt over each quart of shredded cabbage I've packed "gently but firmly" into a crock. The hope is for sauerkraut. I'm taking a break before I peel and pickle the beets I dug this afternoon. It's almost time to milk.

Four hours have gone by. Daniel is up. After milking, we took the washtub to the creek and filled it with our buckets. He plopped the beets in the tub one by one, and I scrubbed them off. Water the color of beets and sunset. We trudged the beets back to the summer kitchen where the lantern light on Daniel's face was straight out of Rembrandt.

You should see the place now—it should be bulldozed. But there are fourteen gleaming pints of pickled beets on the counter next to the crock of someday-sauerkraut. In a fort made of chairs and blankets, Daniel is communing with his imaginary friend Michael.

Last Saturday, Clayton's girlfriend Deb slumped into one of our kitchen chairs and said, "Clayton is in jail."

Seems his truck suffered some electrical incompatibility with itself and while limping it home, he got stopped for having no lights. Turns out Clayton doesn't have a driver's license, and turns out the reason why is related to the snippet of his saga that's about "doing hard time in Texas." When he got out of the joint, he just started walking. Probably walked all the way to St. Maries. Not the kind of thing that goes over with your parole officer. I asked her how Clayton was feeling now and she said, "Real dumb."

Two days later, Robb was heading home and there he was, on foot, shivering, drenched, wearing only a t-shirt. A man with a whole new lease on life who is going to get a driver's license, marry Deb and do everything right from now on. A man with a social security number and a library card. And, spare us all, a man who can't set foot in the state of Texas.

SUNDAY, SEPTEMBER 22, 1985,

Robb has so many reasons why he is ineffective. He will always have reasons for being ineffective. I don't think he can get himself together without therapy. At present, anyway, I doubt he'll do it.

Last winter, he promised me he would find someone to go see, which allayed the fears that were crippling me. He didn't do it, but he had reasons. Good ones. Illness mostly. But his reasons are always good ones. He's smart. So am I. He couldn't get stupid reasons past either one of us.

Fact is, he threw a lantern on the floor, lit the kerosene in a rage, said he wanted to burn the house down. He splintered a chair across the stove. Nothing has happened to change what caused all that, except that he promised he'd get some help. Joke's on me. He didn't promise *when*.

I don't like living under the shadow of his instability. I don't like being the one who has to absorb or deflect shit for him so he doesn't get too pushed or stressed.

They are *his* mental problems, but they are over here on my side. I don't have many choices. (a) wait for him to solve them (b) be governed by them (c) learn to live with him (d) throw him out (e) issue another ultimatum (f) act on the last ultimatum.

Scares me to write these things. If he read them, he would smash another lantern.

Crying won't help.

Later. Insight of the day.

I have to use something other than Robb's approval to measure my competence. He doesn't give approval. He never got any. He doesn't know how it is done.

I live for approval.

Love is the thing I don't know how to give.

Of course he needs lots.

Fine pair we are.

TUESDAY, SEPTEMBER 24, 1985

You stay comfortable in a world of words by talking.

Or writing.

THURSDAY, OCTOBER 17, 1985

Swimming in the talka-walka river. Strolling down talka-walka lane. Soaring in the talka-walka sky.

Two things give the talka-walka the urge to talk. The sound of someone else's voice, and silence.

The music of its own voice talking is the sound that soothes the tal-ka-walka life. The talka-walka spills bubbles, casual and continuous, that accumulate on the surface of the brain. To you, a listener, this may seem a mental overload. Remember, he is talking about this stuff because he is *not* thinking about it. No obligation for you to think about it either.

The talka-walka is too busy talking to notice if you are listening. So concentrate on something else while the noise is going on. Read. Do long division in your head. Walk around. Walk out of the room. Listen to the radio. See how much you can get away with. You can develop feedback habits based on intonation alone—when to laugh, make a flick of eye contact, or murmur assent.

If the talka-walka starts up in another room, don't talk back. He will be in to find you soon enough. Above all, never, ever call out, "What did you say?" Don't worry about missing anything. The problem with these people is that you don't miss enough. Anything important will be repeated and repeated over the course of the next several days or hours.

If you have something truly important to say to the talka-walka, think it over carefully. Get it down to five words or less. Wait for an open-ing. Do not speak unless there is silence. Say your words and do not volunteer any more information. Your sentence has been swept into the record-and-playback mechanism and once it's played back frequently enough, it will make an impression. The talka-walka will call it a realiza-tion. Do not waste your breath by identifying the sentence as your own. You've made your point. This is all you are going to get.

For the last hour, my resident talka-walka has been reading aloud to me from *The Man Who Mistook His Wife for a Hat.*

FRIDAY, NOVEMBER 29, 1985

So this marks the weekend that... The water froze. Because he forgot to leave it running. We all make mistakes. Some of them have bigger con-sequences than others. Period. It's not that big of a deal. Carrying water is inconvenient, but so what. Lots of things are inconvenient. I'd rather the water froze than the drain. It will thaw and it will either break or not break and if it breaks we'll fix it.

SATURDAY, NOVEMBER 30, 1985

"Don't you love me?" he asked. I just don't know anymore. I don't know what love is, or what it is supposed to feel like.

TUESDAY, DECEMBER 3, 1985

What kind of a tongue-lashing can put you fetal on the floor, sobbing, begging him to stop, protecting your head as though you are being beaten? As though you can't get up and walk away. Where can I go?

Write the words down and they will lose their power. I don't remember a single one.

It began as an argument over whether I had the flu or was just lazy.

Oh, he tried to be nice later. He loves me, he keeps saying over and over. Love isn't the issue. I wish he'd pick up his fucking trash and not be such a pig. I wish he didn't demand attention all the time for lack of anything better to do.

Oh, I am so tired of him.

Give him a break.

I can never figure out which should be the last word.

SATURDAY, DECEMBER 7, 1985

Try to think of depression as an illness. This is a guy who gets depressed and angry and hurts the people closest to him. If he isn't going to take steps to get un-depressed and quit blaming me for it, he should leave.

Because I don't care about him?

Yes, I do, but the bigger issue is self-preservation. In its name already I've put up the big walls, thick as can be. No love can get out, but no hurt gets in either.

I want to let some love in.

I've gone too long again without anyone to tell me I'm worthwhile.

I want to be comforted and soothed by someone who isn't asking, "Am I done yet?"

Four years we have been together. This is only the beginning.

People with little hippie cabins and preschool children do split up, you know.

Oh, it's pretty amazing how little I have to say when I quit bitching about Robb.

Go fetch some water.

TUESDAY, DECEMBER 10, 1985

If he's going to walk on me and be critical and unfair all the time, well he is, and there's no sense making that the focus of my life.

A doormat is a doormat is a doormat. Might as well be a cheerful one.

I keep thinking that if I give him enough room, maybe he'll grow up a little.

I can't figure out how he manages to make coffee that tastes like aluminum oxide, time after time. After time. He doesn't mean to. The living room is clean. The kids meet me at the door in their smocks, covered with paint and laughing. I'm in my corner. Alone.

What's the rub?

SUNDAY, DECEMBER 21, 1985

Do we understand better now what the reasons were for initiating this experiment? When we started, I think we were afraid. Running from thermonuclear reactions, either The Big One or the ones in a nuke plants and waste dumps. Not realizing until we got here that this is dump country.

Me and my notebooks. When they get to be full, I do love them. Little volumes, records, of ups, and lately, mostly downs. What I choose to write. What I choose to see.

SATURDAY, JANUARY 11, 1986

Dear Everyone,

Clayton is driving Robb to Coeur d'Alene to get his arm checked out. (It seems to be healing nicely—details to follow). The kids are asleep. I should probably check the downstairs fire—and wash up the last of the dishes, and carry a little more wood into the basement, and take some clean water up to the chickens, and fill the lanterns with kerosene... But enough is enough. The plan was to start this letter when all of the chores were finished. I did the breakfast dishes, fed the horses and the birds, swept the floor, carried in some kitchen wood, put innumerable things away, dusted a little, fixed lunch. *Just these few little things and then the rest of the day will be mine.* The next thing you know it's time to light the lanterns and serve dinner. Story of my life. Well, story of my Christmas vacation, anyway. I'm back to school. Now it's the story of my weekends.

Weekdays, I rise first, build the kitchen fire, and do yoga until the house is warm, the coffee water is boiling and the oatmeal is cooked. I spiff myself up for school while the car warms up, and head down the road just as the rest of the household is coming to life.

Daniel and Mary have figured out that I'm hanging out with other kids when I go away every day, so the new household rule is that I must deliver up all the songs I sang and stories I told for the kids-at-school. I've arranged to "store" the school piano in my classroom and added Joni Mitchell to a poetry unit so we could sing "The Circle Game." Mary and Daniel call it "Round and Round" and twirl themselves dizzy when I play it for them. When the class was trying to delve the secrets of "American Pie," I invoked artistic license and stuck to Doc Watson and Malvina Reynolds at home. They think the kids-at-school read Winnie-the-Pooh.

I've tried to explain to them that when Christmas is over, you don't sing the Christmas songs anymore. My refusal to participate just makes them perform with compensatory gusto. In fact, as I typed the last paragraph they were singing Rudolph (also known as Froggie Christmas E) in their beds. We always call it a night with Brahms' Lullaby—the John W. Schaum version from my long-ago piano lessons—sung in the slow dance of final smooches and my crawl across the loft, with the last syllables delivered standing on the ladder. Froggie Christmas E is their encore.

The broken arm. It was not part of the plans I had made for my Christmas vacation. Plans like sewing, writing this letter, and other things you might do sitting down, including riding the new horse.

During the week I was counting the minutes until vacation, Robb was working on Christmas dinner—a roast suckling pig. Daniel and Mary, the detail managers, appreciated every aspect—butchering, scalding, scraping, trimming. They had questions galore, mostly having to do with the particulars of how you turn a dead pig into something to eat. They were truly bonkers on Christmas Eve, running around the kitchen, reporting to one another, to Robb, to me, to the dog, to the walls, and even perhaps to the pig, every detail and possibility for its final presentation. "Now he's putting *pineapple* into it." The apple in its mouth nearly made them swoon.

The next day, our guests began to arrive in the afternoon. We chatted and relaxed, slowly trashing the house, dirtying every dish and flat surface the way you do when it's Christmas and you don't have to go to work again for ten whole days. We ate quite late at a large saw-horse and plywood table in the new addition, which, over the course of the fall became Robb's studio (below) and our bedroom (the loft).

Of all the smiling faces admiring the pig, the two sweetest ones, by far, were the ones with the round eyes and fat cheeks. They were radiant and giddy, squirming with excitement. Wearing their Christmas socks, Christmas slippers, Christmas pants, Christmas shirts—even Christmas underwear.

When Robb began to carve his masterpiece, Daniel made a speech.

"That pig is *dead.* It was *really sad* to get dead. The blood ran out and ran out and ran out until there wasn't any more blood and then it couldn't be sad. Daddy pulled *all the hairs out* and he took out all the guts and Jake got 'em and ate 'em and he pulled the *backbone* out and its *eyes* because those aren't the pig's eyes, those are cherries. And then he p*ainted* it with honey and soy sauce and cooked it in the oven *all day* and now it's *pork.*"

Mary didn't distinguish herself until later in the meal when we became aware of a silence from the place of that little girl who barely stops talking to breathe. Not exactly silence. Quiet grunting and slurping. Face in the squash and gravy and potatoes, she was eating "just like Jake."

After dinner, the adults sipped and digested. Mary and Daniel stole to the bread counter and feasted on Christmas cookies. It was really late when the last folks left. There wasn't a clean dish or a stick of wood in the house, but we didn't care. We blew out the light and went to bed. We knew where the grindstone was. We'd throw our shoulders to it tomorrow.

Robb got up early because a friend was coming by at seven o'clock to help move some hay. As he rumbled from the covers, he said he'd build a fire. I sank back to sleep knowing I would open my eyes when someone placed a cup of steaming coffee in my hands. The next instant was the crash.

From the wreckage below me, I couldn't tell if Robb or the ladder had fallen through the table first. Under the spatter of broken dishes, squash, and black-eyed peas, was a bleeding pretzel-shaped figure on the floor who was moaning, "I think I broke my arm. I think I broke my arm." The first problem was how to get me down.

It was nearly noon before we showed up at the doctor. While Robb packed snow around the purple lump rising on his forearm, and the kids admired the cut on his head, I dealt with the horses. The addition of the new horse had caused a lot of ruckus and broken fence, and they needed to be secure before we went away for the day. Somehow we all got in the car and headed away just as Robb's friend was showing up, hours late.

Not until the next morning did I begin to clear what was left of Christmas dinner off of what was left of the table. Hay to move, wood to chop, horses to manage, fence to fix… Poor Robb, lying on the bench, holding his arm, reading a book, napping, taking his pain pills. *Oh, Honey, you poor thing. I wish it could have happened to me instead of to you.*

What a vacation! Makes me tired just remembering it. I'm going to bed.

SUNDAY, JANUARY 12, 1986

A wrong-season housefly traversing the wintertime pane. Contemplating taking off backwards?

MONDAY, JANUARY 13, 1986

Trivial Pursuit last night. Lost two out of three. I was surprised by the impulse to cheat. It would have been so easy because Robb doesn't really pay attention.

It's like Scrabble and other so-called games for smart people—inconceivable that I don't win.

Hmmm.

TUESDAY, JANUARY 14, 1986

Twisted Sister, Boy George and the rest. Being odd, being startling, being brief. The instant obsolescence that television makes.

Who is under the Big Bird costume? Who is C3PO? Where is the pulsing human light?

WEDNESDAY, JANUARY 15, 1986

Mathematical chaos contains zones of lovely regularity and tantalizing predictability. You follow the trails, and the regularity always dissipates to a random unpredictability, from which a new regularity emerges. You cannot go back.

You think it is a road, but it it's a one-way mathematical lock.

You think it is a road, but it is a door.

You think it is a road, but it is an encryption.

Sooner or later you can lock and lose so many keys that whatever you had is beyond irretrievable, and forgotten.

Like that precious inner glow I always used to sing about.

Tee-hee. Here comes Clayton. Hahaha. I'm up here. He can't find me. I don't have to listen.

FRIDAY, JANUARY 17, 1986

I feel like a matrimonial chariot designed by Tom Sawyer and Huck Finn. Trailing baggage and garbage attached with cheap string and good knots. Plastic toys. Students. Laundry. Waves of words. Need to pull off this outer layer, leave my boots in the mud and run away barefoot. Shed my locust skin and somehow trick the leeches into not noticing it's hollow.

SUNDAY, JANUARY 19, 1986

Splitting wood and thinking. Being angry because I couldn't find the ax or the maul because he had no doubt come out here to "help" by putting them someplace artistic. Resisting the urge to tell Mary her daddy is a fuckhead. They were leaning against the wall right where I'd left them, hidden by a little dusting of snow.

I split all the wood. What a bundle of conflicts. I wasn't willing to work very hard, but I wanted him to think I had. Why didn't I want to do it? I *like* splitting wood. Why was I such an asshole about it?

MONDAY, JANUARY 21, 1986

Does Robb need a life of his own or what? He doesn't even *like* mine necessarily. He doesn't dislike it. Up this close and he doesn't even see it. For him, there's nothing there.

Loud? He calls himself loud. That's a riot. Not a simple question of vocal volume, but physical volume, too. Oppression.

But oppressive men have always been oppressive. They didn't suddenly become that way a year after you met them.

But he told me! That I was someone worth listening to. I believed him.

He lied.

Not really. How can you lie if you don't listen to what comes out of your mouth? If I tried to tell him he said that, he would either say that was back when he was pussy-whipped (no more!). Or that I had him mixed up with one of those dirty ass-licking hippies I'm always wanting to fuck.

His identity is so tangled up in what I do, how others see me, it's absurd. There are parts of me he thinks other people might reject. So he stands close to my elbow in public, explaining my jokes, interpreting my words—screening me.

Drives me nuts!!!

But that's just the way it is.

TUESDAY, JANUARY 22, 1986

I've got to quit disliking Robb. Of course, he's not going to make it easy. I have completely confounded disliking the things he does with disliking him.

Maybe we're just doing what all these old couples do, and that's grow apart, apart, apart while raising children. Sometimes someone with her hair dyed superblack to the roots will say he was "onry" when they were younger. Then she'll give a sideways look, and legs crossed, arms folded close to her body, lean forward and flick her cigarette ash.

FRIDAY, JANUARY 24, 1986

I think I got problems. Poor ol' Robb. Roaming the woods, the whole fucking woods, for a cigarette butt. As I write.

Saturday, January 25, 1986

Relax.

I am beginning to. For the first time in…months? Years? I have no idea. I have no idea how safe it is to let go. I just know that the thing pouring in when the walls come down is Anguish.

It can wash over me in waves while I sit on the bench, back to the woodbox, breathing. It is my secret, having this feeling. My own Anguish and no one else's.

I need to relax, I told Daniel. Want to relax with me?

He chose, rather, to drive his truck "up the hill" of my chest. I told him I didn't like that, not when I need to relax and he said, "Yes you do," and adjusted his position, digging his elbow into my thigh.

I retreated into pure feeling. What can you say when the words aren't working? I started to cry, said, "See you're making me cry." Not exactly, not really, but you're tipping the scales.

And he hunched over—blue pajamas, face in hands—and started to cry. A real cry, but adorned, too, with an edge of "I bet you can't console me."

I didn't want to do a consoling act, wipe frosting on him until he looked okay. We needed to do something together or separate.

I am so weary of being jangled.

I stood up and sat down over in the green chair. He came over, crawled up, and we cuddled. I think it all turned out okay. Who knows?

How do we all learn, the four of us in this house, to be respectful of one another's needs for privacy and consolation? To communicate our needs?

How do I overcome this feeling of Robb jamming my airwaves?

Switch to FM, but how?

A seed is a seed is a seed and it falls. But what to do when a bad seed falls on you? Be infertile ground. And when zapped by a bad ray? Deflect, reflect. That still necessitates involvement, maybe even aim. I guess you just try and be transparent.

New Year's resolutions. Nothing bothers me. And also to avoid listening to the news, and when I hear it to try not to take it so seriously, to try not to use what I hear to reinforce the notion that the world is marching towards hell.

Writing down words. Dopey, spewing, unimportant, rational, but not particularly crystalline words. Why?

Because writers write, that's why.

I'm late for bed.

Or something.

WEDNESDAY, JANUARY 29, 1986

Clear frosted mornings. The hillside remains white, which is every color, finishing in afternoon rose. Sleepless nights warmed green and blue in the moonlight.

A lady in the woods for a January moon. An Aquarian moon. An inaugural moon. A champagne and weenies moon.

SUNDAY, FEBRUARY 2, 1986

Don't understand, down in the basement, Daniel and Mary helping, bringing oranges and canned goods up to the kitchen. A sudden lump in the throat, hard to breathe, want to cry. Sudden. Sudden. Why? Why?

Happened to me the day before yesterday, too. Borders on panic. Instead of anger? Resigned to doom. Wish I knew. Wish I knew

Or do I?

The reason why Kentucky is such an incredible place peopled with unique individuals, families, and lifestyles about which all of us deserve to be educated, is that he's been there and no one else has.

Just like Clayton's Wisconsin.

Drives me nuts. But I'd rather hear that than a discourse on women's sexuality.

TUESDAY, FEBRUARY 18, 1986

When he fixed himself a sandwich and ate it in front of me while I was helping the kids with their pajamas, I just wanted to cry.

This guy doesn't have any tact.

Oh shit, I'm mad as hell I am in this mess. This relationship.

I'm sick and tired, and in *sick from* and *tired of* placing his "satisfaction" first—not for him, but out of self-preservation. Out of fear. Fear of the unknown, this huge part of him that is destructive and determined not to be self-destructive again.

On the other hand, he doesn't want to make any waves, so there's no reason a creative person can't navigate around him.

Always end on a positive note.

THURSDAY, FEBRUARY 20, 1986

Things I can't do by morning:

• Play "Roll 'em Pete."
• Understand my professional life and feel comfortable in it.
• Feel safe.

TUESDAY, FEBRUARY 25, 1986

I've been getting away a little for myself lately. Little private secrets all my own, mostly in the form of a quilt whose pieces I am sewing together unbeknownst to Robb. Not that there's anything to hide, but I am figuring out this feeling of transparency, of my life being a wide-open book awaiting fingering, violation. I can't retrain the fingerer, but I can put private pages in the book.

Sad, but true—between him and the kids and my always being either within earshot or out in the cold—there's no privacy for me in this house.

But I can make privacy inside my own mind.

SATURDAY, MARCH 8, 1986

Irelands Café. Potlatch. On the road to Moscow.

"Oh, I'm sorry!" I said. It's as good as anything to say, I guess, when one is on the throne of the WC and the door opens. One *is* sorry. Sorry one forgot to latch the door.

Sorry it made me hurry. Upset my aplomb. Forgo hunting a comb for my hair, or scrubbing the dirt from my nails. I couldn't make the soap work. I could see the soap in the dispenser. I pressed the "here" of "Press Here." It had to be true. They wouldn't lie about it unless this was *Candid Camera*.

A single iridescent yellow glop oozed out. Guess that's it folks. I flipped on the water and the misdirected spray ricocheted off my hand and soaked my jeans right below the zipper. Great. Looks like…well, you know. I pulled my sweater down tight, looking like I was trying to hide something, with the something I'm trying to hide clearly visible.

Talk at the next table. Golf, pool. Rumors of corporate maneuverings at "Allied Nukulur." Interstate Trailer going broke. So-and-so's been on the wagon nigh on seven years. Never knew him to take a drink. Never missed a thing. A hundred and twenty million it would take to get the mine in Kellogg on line again. Price of silver'd hafta go way up. Oh, it will someday. Silence—their food arrives.

A whole languid University of Idaho library afternoon.

Now a short stop in the trendy café before driving north. It's Mardi Gras. All of the trendy Moscow people dressed in trendy black and white, sipping trendy chablis before they make their trendy way to the Black and White Ball. I'm wearing a red sweater and drinking coffee. I behave as though I am not out of place. It is an act.

Yuppies. Clean fingernails and shiny hair, long on one side and short on the other. It's way too much for me, this city life, this being hip. They are fun to watch, to frame in imaginary photographs. Pair after pair of eyes catch you. You duck, smile, parry. Don't want to deal with their picture of woods mama and earth muffin, or English teacher in Frederick.

The *Utne Reader,* the verra-verra best of the alternative press. Not for dimwits, either. All the must-must know for a yuppie-on-the go. In flight bags. The outhouse. Quotable.

You read it here first.

Either here or in *CoEvolution Quarterly.*

Have *you* got the whole collection?

These noisy, noisy men and the relentless engine of their ego trips.

Thursday, April 3, 1986

Jake barks. Robb, "asleep" upstairs, bounds down and outside. When he comes in I get a lecture on why it's important to go see what the dog barks at. With footnotes on the type of bark it was and ergo the precise critter it must have been—scent only, of course. Otherwise he'd have seen it.

Oh, I dunno. This is getting out of hand. I just don't have anything else to think about. Everything on the list of interesting topics in this household (the south, politics, painting, horses) bores me to tears.

Yes, tears.

Chew off your foot and the trap will stay behind.

MONDAY, APRIL 14, 1986

It's a little hard to believe I'm sitting beside the coldframe in the afternoon sun, Mary and Daniel splashing sticks in the buckets of water, some seeds already planted in the garden. Another summer within reach. The same yard that had so much snow. The life grows larger. To the garden, to the clothesline, to the ponds and the summer kitchen.

Mary in sneakers and overalls. Daniel the ringmaster. *Who's doin'? Wanna help me throw rocks?* Two very busy people

It's feeling better again.

Last Saturday, when Mary cried and spurned all my food offerings, I slumped into the green chair with the intent of sulking over a ruined morning. Somehow I got myself outside, turned dirt in the garden, planted lettuce, spinach, radish, carrot, kale, broccoli. The day regained, the bad start forgotten. The moral of the story is: if you want to feel good, do things that make you feel good. So simple.

TUESDAY, APRIL 15, 1986

Journals. He says they're only for angry feelings. Not true. At least not all the way true. But he knows everything, so...

So... what???

The taunts in my head when I write such things. The taunts from the part of me that's afraid he'll read this and get angry. I am afraid of his anger because I have seen how angry he can get. He's promised he won't hurt himself again next time.

THURSDAY, APRIL 17, 1986

I have been in this spot before. If I've learned anything, it's that I can't fill the hole inside of me by running out and getting a new boyfriend.

I don't know what it will take to make me feel better inside, to laugh and have fun.

When I'm not blaming Robb for everything that's wrong, I'm blaming my mother.

SUNDAY, APRIL 20, 1986

Sure was bitchy this morning. Started up last night. I get bitchy every time I work hard. (True? Dunno). I sure worked hard yesterday. Got going and couldn't stop. Four wheelbarrows of kitchen wood. Filled the basement with big wood, only two at a time because my arms were so tired. Diaper changes...

Transplanted seedlings with Mary and Daniel. Get the shovel, not the woodbarrow, diggen inna dirt. Finda hoe, throwa stick inna water. Looka broken goose! Bangen onna barrel, climb-a stairs to the smoker. Looka nother one Jeep! This goose not broken. Scoopen onna compost, cover the loveage. Love-itch.

So it goes. Checka spring. Looka wood pile. Can I throw rocks in this one water? Saw Jack Matthews. Biscuit crumbs. Kitty walken onna log.

So many topics of conversation. Uppa hill and back arounnn! Goodbye house! Goodbye summer kitchen! Runnunn downa road!

A visit from Delbert. Dinner flopped. Maybe that's when I began to get bitchy.

I get crabby every time Robb starts to talk. I am so angry and resentful for all the times I have listened to him when I didn't need to, or when he wasn't making sense, or when he wasn't listening to himself, or when I just would have rather it was quiet. Now I keep score. That's not fair.

SUNDAY, APRIL 27, 1986

Whole family on a spring day, helping out in Glenn and Virginia's garden. What have I learned since the last season?

I think I am a lot less frightened that my life—friendships, obligations, what people think of me—is going to fall apart on me if I don't keep every aspect of it clamped in place.

FRIDAY, MAY 23, 1986

How are you today? Just fine. Feeling jolly. Woke up with a stiff neck headache, but that was this morning and some tylenol put it behind me.

Change comes so slow. That's what I mind. I'm also always wondering if I've compressed myself into a nobody. Yes, dear. Of course, darling. Sure you are, honey—so bright, wise, witty, wonderful. Love to hear whatever thoughts are coursing through your head tonight. Anything you say, sweetheart, as long as you don't throw another lantern.

Eat it, mommy, eat it.

Full moon.

11:46. What am I doing awake?

Sunday, May 25, 1986

There is a messenger service of black ants running the wall next to me. Up and down. Up and down.

A bird works all day and in the evening sits on a branch and sings. I work all day and sit on a bench and fret.

If Robb is going to talk so much, I wish he would say something. I still wonder why I let it bug me so much.

Because he knows everything and I don't know jack shit and I'm tired of it. The only time he ever gives me any credit for knowing anything is when he brags to someone how he's caught himself a smart woman.

Caught is right.

I want to be light-hearted and funny again.

The breeze tonight is warm. The moonlight is exquisite.

Saturday, June 20, 1986

You won't get it together to build a barn and a fence before winter, I nearly said. Not if you won't get started before ten, won't work in the hot part of the day, and have a beer on your breaks.

The reason why you don't say such things out loud came strolling up the hill yesterday in the form of Poli.

Domestic troubles. Such a clean phrase. It leaves out the feel of being on the receiving end of the backside of a shovel. A sound—and then is it black or all colors?

Domestic troubles. Visible and invisible scars and bruises. The excuses you make for them.

Men can be tyrants with impunity. Not until the walls blow off the sides of the neighbor's house and we fear getting hit by shrapnel or a stray bullet do we intervene. To protect ourselves. To stop the racket.

I can see where these men are coming from. Wounded, confused, insecure, trying to do OK, trying to be a success, trying to grow a big long dick. A woman can dazzle him, touch him in the parts that crave mystery, that nurture. If he accepts her kindness, she has gotten too close. A crossed eye or a furrowed brow is now a threat. All he can feel in the spot she touches is a knife. He thinks she's twisting it. He's given up his most important secret—vulnerability—and the only way to get it back is to make sure she's the most vulnerable one of all.

Helplessness. A thin, steady tone in the soundtrack. Locked up alone with this person. Hoping it won't happen again. Knowing it happened once. Wondering how you can turn the hope into trust without a blind-siding having a probability of one. Being afraid. Especially when the sun goes down.

MONDAY, JUNE 23, 1986

What horrible door opens up inside him? Don't remind him. Don't take him anywhere near the incident lest he get too much in touch with what triggered it. You might not be so lucky next time.

TUESDAY, JUNE 24, 1986

Tell me, where do you live? In the skinny space between the wall of fear and the boundaries of our lives. A small submissive corner. The only way out is to disappear. If I try to end this, he will become more violent.

How long ago, the lanterns? His promise soothed my fears. He didn't keep it.

Day after day, from fear to hope to trust. And here I am.

TUESDAY, JULY 8, 1986

When I came outside, Jake had laid waste to the beans, making himself a bed in the warmest spot in the garden. Robb had left the gate wide open while he was currying his horse. Jake always does stuff like that if you leave the gate open. I was upset.

At least he backed off from his original only-and-obvious solution and didn't shoot Jake. (Although he shot Clayton's dog last spring for less.) He dropped everything he was doing, tied his horse up where she could eat some grass, and built me a new fence to protect those dead beans. The finest fence you ever saw. Bisected the space. Five feet high. And just to make absolutely sure there weren't going to be any more accidents, no mistakes on anybody's part ever again—he built it without a gate. "You can make a ladder," he said. It's so fucking unbelievable, it's art.

A certain satisfaction did come to me, after I'd endured, "I thought maybe I could have myself a pleasant afternoon, but woah-no, first sign of a guy starting to relax, you…" And on and on. (Stupid cunt.) He finished the fence (and the tirade) in plenty of time to go ride his horse after all, but when he went back up the hill to where he'd tied her, she was gone.

Now a rhapsody on the possible tragedies lying in wait for that horse. (No discourse on techniques and effectiveness of knots, mind you.) First she'll eat enough to bloat up with grass founder and die, but before her stomach splits open, she'll step into a brush pile, wrap her lead rope around a branch, fall, thrash, break two legs and her neck. It's all my fault.

I gotta quit. Writing this is like building your own scaffold. And all the while you thought it was a trellis.

WEDNESDAY, JULY 9, 1986

Poli is, for some reason, putting herself in a position where there is very little escape. But why? Maybe she wants to die. Incredible she would go back. But she did. Why didn't they talk her out of it at the shelter? What is she so afraid of that is worse than being beaten with a shovel?

So many things to fear, from falling off the studio rafters to meeting up with Charlie.

THURSDAY, JULY 10, 1986

Jim and Hazel Caldwell.

They were married 54 years ago. She was 18 and he was only 16, but her mom said, "Go for it. He's a good one." She seems to think she was right.

He's a worker—a shrewd, practical, deliberate, smart guy. A thinker. Cattleman. Cowboy. You family follows you, he believes. She followed him all over creation.

"We didn't raise kids like you do today. They just came along while you worked."

A ranch in Nevada where she was the only woman on a hundred

thousand acres. She told the man politely she didn't care what he paid the last cook-and-bookkeeper, she wouldn't do it for less than the same pay as the men got. She started work before they did and finished later.

Now she's losing her memory. Getting frail.

"Goes down for months at a time," says Jim.

FRIDAY, JULY 11, 1986

When will this be over? When Poli comes out in bits and pieces? Shouldn't someone go down there and make sure she's all right?

Somehow the hole turned into a pocket. There she is still, back to the wall.

SUNDAY, JULY 13, 1986

Fearing
Daddy's tools
and daddy
fear itself
doan wanna get hurt
never really got hurt
world without end amen
the end

TUESDAY, JULY 15, 1986

Poli says she would never, never go back to Korea. "Too a-shame."

TUESDAY, JULY 22, 1986

Vietnam. Ten years after. After the famous last helicopter lifted off the roof of the embassy in Saigon.

Triumphant she walks, the winnah!!! Struts across the deck of the summer kitchen with a clean empty bread pan in her hand and the perfect loaf standing on edge amidst the rolls, the flour-covered rolls.

Anyway... There are yo-yos in the Pentagon who say they're prepared for the next one, know what to do in the jungle and are eager to have a hand at tunnels again. So stupid. Can't they see that their next war will be a terrorist one?

MONDAY, JULY 23, 1986

Saw Teresa. Get together with Jan Matthews to play music at the Silver Buckle? Gotta be kidding. Robb would go through the roof. If he gets jealous over the imaginary Michael or my spending a day making sausage with Virginia, well, I can already hear it about playing music in a bar. That particular way to pass the time isn't of major importance to me, but the issue of doing what I want with my time and being trusted sure are. Why wouldn't I be trustworthy?

But I also have to accept this man's limitations. If I don't want any more lanterns broken.

THURSDAY, JULY 24, 1986

Full moon two nights ago. Bright light all night still. Sleeping badly. Not his fault.

He brought up my journal again. "People read it, I'm sure." Mild accusations of leaving it around. Anyone who comes in here picks it up like a magazine. Not true. I keep it out of sight, always.

I'm sure it threatens him. He certainly doesn't like it.

So he gives me the creeps about it and maybe I'll quit.

If I really wanted to be a writer, I'd not have set myself up against these odds.

SATURDAY, AUGUST 9, 1986

OK, so I did it. Met Jan and Teresa and played and sang in the Silver Buckle. Without a scene. Without shouting. Without insults. Without slandering my mother. It's progress. I couldn't picture that happening a year ago.

Of course they would like to see me defy him and play every week. Maybe I would if I wanted to bad enough. I want to finish the needlepointe, too.

TUESDAY, AUGUST 12, 1986

Mr. Crisis rides again. Gee whiz, drive me nuts. When he's not handling one, he's averting one. And all the rest of us just hang around and cause them when he isn't looking.

While I make my daily rounds of food, diapers, kids, dishes, laundry, and garden, I am unmercifully insensitive to the extreme tension under which he is required to work at all times.

Monday, August 18, 1986

This is one of those passionate, arty, dynamic 5-dimensional relationships wavy-haired women in twin sets and pearls had with cigar-smoking mustachios in tweed pants. Candlelit cottages on windy nights in Maine. Before Roosevelt. We're trying to do it now. In Idaho.

Wednesday, August 20, 1986

We spend whole days walking all the way to the bitter edge of giving up. We cast a glance over the railing, and by nightfall have plodded back to the cave. What we do for foreplay.

The Valley — III

We always made it up in bed, but I've had enough...

—Katrina Benasco
Willow Field by William Kittredge

ENGL/HIST 504: The West and the American Imagination
Weekly response
Week 3: The West in Film
July 23, 1987

Since this course began we've traced the gaze of Manifest Destiny, questioned the motivation of photographers, and peered into scenes conjured by Flannery O'Connor, Eudora Welty, William Kittridge, and Edward Abbey. John Muir has clung to the top of a wildly storming pine. Lewis and Clark have pissed on the continental divide. We've stopped to analyze images: clothing and landscape, the use of black and white. We keep asking the same questions: How was/is the West imagined? What are the roles and symbols?

Examining the West of my personal imagination, I'm sheepish to find it's drawn from my childhood reading of the *Little House* books, *Caddie Woodlawn*, and *Marilyn and her Kettle Named Maud*. This is a West of fresh air and deep snow, where the work of housekeeping is arduous and satisfying, and the most magical roles of all are played by resourceful girls who live happily ever after. I headed West feeling brilliantly original, but it turns out I'm just one more in a two-centuries old caravan plodding towards the wide open spaces beyond the sunset. The plan is always to do better than those left "back East," and better than whoever it is that's already out there, scattered in the few outposts between vistas.

Next stagecoach stop in our quest for the West—a screening of the film *Heartland*, which I have already seen.

Heartland is the story of a woman from Denver, a widow with a six-year-old daughter who answers an ad to be a housekeeper for a homesteading rancher in Wyoming. It's not easy. They are both headstrong. They live. I saw the film six years ago, before I moved to Idaho. It helped inspire me to seek meaning in a life that was rough-hewn and terse. I didn't want to watch it again. I didn't need to watch a woman collapse into sobs at her clothesline while her man and child watched.

I crept into the auditorium as Annick Smith, the film's producer was introducing herself. There stood a woman who had everything: a ranch in Montana, the company of poets, integrity, recognition, and a dead husband. Her tone was personal and her presence, authoritative. I, too, have round glasses and a big carpet of hair. The rest of what she was wearing—long denim skirt, leather vest, boots that wrinkled softly at the ankle—would have made me look like a pack burro.

Heartland is based loosely on the book, *Letters of a Woman Homesteader* by Elizabeth Pruitt Stewart who really did go to Wyoming with her young daughter, and did marry the rancher with whom she'd contracted as a housekeeper. Smith describes her as "a woman with literary pretentions" (note she doesn't say "talent") who wrote letters to friends back in Denver, hoping to publish them, which she did, in *Harper's*. In doing the research for the film, Smith found the daughter—by then frail and aged, living in New Jersey. Her recollections revealed dimensions to her mother's story that were much richer than what the letters alone revealed that Smith took the film in a new direction.

Smith spoke of Elizabeth Pruitt Stewart's choices with respect and compassion. She worked hard without complaining, cared well for her daughter, stood up to the rancher when he was obstinate, even when he was angry and tried to make her feel dumb. She birthed a baby alone, a baby who caught fever a few months later and died. That same winter, they lost most of their cattle. If they were a comfort to each other, this wasn't apparent from the movie.

I went home that night and began reading *Letters of a Woman Homesteader*. I was chagrined and appalled by the false and self-deprecating tone in which she wrote about her life. The way she chirped for comic effect reminded me way too much of the spunky letters I send home, stories scented with woodsmoke and larded with antics of children and chickens. Stories of making bread every week, cheese every day and jam every summer. Stories that skirt the dimensions that are unexpected and rich.

Smith attended our class the next day for a further redux of the film. She fleshed out a postscript. The couple stayed on the ranch until long after the daughter grew up and went away. At some point, they had too many bad years in a row, lost the land, and moved to town.

At the end of class, I hung back from the clot of devotees and aficionados in animated conversation with Smith. With little to add to the literary and filmmaking chatter (but enjoying what I heard) I waited until the crowd thinned and it was my turn to say something.

"I am living this," I told her. "Right now."

"Write about it," she said.

ENGL/EDUC 516: WRITING FOR TEACHERS
WRITING ASSIGNMENT
WEEK 4: POETRY
JULY 30, 1987

Poli

We built the bread counter around
my shape kneading, this dough not yet
elastic, rock on my heels, my Sunday
bread chore island of sanity.

Poli, solid and skilled in farrowing and
hogs, walks bent-shouldered
yellow slicker and pig boots
clean colors on the just-rained-
road, a return from a coinless trip
to a telephone swallowing shame and then
cries staccato shrill for rescue.

She doesn't look up.
I withdraw to my kneading.

In four more bends she
and the soft washed road reach
Charlie, the fenced compound and Charlie's
bald dot eyes and I
annotate my life, the dimming light
my reflection, in a bound journal
a gift, while my loaves rise.

SUNDAY, AUGUST 8, 1987

Home. Home. Home. At last. Robb's turn in Moscow now. Home
alone.

I wanted to go to the support group that met on Wednesday nights last
year at school, but I didn't feel I had a right there unless Robb beat me up.
Maybe I could have run and tattled after that Saturday morning when he
kicked me in the shin. So they could say, "Is that all, Hon?" and send me
home to try harder.

Now I don't know anything.

I used to like to write things down because I thought I was so smart.
Then I woke up and found out I was stupid, and enjoyed writing about
how stupid I was and how smart I am now. Not to mention how stupid
everyone else is. I reread it all and I just feel dumb.

Do I make any progress? No! I'm still just Nancy Nugent who doesn't
have a date to the prom. Eating sterile dinners under a chandelier. The
wallpaper mural of a plantation scene was scraped off the wall by the
new owners when my parents moved to Dallas. There was only one
house with four white pillars in the whole subdivision. There was only
one discounted Priscilla wedding gown, a sample, our price range, size
little. Of course it fit. When you are trying to lead a charmed life, you
stop for everything that seems to fit.

These aren't the things I sat down to write. I was going to pen the
beginnings of a masterwork about a woman who is dumb, dumb, so
deeply dumb, recognizes it, writes oh-so-elequently about it—oh look!
the smartest kid in her class. The only kid in her class. The rest have become adults.

Clever, clever pittycrap.

I have a yeast infection. The first one since a long time ago. *Nature's way of telling you something's wrong*, the radio sings at me. I don't see why I should listen. At least I have some yogurt tabs to treat it with. Capsules, acidophilus would have been better. I'd order some, but I'm never going to need them again, am I?

Oh no, of course not. You're never going to do that again, are you?

Do what?

Make a conquest? Prove to myself I could still get a date? (When will I learn that anyone can get a date?)

Feel lonely and confused and give into it?

Seek relief where it ain't? In a diversion, an amusement, an experiment, a dare. In a reaction to something.

Demand to know the rules of our relationship.

Ruby don't take your love to town.

What a stupid story this is, and what a stupid storyteller.

Boy am I fucked up.

So what was it I got to do with that laughing boy? Lie naked in the starlight (streetlight, my dear) and reassure each other that we were essentially loveable. Kiss and snug and pretend we were in high school. I kept detaching myself, asking if I was enjoying The Forbidden. Was it worth it? At that point it didn't really have any consequences. You never get a very clear idea of the consequences when someone is stroking you and telling you how beautiful you are.

So what'sa matter with curling up with someone who'll say you're wonderful and only show you enough of himself to make you feel the same about him? It was great. I never made a mistake that didn't start out fun. All fun things end up to be mistakes? All fun things don't stay that way. Life is hardship and pain, you endure, and when you're old you look back over it and say it was all worth it because you don't want to die a fool.

What was so great? Having a man look at me and smile. Yikes, I ate it up. It surely wouldn't have been the same if he had bad teeth. I was careful about what to look at.

Is there a way to be sorry without needing, wanting, oughting to punish yourself? Is it possible to have other things to write about than whether I am right or have been wronged?

If only Delbert hadn't grabbed at my ass at the hay barn. I was angry because I felt maneuvered out to the barn alone with him. Somehow going alone with me to the barn was the price of the favor of his help with the hay while the other visitors entertained Robb who was flat on his back. It wasn't like all those other times in the kitchen when he'd tell me how I'd-a not been able to resist him if he was just a little younger. That you can laugh off, wave him out the door with a dishrag. This, I felt like currency in a deal. If I didn't stay there and do the hay, I'd have to tell Robb why.

If only all the school weeks could have been like the first one: leaving for Moscow early on Monday morning, staying focused on school so I wouldn't be bring work home on Friday. Playing with the kids all weekend. I actually enjoyed hearing Robb read me the highlights from the course packet about the West. Night-rocking in the source of our connection. Then what? If only.

If only there hadn't been a note on the table when I got home the next Friday saying he was in the hospital with screaming back pain. If only.

If only I didn't have to do the next two weeks at school in Moscow with Mary and Daniel and day care and breakfast and dinner and cuddle time, reading and writing late, not enough sleep, all in one room. If only. If only.

If only my life wasn't a magnet for chaos.

If only he wouldn't roll over and play dead right when everything promises to open up and be smooth.

The plan was working, *is* working. He'll mellow out after he's had a turn in Moscow. The classes for the teaching certificate are done. Slow down. It was harder than you thought, but it'll work. He'll find a way to show his paintings, and maybe even find an outlet for his chronic excitement.

If only the pieces of his life and past would settle down in a way he can manage.

In this interim time, I want to scrub my kitchen and gather the rooted peace my home and my children bring me. I want to drink from this life I love.

Daniel and Mary shriek with laughter and throw themselves backwards onto the bed. "Seven, eight, nine…fourteen!" I wonder how it feels to inhabit a world where that is such a terrific joke.

MONDAY, AUGUST 9, 1987

Shut into the studio looking uphill to the light on the trunks of the cedars near the creek. Mary and Daniel in the kitchen doing the dishes and cooking ramen noodles for a surprise. After I helped them get everything set up, they said, "Now you go into the studio and *forget!*"

TUESDAY, AUGUST 10, 1987

Virginia has 50 chickens, about 4 weeks old. We go inside the tiny shed when she feeds them. They are adolescent-homely, sparsely-feathered. The smell of chicken shit is stifling.

Daniel: Wow! That mama had a *big* tummy!

Mary: Hey! They're only walkin' on two legs!

Daniel: That's all they ever get, even when they're big.

Mary: (After a pause.) That's all we ever get, too.

WEDNESDAY, AUGUST 12, 1987

Oh shit.

That's what came out of my mouth. Deepening the transgression. I wonder if there's anything I could have said that wouldn't make it worse. Oh shit. If only.

If only the laughing boy hadn't slipped a note into the bed.

Before this gets too out of hand, show me the constitution. What are the names and the numbers of all the laws? Write down a list of all the rules.

Everyone was telling me to leave him. Not with words, but with their sad pitying eyes. Inside, I raged. At them for not understanding. At their shrugs of shoulder and twists of eyebrow. As if I don't already know that not to decide is to decide. Every concerned question about how things were going at home made me feel like a fool. Everyone thinks I'm a fool for believing in him. But I do.

Why? Why? Why? The never-ending question. No reason is ever good enough.

What if I said it was because of the way his cold back feigned sleep that last Sunday night? No entwined limbs. No hymn to my body. No glow from our promising future. A sleepy pillow-stifled goodbye in the morning instead of a gesture of reconciliation.

A whole big nothing to buoy me on the silent drive to Moscow through the dawn. No gentle wind at my back blowing from the direction of home. Sliding the car between the trunks of those two front-yard trees, branches on the windshield. *Must get out, unload the stuff, take a shower, walk to campus…* Head on the steering wheel. Not enough momentum to reach the high road. A doorway. I didn't step through. I wasn't pushed. I rolled.

I knew whose laughing eyes I could meet over the course of the next week.

Friday, August 14, 1987

So the sheriff shows up and says he's not the one to talk to about whether it's fair or not. Here's the papers and the collection agency that has Robb's medical bills is seizing all of the artwork in the show in St. Maries, along with any completed works stored here or elsewhere. Everything.

Saturday, August 15, 1987

Mary cuddles a purring kitty which she has dressed in red jammies and a baseball cap.

Monday, August 17, 1987

What a delightful time I had with Daniel yesterday. A friendly little companion. He talked seriously about wanting to learn to read and know all the hard numbers, like forty. Says he'll really need to be going to school. How else will he be able to remember past 13?

Daniel and Mary play "Back to Kentucky" which entails marching all over the hill hollering "Back! To Kentucky!" The imaginary Michael has moved back to Kentucky. He went there to build pig pens. Now he's a Manufacturer. He's making little plastic pigs.

WEDNESDAY, AUGUST 19, 1987

The jeep rattles and wobbles. No tunes. Torn plastic seats. Ran out of gas outside Frederick. Math problem: starter, odometer, gas gauge all broken, a leak in the gas tank. How much gas do you have left? If you know, it's because the tank is empty. Pull over, unhook the jerry can. Push the starter button against the engine, hold your hair clear of the fan and your skirt clear of the fender. Stay alive, stay clean. Didja prime the carburetor?

Afternoon blast of dirt-scraped August heat off the terraced ridges of the roadcut. Thin brown-needled seedlings asphyxiated by petro-fumes. Plucked-chicken hillsides going for their fourth growth. The steam-belching, metal-grunting mill—piles of disismembered tree corpses, log home kits. Heat of the asphalt highway. Nothing is pristine. There is no empty space.

SUNDAY, AUGUST 23, 1987

I am attached to a box that is visible to everyone but me and does not belong to me. Out in the world whatever I do, I must always be aware of the box. It is in constant danger of being opened by someone who is not the owner. I wish I could cut it off and throw it to the world, to everyone who has a stake in what's in it.

What am I supposed to promise him? Never to fuck anyone but him again? Are there any other pledges that get made in relationships? He tells of his daily struggle to trust me, which a person like me could never understand. Talks about the behavior of "decent people," a community to which I no longer belong. Have I committed the only crime that matters?

What did he say when he lit out at me last night? I walk around with a lousy superior attitude without the least foundation for it. Do I think anybody would *want* to look at my fat ass and stringy tits night after night? Lousy piece of snatch. Wag my smelly twat at every gizzard-fucking hippie boy with a joint in one hand and a reggae record under his arm. Everywhere I wipe my greasy cunt…

Oh he's such a fool. He sure can't see that. It's hard. Afterward, when he apologized, all I could think was, "I'm OK and you're not." Somehow in the structure of things, this is not a valid statement. Finger-pointing is not any kind of step toward resolution.

THURSDAY, SEPTEMBER 10, 1987

Susannah. New counselor in Coeur d'Alene. Write down what happens and how you feel, she says. Imagine that. Somebody says I should do something I know how to do.

Dismayed. That was a popular feeling today. Talking to Cynthia in the lounge, Poli at the mailbox, feeling hopeless, doubting I could get through the moments.

Feeling hopeful, too. Leaving this morning, waving goodbye and honking to happy faces in the kitchen window. Feeling like it might all work out, and then feeling just the opposite as I entered the final tunnel of uphill curves before home.

Feeling a little surprised and disappointed there were so few feelings. Or that their intensity was so low. Almost no feelings at all.

I remember "stuffing" some angry feelings, and wanting to cry here and there during the day but not doing it.

Struggle for Intimacy—Introduction: Family Interactions.

Interactions between my parents: Sometimes my dad would get angry at my mom. Never the other way around. It was always pretty controlled—nothing in front of us kids that wouldn't have been OK in public. Communication was about people and events, not feelings. No friendships in my family. We were acquaintances—sometimes allies, sometimes enemies. It was clean and clinical. If my dad was being unpredictable, well, we backed off, remained polite, maybe a little embarrassed. We bore with it until it was over.

My dad's "dysfunction" is alcoholism? It's hard for me to equate it with the kinds of alcoholism I see around me these days. I think of alcoholism as "drunk and mean." What I witnessed was "drunk and out of reach." This is just as damaging? No bruises on your pretty face. Just worry lines.

FRIDAY, SEPTEMBER 11, 1987

Struggle for Intimacy, Chapter 1: Family roles.

Everything is going wrong in this relationship. I used to think I could change myself enough to make the relationship OK—or at least not damaging to me. I was willing to settle for that. Now I am not very willing to try like I used to—being meek and submissive, swallowing angry feelings, feeling one way and acting another.

Superperson. That's me. I'll take all the responsibility because I think it will get me control. Everything is always out of control and I never feel like I get the credit I deserve.

SATURDAY, SEPTEMBER 12, 1987

Struggle for Intimacy. Shared relationship issues.

Vulnerability. Why do I feel vulnerable? Do I? Why else would I have gotten so angry yesterday when Robb reported that Reardon proclaimed him vulnerable and me not.

The feelings I am most unable to share are negative ones—and that seems to be all I have lately. When I have shared negative feelings with Robb in the past, he has become unbelievably, unpredictably angry. Everything, anything I have ever shared with him is available to be flung at me. I have tried my hardest and given my all for the last month. In return I got a bunch of pain. And I got tired. Never could I give him a "satisfactory explanation" for the affair. If I try to express how beat down I felt, how empty I was, my needs—he just has that many more phrases to mock me with.

Reading this whole damn book about children of alcoholics is strange. Sometimes the person being described is Robb and not me. Other times, it seems to describe a person I have been pushed and mashed into, not the me I was ten years ago.

But who got herself into this relationship?

The "alcoholic parent" doesn't remind me of my dad. Reminds me of Robb.

MONDAY, SEPTEMBER 14, 1987

Angry is what I was today. Oh yeah, and relieved, too, when the car was cheap to fix. Angry, sitting in a staff meeting that felt pointless.

Afraid last night in bed.

TUESDAY, SEPTEMBER 15, 1987

Tirade of the day: It just kills you, *kills you,* KILLS you to be nice to me doesn't it, bitch? It kills you to give anything to anyone, doesn't it, bitch? It's one thing to be unloved—and believe me bitch, I don't love you—but you, bitch, are just plain *unlovable.* Except to one of them gizzard-fuckers sniffing around for any willing hole.

Sticks and stones?

Wednesday, September 16, 1987

What do I feel now? Relieved with Robb gone for the day and a little apprehensive, too, that he'll come home early. When he takes my hand and looks limp and helpless, expectant in his love for me, I feel angry, crowded, impatient and *just plain bored.* His eyes don't quit begging, but won't say what they want. I hate it.

Last night, the kids tied all of their dolls and teddy bears together and whirled them around in the air. "We're having a circus!"

They've been telling Santa Claus jokes. Tedda saw Santa Claus break a hole in the roof and jump on your bed! Monka saw Santa Claus come in through the bread counter window and eat all the granola! Raucous paroxysms of laughter. Every creature in the menagerie has spotted Santa making mischief. Santa Claus came down the chimney and gave everybody a cold! Santa Claus came up the ladder and pooped on the Christmas tree!

Friday, September 18, 1987

Let's do something fun, huh? Yeah, when we gonna have some fun? Let's go fill out all that bankruptcy paperwork in the Silver Buckle, make a night of it, just me and you, prove ya love me while you're at it. Oh yeah, all you ever wanna do is write in your damn journal. Well I'm going then, have me a little fun. I made a resolution. I owe it to myself, I decided, maybe take my guitar, never know who I might meet…

Go ahead, go. But don't try to drain me at the same time. And if you leave at four in the afternoon and say you're not coming back until midnight, then don't show back up at eight o'clock, when the kids are just tucked in and the dishes finished. Don't leave all the work to me and come home to yatter just when it's all quiet.

Oh who cares.

SATURDAY, SEPTEMBER 19, 1987

"I hope the fuck you find somebody who is attractive enough for you someday. You're not always gonna be able to get them, you know. You'll sag, and you'll…"

My heart pounds in my chest. It shouldn't. But it does. He promised.

I hear something shatter. A beer bottle perhaps.

I'm afraid again. Afraid for my safety and well-being.

Why does he scare me? Does he try to? Does he want to? What does he want from me?

Oh, it just doesn't make sense.

Here I am, wanting to get up out of this chair and get myself a cup of tea and go upstairs and read myself to sleep to try again tomorrow. But I'm afraid to get up, to call attention to myself, to exist in his world. I have to exist somewhere where he can't get to me, someplace he doesn't know is there.

What am I supposed to do?

What do I want?

For my heart to quit pounding.

TUESDAY, SEPTEMBER 22, 1987

A poem by Adrienne Rich, "Afterward." How does it feel to be reduced to the level of pain and turmoil you thought you were programmed to escape, the kind reserved for the riffraff?

WEDNESDAY, SEPTEMBER 23, 1987

How did I feel when I jumped out of the car last night on the way home? Pissed off, but good. Daniel and Robb were in some hassle. I thought Robb was wrong and he knew it. He wanted to discuss it. I won't discuss the kids and their motivations in the third person in their presence. I said I didn't want to talk about it until later. He persisted. I was silent. Then he and Daniel got into a tattling match over what the other had done. I told them calmly I didn't want to be part of their argument. Robb slammed on the brakes, grabbed my arm, enraged, "Don't you dare talk to me like I'm a child!"

"I'll walk home," I said, and got out of the car. He sped off. Three miles from home, stars, a country road. I was dressed warm and had my boots on. I felt pretty good.

Right before I got out of the car, I felt…cornered, trapped.

In bed, later, he had a proposal. He would borrow some money to get a start someplace so he can move out. "I'll be out of here by the end of October. What do you think?"

Nothing, absolutely nothing. The end of October is a month away and he changes every four hours. He wants me to say the words to make him stay. His gyrations are getting more and more extreme. I'd say what he wants to hear but there is no right combination of words to satisfy him.

How do I feel? Trapped. Trapped with a nut. He thinks I'm the one who should check herself into Cedarcrest now.

To get myself more room, it feels as though I have to do things that are overblown and damaging—like jumping out of cars. That's why I feel trapped. Are there no choices for me that begin with something I do that feels good?

THURSDAY, SEPTEMBER 24, 1987

I am tired of this period in my life. I want it to be over. I want to concentrate my energy into something other than changing my behavior, being patient, and helping this relationship work.

The road is so damn long.

SATURDAY, SEPTEMBER 26, 1987

I knocked down the woodpile. Karate-kicked it. With each blast, I muttered, "This feels *good*." My teeth were clenched.

I'm all by myself now. The kids are napping. Robb's been gone all day. Who knows when he'll be back. The other night when I got home, not even late, he accosted me on the porch. Demanded to know where I'd been. He already knew. I said so. I have an appointment with Susannah every Thursday. We'd talked about it that morning. I reminded him of how I'm not allowed to ask him about any of the particulars of his whereabouts. He says that's because he can be trusted and I can't.

He put his arms around me. Tight. I was still holding my purse.

"C'mon," he murmured, "Let's snuggle up and be intimate."

I seethed.

Munching at Arby's all-you-can-eat salad bar after I left Susannah's, I filled pages with words and tried to remember what she said that made me so upset. As she talked, I fought tears and held myself apart from what she meant. Was it a complicated point? Something new? I made a note of each one of the sentences, but kept them separate from each other until I could get somewhere alone to put them back together and think it over, somewhere with my defenses in place, so it wouldn't have to rush all over me at once. That's why I stopped at Arby's. Inside, at a table with some food, my defenses were so good I couldn't remember a thing she had said.

On the way home, it came back to me. The long drive from Coeur d'Alene in the dark always makes me lucid. The tire sounds and the rhythm of the hills and curves are soothing. Gliding down the steep and twisty grade to Ridley Creek, I feel weightless.

Susannah and I were talking about how I am supposed to write down two things each day that are, if not lovable, then at least right about Robb. It's a good idea. The thing I was refusing to hear her say is that if I can't look at him and find a single loving feeling, then things are grim. Coming up with two things he does right each day will be the key to reconnecting to those feelings. Then I get home and he meets me on the porch steps with accusations.

He sure doesn't make it easy.

I've written a note to put on the demolished woodpile.

I went out to work on it, not tear it down. Robb has been sawing the logs and splitting the big rounds in half. When I get home from school, I split them some more and stack the wood. When we started, I could barely hoist the half-logs onto the chopping block, they were so heavy. Then it took a long time with the mallet and wedge, *tink, tink, tink,* before the log cleaved in two and I could whack the halves into pieces with the maul.

Robb taught me how to use wedges when he presented them to me one afternoon the first spring we were here. "These are for you. In case I ever go to Spokane for work and there's a snowstorm and I can't get home. You'll say, 'No good bum left me here with a baby and no firewood.' But you'll be able to split your own..."

I thought that was dumb. He'd never leave me without firewood.

Why would he go all the way to Spokane for work?

I love to split wood. With wedges you can split huge logs if you take the time. No matter how little you are. It's not hard to learn how to see, in the way the log has checked, where to strike to make it cleave. After that it's *The Inner Game of Tennis*. Look at the spot you will strike. Propel the maul with the weight of your body. Follow through.

I work that woodpile every day after school, rain or shine. Stress-relieving physical activity for me, and the kids enjoy it a lot, the three of us together, robust in the cold twilight. I've gotten faster and stronger, am wicked accurate with the maul and seldom need the wedge anymore. What better project than firewood—we do it together and it brings our lives forward.

I know about stacking wood. The first afternoon, I dragged some slender poles to the pile and laid them out in a frame. It was well thought-out, supported properly with rocks so the woodpile would be flat, despite the angle of the hill. I laid the crosspieces the correct distance apart so the lengths of firewood would span them perfectly and be held off the ground so they couldn't wick up moisture.

When I got to the woodpile this morning, it listed, slumped. Every piece of frame he could reach had been yanked out, all the poles sawed into dinky little sticks of firewood. The wedge was on the ground in front of the pile. I picked it up and heaved it. I wanted it to end up "lost." It landed, *cling!*, with the maul and the axe, where it belongs. That's when I started kicking.

Oh, it didn't feel good at all. I knocked it all down and kept on kicking until I felt stupid. I thought about burning his shop next, or scribbling on the painting he started yesterday. When I act on this kind of rage, I feel sad and helpless. Even from the searing center of a rampage, I remain aware of how every path of destruction leads straight back to me. On the way back to the house, I up-ended the feed barrel. And picked it up. I was careful, too, not to rip the tarp that covers it. That's how I always am in my angry displays—attentive. I never wreck anything so badly I can't put it back the way it was.

I came in from the ex-woodpile and wrote a note. *I did this for you. So you can know how it feels when your partner is someone who makes promises, talks like a helper, and then tears down your work as soon as you aren't there to guard it. Oh yeah… I didn't really do this. That was anger talking. All I want is your love. I am a changed person now. I'll never do such a thing again.* He's always telling me the mean things he does are "just depression talking."

When I go out there next, should I leave the note, or just start stacking?

We talked the other night about commitment. He talked. We were having a sandwich in town at the café. He told me how Reardon said we goofed up in coming here because we didn't have any plans.

That's not true. We did so have a plan. We were going to work together and build this place up into something. A "new ancestral home" he called it. We pledged to live simply and try to achieve some spiritual peace by coming closer to the earth. We promised each other that when it was incomprehensibly hard we would stand rock-solid beside one another. He would paint. I would write. We would be surrounded by the art that grew out of our lives. We had all kinds of dreams. Now he says anyone knows this can't be done, and only dirty hippies try.

I don't have to give up just because he does. I'm staying here and moving forward.

SAME NIGHT

What happened? Robb punched me. How do I feel? I dunno.

He saw the woodpile this afternoon as soon as he got home. The note was there, stuck to the chopping block with an axe. As we walked towards it, I hurried ahead and ripped the note away before he saw it, burned it later. I was glad I did. We restacked the pile together and he looked into my eyes and said he was sorry, sorry for me, because he understands how that kind of rage can feel.

It was 6:15 when we came back inside, and I knew I'd have to step into high gear to do everything I had committed to do before bedtime. Kids in bed by 7:30. Private time for each of us until nine, after which we would be together. That's what we agreed to in the café the other night. We even signed it.

The kids and I had started a batch of bread earlier, another commitment, so the rest was a dance, a clever balancing of bathing and putting on PJs, interspersed with dough-punching and loaf-shaping and sculpting. Even when Mary toppled her dresser, its contents and the two-gallon avocado plant on top of it by climbing into her top drawer for her PJs, I was a paragon of calm. We cleaned it up together and kept to the schedule.

The kids were ready for bed and their bread was baking when he leaped from the couch and pulled me to him. I was tidying the kitchen so I wouldn't have to spend my private time cleaning up the bread mess. I didn't want to talk to him or look into those eyes and watch them probe for sentiments that just aren't there. I didn't have to do that until nine o'clock. Still, I felt like I owed it to him to try a little and not just walk away. I hugged him with the dishrag still in my hand, held out wide so it wouldn't get his shirt wet. He clung.

I was saved by the timer, took the bread out, got the peanut butter, and set the kids up at the table with the bread-creatures they had made. While they munched, I started cleaning up again. No dice.

He kept trying to suck words out, only I never said the right thing. Finally he said all he wanted was for me to tell him I love him.

"I do," I said, "I love you. And I don't want to hear any more about it." I was quoting the legendary line spoken by his grandfather to his 16-year-old bride when they arrived with a buckboard and a team on their empty quarter-section of land. He didn't like that. He didn't like my tone of voice, either.

"Do you think I would go to all this trouble if I didn't love you?" I asked. Good question. My hands, I admit, were on my hips.

Earlier, in the calmer part of the conversation, I had said that when you fish for feelings you can't control what you catch. He told me to tell him the truth, he could take it. I didn't really believe him, but I know it's not fair to wall him out every time he encourages me to express what I feel. The conversation about why I kicked down the woodpile seemed sane and fair and that probably made me bold. At any rate, I started out calm, but once I began to open up, it was as though a locomotive inside me began to chug its way up to full power.

"There's nothing, really, that I can say that will be good enough for you. First you only want me to tell you I love you, so I do. But then it turns out I haven't said it *right.* Look—here I am. Take it or leave it. You don't like my peaches, get your grubby hands off my–"

I didn't get to say "tree." Next thing I knew, I was breaking my fall against the cold naugahyde of the green chair, trying for a landing that wouldn't smash the guitar on the seat. I didn't see him cock his arm or swing, or what his face looked like or anything. He clobbered me in the breastbone and I was surprised it didn't hurt more. I cowered, but he didn't come after me.

Ye gods. I've always known what you're supposed to do if *this* happens. Kick him out. If you don't, you become a Battered Woman.

"You gotta get out of here," I said.

"Don't worry. I'm leaving for good right now."

For good? I fought the urge to point out that he was being unnecessarily extreme. The important thing was simply to get him out. Now.

"You gotta help me," he said. "Help me make a plan for getting away."

For Christ sake, I thought. Make your own goddamn plans.

I leaned back against the counter, arms folded. He accused me, angrily, of killing him. Soon he was on his knees, sobbing into my shins, just like all the dysfunctional family books say. I told him straight, firmly, I was not killing him, but something else was. I felt calm.

He wailed about losing his family, telling me how all he ever wanted was gone from him because I had taken all the love away. I looked across the dim room, noted the position of every object, listened for sounds from the kids at the table, waited for this part to be over.

He got himself under control and we went to the kids and held them. They continued to munch, upset. Mary began to cry, said she was scared. Rough night for her. First the dresser now this. Just as rough for Daniel, but he won't lose until morning when he can't get his sock on. When he left, Robb promised to call Reardon right away.

I feel anxious, but also like my life is new.

SUNDAY, SEPTEMBER 27, 1987

Now how do I feel?

I see how it happens. I am a character in a domestic violence pamphlet.

Just as I was getting into bed, he came back. He called Reardon, who helped him understand the dynamic that made him lose control. It won't happen again, he said. Reardon assured him this was an isolated incident. The tests they've been doing together show he is not the type of guy who resorts to violence in an argument. It was late. We were both tired. Tomorrow he would find another place to stay for a while.

All night long, I was aware of the weight of him next to me in the bed. This morning when I woke up, I felt like a volcano.

Battered Women are stupid. They are supposed to *get rid of The Bum*. Throw him out. And they don't.

Why? I'm afraid to. Alone here in the woods, no phone, no neighbors, him facing ultimate rejection, stewing on his misfortunes in the bar, deciding I was stealing his soul. He might be out of sight, but how can I ever be sure he is really gone?

I can leave, of course, but I would have to disappear to someplace where he can't find me. Seems extreme. If I've already considered what I'd do, how I'd take the kids and split, where I'd go, who I'd borrow money from, how I'd get there, what the note would say, what I'd bring—does it mean I am really just setting up a drama so I can be in it?

Still, I refuse to be in the movie where I get bashed, believe an apology, lie about the bruises, and pretend it won't happen again.

Or so I say. That's exactly what I am doing, only so far, it's not bruises I lie about. And I don't exactly lie, I just never tell anyone the whole truth. That's what Battered Women do—organize what they say and what they show to protect The Bum. If I tell anyone the whole truth, they'll tell me to get the hell out.

And then what will I say? Oh no, I can't. Don't you see? It's real complicated. I don't want to give up my house and the patch of dirt it's on. I have to keep him right here in front of me, keep him mollified. If don't, why, I'm afraid he'll sneak up here in the night and kill me.

Great trade for a house on a hill.

But there's more. I've always trusted him to straighten out the problems at the root of all this anger. I've always believed there would come a time when he couldn't stand it anymore and he would get some help to really change things. I think that's what's happening now.

After breakfast, he gathered his things politely and left. He's pretty sure he can rent a room from Pauline, an elderly widow in his painting class. He'll be back in the morning before I leave for school to take care of the kids all day while I am gone. I don't want him here, but I don't have much choice. He has a right to be with his children. There's no room for them at Pauline's. They are happy and comfortable here. Daycare is expensive. I have to keep my job.

I am going to play the relaxation tape, will myself to sleep if I have to, get some rest.

I feel stark. Empty. Hopeful. Relieved.

MONDAY, SEPTEMBER 28, 1987

What happened today? The seventh and eighth graders revolted. In the middle of it, I felt awful. Worried, too, when I couldn't stop the shaking, choking sobs. Now I feel tired, and like my insides have been hosed out. My eyes burn. I cried for two solid hours, took a break and started up again. By then I was sitting politely at a table with four other people and I managed to hold it to silent, seeping tears for an hour while they talked over what had happened. Yikes. Promise me that uncorking all of this is useful and not the start of a whole new way of life.

I knew something was brewing in the back corner. The cook's daughters have been pushing me hard—sassing, contradicting. They are good students and used to having their way. I've been strict. At lunchtime today when I showed up at the cafeteria window with my tray, their mom said, almost cheerfully, "None for you anymore!"

"Linda," I said. "What's going on?" I stood at the window while she served the entire third grade as if she had to memorize the mashed potatoes to get them dished up right. Finally, I walked away, empty tray hanging stupidly at my side. I felt confused, but calm. Step one was to figure out what was happening.

I found Cynthia in her office. She greeted me like she was expecting me, like I had been sent there for being a problem. She talked first. "There was a group of people in here all morning demanding that you be fired. We'll do conflict resolution in your classroom. Right after lunch." She didn't want to hear any more.

Am I in some kind of negative energy warp? Does everyone experience this level of drama in their life? Am I bringing this on myself? Do I have any control over my situation at all?

How did I feel? Beaten.

I put a note in Cynthia's box saying I couldn't face this now, and I'd be back tomorrow. I had a right to let the whole horrid way I felt wash over me with nobody looking. I drove a few miles up the highway. It was raining. Where could I go? Home to Robb? To the café for small talk with the retired ranchers? Down a logging road where I could sit in the cold and wait for the day to be over? None of this would be any easier to face tomorrow. I turned around. When I got back to my classroom, the inquisition was in full swing without me. I sat down at my desk. I felt nothing.

Cynthia was in charge. Linda and Coach stood at her side. The conflict resolution procedure is one we all know. We've attended workshops to learn how to use it to debrief skirmishes on the playground. The session begins with everyone telling their version of the story without interruption. It looked as though every student was going to talk. They said I was unfair, made unreasonable demands, and was mean.

"I think she has problems at home," said Marla in an extra-mature voice, "But she shouldn't be taking them out on us."

What would she know about my "problems" at home? I haven't told anyone about Robb moving out over the weekend.

Shelby stood up and said I yell at them all the time, and if they do the least little thing wrong I scream and swear, and on Friday I called them a bunch of fuck-ups. I was so shocked I spoke out of turn—low, flat, and firm—"Shelby, you're lying."

Cynthia gave me her stern face, reprimanded me for disrupting the process, and sent me to her office for time out. Cynthia is my friend, my colleague. She has never spoken to me like this before. That's when I started to sob.

When the shuddering tears let up some, I grabbed a piece of paper and did what every kid is supposed to do when they get sent to time out: Write about it.

How did you get yourself here? How did you feel about it then? How do you feel about it now? Isn't that what you write about in time out?

How did I get here? I ran away and then I came back. Then I misbehaved and I got kicked out. Get in touch with your feelings they tell you. Even if your feelings are shit and make you feel like same. Get them up to the surface, it is okay to cry. But crying is not socially acceptable in most contexts. Most certainly not in the classroom. In the classroom they have another rule—don't let them know they're getting to you, they'll come back for more tomorrow. That's what the other teachers have been telling me. It sounds calm and orderly over there. Is my presence in the classroom disruptive? Can't my troubles at home stay there? Can't I come here and not think about them? Nancy has problems at home. Seems to me she has problems at school, too. What was your first clue? Maybe the problem is Nancy. Nancy is the only thing I can change.

What am I gonna do?

I found out later that Frank—the teacher who also uses this classroom, who is in and out sometimes when I am teaching—he was the one who finally stuck up for me and put a stop to it all. He told them they would be ashamed if they heard the way those kids talk to me. One by one the kids confessed to exaggeration. Cynthia tried to get me to come out, said they wanted to apologize. I couldn't stop crying long enough to make an appearance, didn't want to parade the wreckage of myself, give them my puffy, snot-filled face for a trophy. I feel misplaced, stuck in the wrong life.

Cynthia came back to get me after school when there were no kids around. We sat at a table in the library—Cynthia, Frank, Linda, Coach, and me. Coach was devastated. He never believed the kids would lie to him. Everyone felt sorry for him and was trying to help him get over it. Nobody apologized to me or said I had really gotten the shaft. I don't think they even looked at me. But I didn't care. I couldn't talk anyway. I don't feel anything now and I refused to feel anything then. Not in front of people who won't look me in the eye and acknowledge how I was wronged.

WEDNESDAY, SEPTEMBER 30, 1987

Robb drove up in the dark last night and the first thing he said was that he couldn't help it. He was sitting in the bar when a guy came in all ecstatic, passing out cigars… He stood in the doorway all tearful and told me I am not capable of comprehending how staying away at night is the hardest thing he has ever done. So this was a plea, for me to grant him the privilege of sleeping under the same roof with his children. He would sleep downstairs by the stove. There wouldn't be any weirdness. Just this once.

I was fuming. But also very afraid. It's always the same. This is so hard, he says, I can't do it alone, help me, open up, just give me some love vibes. He presses harder and harder until we get to have a rejection scene.

I never know if I am going to get out of it, and whatever happens, it takes me hours to calm down. I let him in.

I couldn't stand to look at him. I told him I didn't want to talk to him, I was too afraid, I can't trust how he reacts to my feelings. He assured me that these few days have profoundly changed him. That's just plain false.

And the feeling? It was fear. The noticeable part was the physical manifestation. Chatter-tooth shaking. It could have become as uncontrollable as Monday's sobbing. I have no idea how deep this well is, and I didn't want to find out with him looking. So I turned it off. Click. Like that.

What's the use of the freezing shake? Something to do while you wonder if this is the big one, if out of me? If I am about to find out how it will feel when he beats the crap out of me.

After I fell asleep, he crawled into my bed. Neither of us spoke. I didn't move until morning. He didn't get up when I left. When I got home from school, he left without incident. I feel frozen, paralyzed. What is going to happen?

Friday, October 2, 1987

I wonder what happened. I wonder how I feel. A little relieved and more competent at school, but still crowded and rushed. So much is expected of me, but I will never get a chance to meet all the demands.

I am also very unsatisfied with writing all this down. What happened and how did I feel? Where is that supposed to lead? My feelings are nothing but a backdrop for whatever is going to happen next. If anything, they get in the way. I guess I have to learn to understand my feelings before I can ever learn to control them.

Detached. That is how I am feeling more and more of the time. I refuse to get involved any further in this life of mine. I am not laying myself on the line anymore. I don't care and I don't want to care about anything other than my kids and my house. Open up more than that and all I ever find out is that I am woefully inadequate.

Last night, when Robb grabbed me by the throat and shook me, I wasn't even scared. It felt like the next inevitable step. He is right when he says I am cold and distant.

FRIDAY, NOVEMBER 6, 1987

Frank says it's all too unbelievable. He says I need to write all this down. Serious. "Isn't that what made you so excited about the class you took last summer?" he asks.

SATURDAY, NOVEMBER 7, 1987

Once upon a time there were two people who lived out of wedlock. The bankruptcy lawyer explains that for the bankruptcy the law will consider them married, yet for the purpose of the debt the law sees them as unmarried. They are worth going after. They own land. The collection agency lawyer (nasty, rabid) has muttered the word "fraud." The bankruptcy lawyer asks if there's any reason why they don't just get married. "Well, I don't like the idea of...," the woman begins. The bankruptcy lawyer cuts her off. "How do you like the idea of being accused of *fraud?*" he asks.

Robb was going to meet Reardon on a Sunday and check himself into Cedarcrest for a program that would last a month, so we went to Coeur d'Alene the day before to get married. That would make the bankruptcy filing smooth, and take that off his mind while he was in Cedarcrest. After we got the marriage license, we found out we needed a preacher or a judge to finish the deed. The judge wouldn't be in until Monday. If we couldn't wait, we could pay $200 at the wedding chapel across the way. Robb and the wife of one of the preachers in St. Maries have become good friends through the art gallery, so we decide to try there.

When we found the preacher, I let Robb make the arrangements. This was his trip—he needed a paper marriage for his bankruptcy. Fine. I could give him that, but on the condition that it wasn't going to get twisted into anything else. That's what I said in the car as we headed out the valley road that morning—paperwork only, no discussion, no deeper meanings. Just tell me where to sign.

So what did I feel? Somnambulant. Things were such a mess. One more mistake wasn't going to matter, toss it on the pile. If this helped him get to Cedarcrest, I would do it.

I heard him say something to the preacher about "legally expedient." When his wife hustled over to be the witness, she was all touched and brought some roses for me to hold. I handed them straight to Mary, had to hold back to be gentle, and not slap them into her chest. The kids were crabby and dirty from the long day in the car.

The preacher's wife asked, "Why today?"

I froze and waited for Robb to answer. He lied and yattered some stuff about feelings and commitments. I was disappointed, but from a distance. This was a river, and I was in the current. Talking was elsewhere.

When it came to the vows, Robb got all choked up, and I wanted to laugh. I made myself cry instead so my reaction could seem appropriate. To turn on the crying, I let the word "fraud" pronounce itself in my mind.

We had pledged to go get some ice cream afterward. I've soothed other hurts with hot fudge. Instead, the consolation prize was to sit in the preacher's clean-edged dining room and eat from the church basement's bottomless stash of orange sherbet dixie cups with individually wrapped wooden spoons. The kids could have all they wanted. Words floated—blessed union, the meaning of vows, the symbolism of the ring, yes, they really encourage us to consider getting rings. I spoke only to the kids, managing their sticky fingers and faces, feeling the shit pile deeper and deeper around me.

As we were leaving, Robb made a date to teach the preacher how to play the guitar—a convenient 6 weeks away. The wife twisted it into a family dinner invitation. I never want to see this place again. I want to forget this whole hot tiresome afternoon. I didn't have the will to say so.

Robb goes to Cedarcrest and comes home in a month as scheduled. I'm weary, but encouraged. He has medication. He is so much calmer. He recognizes the destructiveness of his depression. His reunion with the kids is delirious. It's great to have him back. My life forgets to get any easier.

We went to the dinner at the preacher's yesterday, Friday. On the counter were cards and flowers. *Congratulations on your wedding.* From the art gallery people. I was horrified, but at least these people were all strangers to me.

After dinner, more folks started trickling in, more flowers, bottles of champagne, presents. *Omigod. This is a wedding reception.* Women keening my name in greeting. *Nancy, you didn't even tell us!* It was agony. Stan and Marsha with tears streaming down their cheeks. The wife of the sheriff who confiscated Robb's paintings. Regrets from Jan and Teresa. Everyone so happy, telling us not to be so shy and humble. There was so much to be said. Nobody noticed that once again, I couldn't speak.

Robb was thrilled. "Now these are real people! Real friends! We've been feeling so lonely all this time, and it's because we were never around the people who really know how to show they care. Isn't that right, Hon?" He pressed me for words of agreement. All I could do was stare. No words would come out of my mouth at all. I thought of all the people who have listened to me, driven miles for me when my car broke down, hugged me like they meant it. Why, why, why does he do lies like this?

Maybe they aren't lies. Maybe this is the first time he's felt the friendship of others. Still, that's no reason to go out in public, grab me and prop me to his side like a dummy while he speaks for both of us.

It makes me angry, but I know I should have spoken up six weeks ago in that church vestibule. I should have known better than entrusting all the communication to Robb. I didn't want to be rude to the preacher's wife, or to embarrass her in front of her guests, and so I just felt helpless, hostile, and stupid.

Nobody accused me of fraud.

MONDAY, NOVEMBER 9, 1987

Guys from Ridley Peak passed through overnight. Robb criticized me cruelly in front of them. Repeatedly. He cut in rudely at all my attempts at small talk. He turned every conversation into how awful our house is, what an undesirable place this is to live, what a disappointment our children are, how dull all the locals. I told him privately he was a little out of line and suggested a walk. He refused. He went back into the living room ahead of me and said, "Nancy says I'm being rude. Do you think I'm being rude?"

Hurt and embarrassed, that's how I felt.

I tried to tell him later. He was really angry with me. Turns out someone at the bar said I look sad and lonely and like what I need is a good fuck. More proof I can't be trusted.

How do I feel? Stupid.

Tuesday, November 10, 1987

Frank asked, "How is everything?" and *poof!* I had to force myself not
to cry. It was the tenor in his voice that was genuine kindness. Nobody
talks to me like that.

Oh they care that I'm propped up in good enough shape to keep
the 9th grade under wraps from two to three on Thursdays, hug babies
on cue, fix dinner, nod at the right part of the conversation and become
"loving and intimate" after 7:30, but no one, no one, is willing to consider the real cost to me of their demands.

Makes me want to cry and fight back. Against what? You're a free
woman, no one is forcing you. All you have to do is speak up.

And so in the end, I just sort of feel the fool.

Wednesday November 11, 1987

I was a cunt and a whore again last night, taking off my pants for
whoever comes by. We were spending the night at Bob and Fran's in
Moscow, because Robb wanted to visit them before he moves back to
Boulder.

I was buried under layers of sleep for the first time since forever, on
the couch. The tea Fran made had silenced my never-gonna-quit cough,
and from the depths of a dream, he's thumping on me, telling me I'm a
cunt and a whore.

Annoyed. I felt annoyed. And distant.

At breakfast he talks matter-of-factly of his life, our lives, the major
theme of which is how fucked up a place and community we live in, how
people like them are the truest of friends and so on. I picked at a sliver in
my thumb and waited for it to be over. Until I couldn't stand it.

"Oh tell them the fucking truth," I said. "He's moving to Boulder."
Then slammed myself out the door.

I feel, frustrated, sad, cheated, enraged, discouraged, and even despairing
at his private cruelties while outwardly he strives to appear wonderful
and sincere. He acts warm and honest, but I don't feel warm, and if I'm
honest, then I'm the spoiler, the one who makes a scene. I am looking for
solace for the sadness in my life, but there's only distance between me
and other people.

Isolation.

How my friendships seem to threaten him. Says next I'll be "lezzing out" with Teresa.

I wonder if he'll actually go.

When he told me he was leaving, and when I didn't fly into tears of rage or remorse, when I didn't plead, he said, "What'sa matter? Isn't Thursday a good day?" I don't want to influence his decision in any way and he wants to give me all the power.

POSTMARK: SALT LAKE CITY, UT
NOVEMBER 15, 1987

Playing guitar in the grey raining bus terminal. Sad twangy strings under fluorescent lights that thin blood. Farmers traveling are embarrassed that anyone would play music here.

Black man in red patent shoes must visit sister in rest home. Fort Worth. "Love will indoor," he says. Young toughs, homeless bums. ("I was in Nam," says one with scars on face.) We are all God's geeks in the bright unforgiving heart of Greyhound.

Will love "indoor"?
Robb

POSTMARK: BOULDER, CO
NOVEMBER 16, 1987

Dearest Nancy: I am so lonely for my family. I want to come back, but I know I must restore myself to what I am born to be. This is painful but there is no growth without pain. I only hope we will find happiness together, though I must be prepared to be strong alone. I cannot come back feeling the way I do now, so distrustful and fearful of what you might do. I love you and my family, but no longer at any cost whatsoever. I hope we will have made a choice by xmas or sooner.

You have my heart.
Love, Robb

POSTMARK: BOULDER, CO
NOVEMBER 18, 1987

Nancy: Just went out with Sam, who treated me to a Thai dinner, wonderful curries with squid and chicken. I can't believe what he shelled
out for dinner, but that's Boulder.

I also saw Mike Larsen and he told me Fine Design has more work
than they can handle and maybe I can have my old job back. I talk to
them at 9 a.m. tomorrow.

I really just want my family life back, only I can't have it right now
I guess. Can't quit thinking of family. Yet I know if I came back we'd
fall into the same traps. What can we do? Write me. Tell me what you
really feel. Are you still so deeply angry at me? I'm learning I have my
own anger to get rid of, but I will. Will we ever be able to be in the same
room together again? Will we trust? Make love? These are the things I
wonder…

Also, I want you to know I am faithful to you here. Why? I don't
know, but I just am. I hope you are the same, for the sake of our injured
trust. Can you be? I think so. You must understand how hard "blind
trust" is for me. Yet I love you body and soul

There is a new life right here in front of me and I want it, yet I'm
afraid of it because the price is my family. I don't want to lose my children and I want you if you will be faithful. Sorry to harp on it, but it
is the thorn in my side every day, along with your anger. I am learning
to let go but only a little so far. I'm being straight with you because I
love you so much. And I loved you too much. So now I'm loving me, or
trying to anyway. Write me and tell me your feelings. I care—I care—I
care. I am also afraid but getting less so.

Let's go away together this spring, if things work out. Let's get it
together by xmas. Can we? I want that, but not at any cost. I'm talking
very simply here, because to me it's a simple thing. We will either try
or we won't.

I'm willing.
My deepest love,
Robb

Dearest Nancy: Sunny and bright here today. I went to see a counselor and had a wonderful session. He helped me see what we've accomplished instead of being so negative. Am starting to meditate, which as near as I can tell is mostly self-hypnosis. It does work. Am very lonely.

All my love,
Robb

Dearest Nancy: I just talked to Daniel and Mary on the phone and feel great having heard them laugh again. I want to take the time to share a thought with you. It concerns my past dependency upon you and I wanted your thoughts on it. Here goes…

There is a common misconception that dependency is love. (My past misconception.) It can be seen in individuals who become incapacitatingly depressed or attempt suicide after being rejected by a spouse or lover. This is parasitism, not love. When you require another individual for your emotional survival, you are a parasite on that individual. There is no choice, no freedom in the relationship. It is necessity, not love.

I think I have been this way and I am extremely sorry for what it has caused. I wanted to say it in writing so you would have it to remind me if I ever do this again. I want the kind of love two free people experience by choice. I am working hard to achieve this.

Other thoughts: I am really excited about pursuing art to the fullest. The market for art is astonishing here. It won't be easy, but I can do it. I am in the process of coming up with a long range plan for a career, part of which will include hitting all the arts festivals and galleries possible. It won't be easy and it'll take a long time, but my dysfunction has been jarred loose by this trip and I'm excited for the first time in years. I envision Mary and Daniel growing up taking road trips with their dad to sell his art. It can be a great life, I believe, but it will take time to put together.

Every day I worry about the work load on you with me gone. Can't help myself. I love you and want to share a healthy happy and meaningful

life together. I know now I can do it all alone, but still prefer to finish rais-
ing the family we created. We both need help from therapists for a while,
but I think we can do it if we try. Seems to me that right now is the point
at which the real work and rewards of the relationship can begin. We are
losing our illusions and becoming real people. Let's go forward together.

I'm really ready to try.
My deepest love,
Robb

POSTMARK: BOULDER, CO
NOVEMBER 28, 1987

Dearest Nancy: I got your letter today and feel it is full of truths. First
of all, the one about how I recorded over all those tapes you made. You
know something? I don't even remember doing that horribly disre-
spectful thing, though I'm sure I did. It goes to show how badly I've re-
spected your rights. I know that now. It was blind stupidity on my part.

Another thing is the way I used up all the space in our lives so there
was none left for you. I don't know why or how it came about, but I
am ever-so-deeply sorry now. The other thing I am sorry for is that I
quit listening to you. Listening is the true work of love and I failed. I
promise you that from now on I will listen even if we have to do it by
appointment. One cannot really listen unless we are alone together, so
I hope you will set aside time for me to listen to you and your thoughts.

As for you being a writer, I think you are a good one already—
though a bit unfocused. I want to live as an artist and with a writer.
And you are the one. Please allow me to support and nurture you in
that endeavor. I'm asking for your trust. In exchange I will be there for
you when you need me. I'm speaking simply and straightforward now,
and I mean every word.

Love is an agreement. An agreement for each of us to be the best
individual we can. I've changed, not totally but significantly. I'm ready
to be a strong individual for my own sake. I hope we can be our best
together. I hope you still want me to return and that you will pick me
up at the bus station in Spokane on November 30 at 10:10 a.m.

My deepest love,
Robb

THURSDAY, DECEMBER 3, 1987

When Robb was gone there was just too much demanded of me. Function at school, with Daniel and Mary needing so much extra—their pain and the stressed, timebound structure of daycare. Feeding the animals, chopping wood, stoking the fire. Had he left me in summer, maybe I wouldn't have found myself crying for his return.

SATURDAY, DECEMBER 5, 1987

I sat in the greenhouse last night sobbing and questioned whether or not the time has come for me to get out, out, out. The answer was a definite yes, but I doubt the solidity of the place the decision came from. For an instant I knew. But the instant passed.

WEDNESDAY, DECEMBER 9, 1987

Robb is exuberant with the kids and rebuffs my attempts at conversation. Curt. Rude. Finally he tells me he's come to the realization that "this thing is never going to work."

He doesn't say he is leaving. He crackles at the edge of attacking me, hinting that reassurance might back him off. He will do me a favor and end this relationship. He can tell I don't want it because I don't show the right signs. He can't name the things I never do.

He still has nothing going on in his life except me. I come home from school, and he is slumped in the living room waiting for me to give him something to talk about. He follows me from room to room quoting talk radio.

I can't say I'll do anything to make him stay because I won't. If he leaves, he leaves. For good. No more back-and-forth games for me. I'm not going to hold his life together for him while he is gone. He leaves and his life gets cancelled around here. The horses go, and I buy firewood.

SUNDAY, MARCH 20, 1988

Dear Everyone,

I have just closed myself in the studio and vowed not to emerge until I have produced one of those "newsy letters" for which I was once famous. News has always been easy enough to come by. If look up, there's always a chicken, or a goat, goose or duck doing something on my door-step that certainly isn't happening on yours, and I have plenty to say. However, since there have been ever-cleverer children on the doorstep and down into the greenhouse and out the porch door into the yard— well, there's even more to say, but less time at the typewriter.

Actually, our animal population has been reduced. We gave away our chickens in the fall, except for one, who is hoping she'll get new friends by sitting on a clutch of eggs under the porch. I must read to her from the poultry husbandry book about poultry husbands so she can understand the futility of her efforts.

Mary feeds the dog and Daniel feeds the cat. Being five, Daniel is very serious about his responsibility. In the mornings, often before any-one is up, he puts on his hat, boots, gloves, and work coat, fills up his cat food scooper, and trudges up to the shop, a hundred yards up the hill, to feed the kitties. I watch him sometimes from the window, holding the food up high while the entire feline population tumbles before his feet. He doesn't let them have any until he's climbed high on the shop porch (safe from Jake and the geese) where he can spread it out in a way that every kitty will get its share.

Mary is still working out the details of this responsibility thing. She is plenty skilled at getting the scooper full of food into Jake's dish, but she thinks the chore is more fun when the geese come and drive Jake from his dish and eat all the food. So we moved the dish inside and let her take a little food out to the geese after she feeds Jake. She always remembers to throw the dog food to the geese, but does she always remember to give some to Jake? He lets us know when she doesn't.

Mary and her Teddy Bear are inseparable. This doesn't mean she doesn't still sleep with The White Doll, The Red Doll, The Unicorn, her plastic horse, her wallet, and her most treasured artwork. It's just that Tedda is special. She sits next to Mary when she eats, and tickles her when she is sad. With Mary's assistance, Tedda can even draw, clear the table, and fly. She only likes girls, so I have to hold her when Mary dresses or bathes.

The two short people in the family have repaired to the loft with a lantern to pass the rest of the evening. The loft is entirely their province now. It's five feet high in the center and runs the length of the house. For a full-grown person, it's a cramped space you crawl around in. For the kids, it's a gymnasium.

Periodically, a playmate who is tiny enough to fit, yet old enough to have mastered the art of Cleaning Your Room appreciates its potential as a fairyland and helps them put the legs back on the tables, arrange the toys, park the trucks, and put their little mattresses side by side. They show it all off proudly. I give the pep talk about keeping it that way forever, but after a few days I'll be making the morning fire and hear them playing a wake-up game of Slide, or Fort, or Train, and they are back to demolition and remodeling.

Right now, they are playing "Daddy and Kelvin." Kelvin is our neighbor who works on the road crew and plows us out in the wintertime. Daniel tells Mary, "You stand there. You be Daddy." He is Kelvin, going, "Rrrrt. Rrrrrrrrrrrt. Rrr…" with his toy grader. "OK now you say 'Jesus Christ that thing throws some snow!'" Mary executes her line flawlessly, and the grader disappears around the curve in a cloud of snow. "Rrrrt. Rrrrt. Rrr…..."

This has been a long-range planning year for us. (We are currently into the fifth year of our original three-year plan.) I have had enough of going away to be a schoolteacher every day, and I miss the time when my life was centered at home. Robb, on the other hand, the one who has been on the home front for four years, wants to be out in the world. His art has come just about as far as it can for one person working all alone in the woods.

After a lot of pondering and exploration—and a job offer for Robb from a weekly newsmagazine—we decided to move to Moscow, a college town south of here. I still exchange Christmas cards with an old IBM friend named Wilson who has moved to California and started a software company. When he heard I was going to have electricity again, he offered me a job testing software and writing documentation at home. So things have rapidly fallen into place to support a big change in our lives.

We aren't giving up our house. We might only do this for a few years, and we always want to have it to come back to. Things are stable and can be left in Clayton and Deb's hands. It's better to have someone living in the house than boarding it up.

Robb starts work June 1. I'll finish off the school year and start packing. We're shooting to do the big move on the 4th of July. A whole different kind of summer ahead for me.

For you, coming soon—I hope—news from a different doorstep.

Second Street

You only have to let the soft animal of your body love what it loves.
—"Wild Geese" by Mary Oliver

Thursday, September 15, 1988. Statement provided to the Latah County Sheriff by Nancy Casey, asking for an Order for Protection against Robert E. Wilkerson:

My name is Nancy Casey and I live at 319 East Second Street in Moscow with my husband and my two children, ages 4 and 5. I am afraid that my husband, Robert E. Wilkerson, Jr. is going to hurt me. In the past, he has threatened to kill me, punched me, set fires, and smashed furniture. It's all getting worse. Last Sunday night, he left the house saying he was going to kill himself and I called the police and told them I was afraid and didn't want to let him back in if he came home. He went to the emergency room. The doctor gave him some medication and then called me and said I had to take him back, so the police brought him home. The doctor said he wasn't supposed to drink alcohol with the pills he was taking, but he drank a lot anyway. Last night at around midnight I was so afraid of him I ran out of the house, and apparently he called the police and told them I was threatening him with a gun because two police cars pulled up and they thought I was the dangerous person until I explained what was going on. The police took me back to the house and had me wait outside until they got my husband out and walked him down the block. I could hear him yelling and swearing the whole way. I went inside and got my kids out of bed and went to a friend's house. The next morning after I was sure he was at work, I came back to our house and everything in it was destroyed. Books and plants were thrown everywhere, furniture was broken, an upright piano was knocked over and smashed up, all the dishes and all the canned goods in the pantry had been thrown and broken against the kitchen wall, everything in the cupboards was dumped out, two guitars were smashed, my clothes were all on the ground in the yard. The whole place is a wreck. You can hardly walk through it.

When he's been violent before, he's calmed down and been sorry, but he always gets violent again. I am afraid of what he will to me next. He has never hurt the kids, but I don't trust him at all. He doesn't know where I am staying, but if he finds out, I'm afraid he will come and try to do something to me.

SATURDAY, SEPTEMBER 24, 1988

Now, the hard part. Go be normal.

The computer comes next week. I need to get the office room set up. It's so empty in here. Just like when we first moved in. The piano looks down-home great on the porch. Well, sort of. A piano could look great—that one looks terrible.

Part of me wants to breathe a big sigh, shrug and smile. "There! That's over with!" As though this has cleared the air and now everything is fine.

I haven't cried about it in the last few days.

I am so glad to be rid of him I've wanted him gone for such a long long time. Only for some reason I wouldn't do it… Crazy.

SUNDAY SEPTEMBER 25, 1988

I tried hard enough. Hayley says not to say I failed. Only that I tried. And I tried. And I tried.

At the Santa Barter Fair—first week in September, cataclysm a week ahead—Robb took on the role of Wronged Husband, the role he couldn't shed, even though it had been well over a year, even though as a pledge to him and the relationship, I had agreed—proposed!—that we leave the valley. I didn't believe, as he did, that I was killing him, that I had forced him into a lifestyle he had never wanted. Leaving that place ripped my heart out, a sacrifice I was making to help him get what he needed if he could not survive there.

A day of blurry heat, the September day of the Barter Fair. 106 degrees on the time-and-temperature sign at Rosauers as we drove north out of Moscow.

That same morning, a farmer's-market morning downtown, Daniel's face jumped from everywhere, life-size on the cover of Robb's magazine, sighting down the plastic scope of a toy gun. He looked troubled, like a child sniper. "Gimme a scowl," the photographer had said. Later Daniel asked me what a scowl was, thought it was some kind of money he was supposed to use to pay for the picture. All week Robb had been talking about the story he was doing about violence and children, how the research linking violent toys with violent behavior is inconclusive. We need a kid for a photo, he'd said.

Next issue, he was doing a story about the historical Jesus, so that's what we heard about the whole hot winding ride over the White Pine Drive.

I didn't have anything to trade at the barter fair. All I wanted from the gathering was to feel rested and connected to the life I believe in. I don't see these folks that often, but they are the ones who most feel like family to me. I'd talk with Esther about having had Caesareans and Gretchen about gender-role-reversal households. Daniel would play with Gabe and Mary with Kelsey. I would fondle Karen's baskets and she'd encourage me to keep making my own. I would ask Janesta how her house was coming and she would give me the details for this year. She'd say why she felt blessed and I'd reconnect with my own blessings. If it was a good campfire, we would play music and sing all night...

I was still helping the kids unbuckle and climb out when Robb rushed up. "I can't stay here. Fuckface is over there."

When would this stop? I so wanted to stay there. Yet he could have a point. But how could we make the kids spend another bizarre day sucking their thumbs in the back seat of the car while we drove all over sweltering hell?

"I'm not playing hippie-lovey-dovey bullshit for you," he spat. "We're leaving before you sneak off for a grope each in the dirt. But first I'm going to kick that motherfucker's ass."

The feeling that something sloughed off me was physical. Like a harness had unbuckled and dropped from my soul. The person I am and what he does bear no relationship to each other. Freedom. A brand new sensation.

From what I heard, while I was helping the kids unload their stuff, Robb strode over, said hello, picked him up and knocked him down. He and his girlfriend left. Robb said the only thing he was sorry about was that they pulled him away before he could kick him. He was glad. The whole thing made him feel better, gave him his self-respect back.

"I'm done," I said. "This will never work."

"OK, then, let's split up."

"Exactly."

"Let's go home right now and split up."

"You go home. I want to spend the weekend here. Just take the car and go. We can get a ride home on Sunday. We'll split up when I get back."

He changed his mind and decided he was sorry and wanted to stay. He spent the weekend in his sleeping bag.

Around the campfire that night in the middle of *Truckin'* Larry Mason and I exploded into some harmony of the heart, shouting "They can't revoke your soul for trying!" It made the others draw back.

I went down to the creek in the dark, took my clothes off and lay down. Fucking cold and freezing. The water lapped past my body and I felt like somebody who was still alive.

MONDAY, SEPTEMBER 26, 1988

I thought my challenging and difficult life would eventually reap deep rewards. Always "making progress" towards Robb turning into a normal loving guy. Someday all this struggle would pay off—but not if we didn't stay together.

I really believed that. I really thought my situation was violent only in some minor way. Enough to make it challenging, but not so violent as to make it dangerous, or even bad for me. I really believed that what he was doing wasn't hurting me. Once I could get my spine to quit tingling, everything would be fine.

Sick. You don't have to learn very much about this abuse stuff to know what the word is for that kind of thinking. Denial.

TUESDAY, SEPTEMBER 27, 1988

Backed to the wall by the American Medical Association. That's how I felt when the emergency room doctor said I had to take him back or else I'd be responsible for what he did. Stupid is how I felt with that cop on the front porch, looking at me and shaking his head (Did he really shake his head? I'm sure he did later.) "Are you *sure* you want to do this?" It was a blurred blue and gray domestic violence scene with flashing police lights.

Hayley says not to be mad at myself for not standing up to the doctor. You feel like you won't have any allies if you don't do what the doctor says. So weird, the bureaucracy of domestic violence. The sheriff has a procedure that says to call the domestic violence hotline. The city cops and the hospital don't. That's why it was so different when I went to the courthouse to ask about a restraining order. It was the sheriff's office. The guy who brought Robb to the door after the emergency room was a city cop.

When I told the cop at the window I was afraid my husband was going to kill me, it was the first time I wanted to cry. He got all flustered like he wasn't being the right kind of host and said I needed to come in and sit down, said he had to call someone who could help out with this. He brought me coffee and donuts and kept fussing, saying everything would be better when she got here.

Enter Hayley.

An advocate is a person who will spend the day with you while you navigate through the hearing and the paperwork, she explained. Hayley says that in a bar fight, broken glass is a lethal weapon. If he smashes a chair over the stove, he's showing you he could just as well smash it over your head. Threatening to hurt you is a crime called assault.

In other words: I qualify.

WEDNESDAY, SEPTEMBER 28, 1988

After the Barter Fair, we had begging-and-pleading.

"Can't you see how I hate myself for the things I do to you? I hear the things I say to you, see you recoil from me and cringe, and I just hate myself. Don't you see?"

No, I don't see. It was too late for me to see.

When he started tearing through boxes looking for the shotgun shells, I told him to get the hell out. He could kill himself and get this over with, but we didn't deserve to find him splattered all over some wall.

It's damn weird to go around the inside of your own house and make sure all your windows are locked.

The phone call from that stupid doctor. *You can't kick a man out of his own house.* Hayley says there will be plenty of time to confront the doctor. If I'm afraid he'll make me feel weak and humiliated, I simply don't have to take that on this week.

After that night, Robb was medicated and crazy. Insane and slow. Once he had the "right" drugs, he was way more scary than he ever was. It took until Wednesday for the light to go on in my head, when I did the arithmetic and realized it was not impossible for me to move. I practiced saying, "This weekend, somebody is going to move out, and I don't care if it's me or if it's you." He didn't come home from work until midnight. He was all sloppy from drinking, and at first I thought I should wait until a better time to tell him. There was never be a good time to tell him. So I said the words.

"Moving out? No…" He spoke slowly—medicated. Insane. "That would be something we'd have to talk about. I'm going to sit down with you right here and we might just talk about this all night."

Of all the things he has ever said to me, why was that the scariest thing I ever heard? Because with every slow, drugged word he was backing me into a corner of the upstairs bedroom, that's why. What would he have done to me if his cigarettes had been in his pocket? If he had kept me body-blocked in the corner instead of going off to hunt his smokes? What would have happened if I hadn't run out of the house?

My mother on the phone. I don't have to tell her anything because Robb has already called. She won't say a word until she's had a chance to talk to my father, but she wants to hear what I have to say about this filth Robb has told her about me.

So clear. So easy. I was only talking to people who were going to help and support me. I said so. I said I wasn't interested in a single thing Robb had to say about me.

I said bye.

FRIDAY, OCTOBER 7, 1988

The minister guy from up the street stops by with a basket of fruit right after Robb leaves with the kids.

He is *not* the one for me. Even if the string of coincidences is "too powerful to ignore."

I give him the chair and sit on the stool, thinking he'll stay for 10 minutes. He talks. And talks. I could be doing yoga. I could be reading *Women Who Love Too Much*, or finishing *Love in the Time of Cholera*. I could be at the computer designing Help screens, or writing in my journal. Instead I hear his life story. My mistake for asking what he did before coming here. I expected a three-word answer. He began with his childhood. He manages to pace around and end up sitting on the floor, leaving me all prim and uptight on the stool. He stretches out with his head propped on his elbow, lounging so comfortably on the carpet. My carpet. He has no right to be more comfortable in my house than I am. Him and his basket of fruit.

"Do you want to have a genuine friendship, or shall it just be a string of brief, shallow greetings now and again?" Niggle niggle. He finds me so uniquely intelligent. He's had deep insights about me that make him like me a lot. No go. I fell for that eight years ago.

I wonder how long before it's going to be over. It gets later and later and I feel more and more intruded upon. The issue of parting looms. Listening to him (or thinking about other things and being angry while he talks) is preferable to kissing him, or having to parry kissing him, or enduring some "meaningful" hug so he can press his dick against me.

He's dumpy and he's 13 years older than I am. I don't want any more daddies. I want someone *else* who was too young to go to Woodstock. This guy has crumbs in his beard and holes in his socks. Who told him he could take his shoes off?

As he talks, he scoots closer and closer to me so he can tap my foot to make a point or announce a joke. I stand up.

"Look, I don't want any romantic involvements." He explains why this isn't one. Because the lesson he most needs to learn is patience, he will be here for me when I am ready. You see, there was a line in the Rachmaninoff C-minor concerto that he knows only someone like me could share his insight about. If he could meet a woman who would intimidate him musically, she'd win him. Was that an invitation to be intimidating? I clearly don't intimidate him musically and apparently I have won him anyway.

Finally, he'll go. Ready, set, hug. Dick in the crotch. I turn my face outward, but he won't let go of my hands. Doesn't leave. Agenda's not up. He kisses me. Eyes open, teeth clash. Mash, mash.

"Look, I'm not up for this," I say

"A kiss???" Clearly I don't know anything about friendships and the role of kissing in them.

I am not protesting at every sick-o juncture because I am afraid of being humiliated.

Then in the morning he comes back! To apologize, I think. Instead, it's a la-la thank-you for what we shared, oh it's so wonderful when two people can truly meet. Today he is so happy and open to the world. He proposes an outing for tonight "so you can tell me your story."

"No."

Why is it so hard for me to say that one syllable to assholes?

At least I didn't let him beyond the porch.

SATURDAY, OCTOBER 29, 1988

At Robb's this morning. He didn't look so terribly awful. Green plaid shirt, jeans, bare feet. Under the clothes, the motions of the body I used to be so involved with. He was fumbling through pieces of paper for the address of where I should pick up the kids. I see the palsied, shaking, hands of an old man and I'm embarrassed for him. Envelopes on the table with doctors' names and "National Health Laboratories."

SUNDAY, OCTOBER 30, 1988

Batterer. It sure depersonalizes them. I can't tell to what degree they are to be depersonalized and hated. The opposite of love isn't hatred, it's indifference.

The big deal in the women's group is "getting out that anger." Anger, yes, I've certainly got plenty of that. But beneath the anger is pain. Wallowing in your anger is a way of not dealing with the pain. What are you supposed to do with the pain? You can't even point to where it hurts.

I don't feel it so much when I'm alone, like right now. But as soon as I'm out in the world, as soon as I have to deal with another person who isn't Mary or Daniel, I'm paralyzed.

I can't imagine I am doing anything right at all.

I'm probably supposed to talk in the group about that and I can't.

SUNDAY, NOVEMBER 6, 1988

Mary and I, looking at a map of the US. I am pointing out some of the shapes of the states. She asks, "Is this the map that has the state that's in the shape of an animal?"

"What animal?"

"A duckbilled dinosaur walking on three toes."

TUESDAY, NOVEMBER 8, 1988

Every time the furnace blower goes on, I remember the day Robb turned on the heat for the first time. It was a Sunday. It had been a bad one. All of the Sundays were bad ones by then. Robb was being a lump.

The kids and I walked to the food co-op and got some apple juice to share. I needed to be out of the house. You couldn't relax. You could sit down and prove you were depressed, or sit down and get ready to be talked at. The act of sitting down was like climbing into a trap.

Walking home, we saw a sign that said "Rug Sale" on a truck outside the Community Center, so we went in. The place was full of rugs—beautiful rugs, expensive rugs. It was a wet day, and I was real conscious of the little feet that shouldn't be walking on these rugs.

"Can we buy one?"

"No we're just looking at them because they're so pretty. The cost lots and lots of money. This one, for instance is six hundred dollars." A throw rug. That sent off a string of "How much is this one and this one and this one." They would have asked me how much every rug in the place was. There were hundreds of them.

Another couple was there at the same time, supposedly getting all of the salesman's attention. But as the mother of two children with wet feet, I could feel his attention trained on us, too. The couple was looking at 9 x 12 rugs, only they weren't talking about rugs, but about "pieces." This piece, and that piece—which was like the piece they had at home. How a piece like this one will grow on you, but a piece like that one you might get tired of. I wanted to check out the price of a 9 x 12 to get an idea of how much they were fixing to drop on their piece. But I felt so self-conscious, like all the other eyes were on me and my raggedy kids, and I was too afraid of showing how tacky and crude I was by peeking at the tag for what could only be the obvious reason.

Before the man could ask us to leave, we tiptoed out the side door.

At home, the furnace was running. Robb was proud and ecstatic. The kids went from room to room—I guess we all did—checking the vents to feel the warm air. My worst fear was coming at me through the walls. Doors and windows closed. Trapped in there with him for the winter. Stale air falls to the basement, is reheated and spat back up. When I wasn't looking, he rose up from his depression couch and closed the gates.

THURSDAY, NOVEMBER 10, 1989

Women Who Love Too Much. A whole book about the ways I shoot myself in the foot. I feel cheated by how she says the only way out of the pattern is to forswear men and relationships. More punishment for being the way I am. If someone comes along to offer some comfort and consolation, because of who you are, you must turn it down.

SUNDAY, NOVEMBER 13, 1988

Papier-mâché puppets. I promised we could make papier-mâché puppets. We have books from the library to show us how.

What is the right formula for making Daniel, Mary, and I a perfect trio together? Exactly how shall I set this up so they behave like they are happy?

Why can't we just relax and do this?

Because I don't know how. I get upset with every little jiggle of the table. Tables don't jiggle when children are quiet and perfect, adoring what I am doing for them. I zip my lips, just zip them. The kids are goofy and messy, as are the puppet heads, but the project gets done. Soon we are putting on PJs, brushing teeth, and then playing in the living room with puzzles. Slowly, slowly I relax. This will all be okay.

Next on my program is for them to go to bed. They want to clean their room. I want to order them not to, except they have already launched themselves into the task—industriously, delightfully. I do not allow myself to stop them. Zip the lips. When they are done and call me in to see, we have warm and joyous tucks and snuggles. We are *all* proud of ourselves.

Here I am now, drinking coffee, canning apple butter.

FRIDAY, NOVEMBER 25, 1988

Picking up the kids left me fried and angry. Robb asked for my phone number. No way.

He says I don't realize how, now that the "burden is off" he's a happy guy with a circle of friends that spans three counties. "Not lovers, friends. People that are glad to help me out." On Friday nights, he comes to the Deli to help cater their banquets, not for money, just for the people. The waiters and waitresses are all into theater. When there's leftover salmon, guess who goes home with a big chunk? If he is living so grand, then why does he always tell me to feed the kids before they come?

I remember the time in Boulder when he had talked endlessly about some wild game specialty restaurant up in the mountains. He'd done a story about it once, and would expound to everyone, everyone (Clayton, my mother, random hunters) on all the techniques for cooking wild game. Mostly he just slopped a jar of jam over whatever he cooked. I was the one who cooked the three bears and the occasional grouse, venison, or elk that came our way. But that was the greatest restaurant, the owner just loved him, they were such pals, we would visit, and feast for free. We dressed up, drove up there, and at the door, the wonderful owner had to ask who in the hell he was. As I recall, we had bread and broth because it was the only thing we could afford.

Anyway, I'm trying to get out of the Deli and he wants my phone number. Like it's unimaginable he'd abuse it as a drunken asshole, or even as a sober one. I want some humble homage, the tiniest recognition that he wrecked my house and everything in it. What does he say? "You're not the only one who got burned in this deal, you know." Fucking asshole. What the fuck did I do to him that he didn't top?

Which is the whole deal when people get divorced.

Might as well recognize the bit of Nancy Nugent operating here. Can't bear to be told she ever did anything wrong. What? Me? A mistake? Well, certainly nothing in comparison to the mistakes somebody else has made.

A discussion with Robb is like one with my father. The rules of good taste and decorum guarantee you'll lose. Innocent little clods like me, we expect something fair. We have practiced all of the principles of forgiveness and honesty, rehearsed our speeches in good faith, purging nasty, vindictive thoughts with positive affirmations. Fill your heart with love, leave your weapons at home, expose your neck. Get creamed every time. Get told you brought it upon yourself.

The whole sidewalk way home, my mind boiled with frustrated thoughts. How could he? How dare he? All that crap. I ought to just be thankful I am no longer saddled with him and move on.

My goal for the day was to have a pleasant Thanksgiving time with the kids. Not yet realized. They've been asleep since we got home at noon. That means we can have a long and nice evening together, I hope. Make placemats and place cards, pumpkin pie. Eat turkey, squash, mashed potatoes.

And we did.

I thought about inviting other people and couldn't come up with anyone to invite who wouldn't be someone to worry over. Who'd make me have to cook and think at the same time, while the kids were shunted off to the other room.

Could there have been two more perfect Thanksgiving guests? They didn't know what the schedule for eating ought to be. They woke up at 5 o'clock all excited about the turkey, regardless of when I thought it should come out of the oven. They made bread. They made placemats. I cooked and fooled around, enjoying what I was doing, struggling not to think of Robb, and winning. They didn't hassle me, ask me complicated questions, offer to help, ply me drinks, or roll joints. They were busy and excited. I suggested they invite their dolls and stuffed animals to sit at the unoccupied end of the table.

"My puppy has never had turkey before, and besides, I haven't played with him in a long time," says Daniel. Then they all have to have place cards. "How do you spell Rubberfeet?" The place cards had to have paper feathers. So they'd look like turkeys.

Daniel has learned about Thanksgiving in kindergarten and he told the story after we all sat down: "A long time ago, the Pilgrims came from somewhere, I can't remember where, but they came on the Mayflower. When they got here, they only had a little bit of food in the basement of the Mayflower and when winter came, they were hungry. Then some Indians brought them some food and they ate it all. All this happened before there were any people. The people didn't come for a long, long time. Thirty summers."

We ate. The food was terrible. They didn't know. The pumpkin pie was good.

Looking at Tedda, Smidgel, Puppa, Monka and Rubberfeet at their end of the table, it hit me—Daniel's "Pilgrims." From *A Visit to William Blake's Inn*, a poem I've read to them so many times, where Tiger, Rabbit, Bear and Mouse sit at the hearth and "toast their toes in praise of fire." The last line: "Keep all these little pilgrims warm."

Oh my little guys. So precious. So precious.

FRIDAY, DECEMBER 9, 1988

Reading old journals has turned me upside down. The slow-tornado chaos of the whole last year—Robb in bad shape, me struggling. In some ways it was boring to read. Then I started on the older notebooks. I'd never read back over some of that stuff before. When I was writing it always felt like junk, junk, junk–nothing worth reading again. I guess that's even part of the denial. It's all there. The incidents, the fights. They started early and never stopped. If I had read it back then, would I have noticed that, picked up on the pattern?

I had no idea how much I blamed myself for the way he treated me. Blamed myself for not loving him enough to overlook it.

SUNDAY, DECEMBER 11, 1988

Anyone who tried and worked as hard as I have in the last seven years ought to have something to show for it.

When I say that, people point to the kids. Like they are the reason I shouldn't feel empty.

Kids aren't "something you have to show." They aren't a reward. They are barely a product of your efforts. You certainly don't own them.

SUNDAY, DECEMBER 18, 1988

Dinner was eggs and toast. They told me they only had candy and chips at Robb's. I wonder if it is true. They both opted for dessert rather than another egg. When the meal was winding up, I had an urge to get up and go into the living room and play the piano. So many parts of my life have opened back up now that Robb is gone, it seemed like that part could open up, too. The urge was so strong and so real, it seemed as though, if I walked around to the other side of the wall just right, I'd see the piano and not a paper-plate reindeer and Christmas stockings.

"Y'know what I wish," I said to them. "I wish I could play the piano." I tried to talk adult-to-kid fashion about why a piano is a nice thing to have. They told me ours has fourteen keys that still make sounds.

"We'll get another one someday."

"When?"

"Well, when we can. They cost lost of money."

Daniel wishes someone had a piano that cost one cent. "I would go into my dresser and get a penny and I would say here it is, here is your money." He pantomimes reaching into his pocket and thrusting the coin high into the hand of the imaginary piano seller.

I could have changed the subject. I could have stood up, cleared the table, and gone into the other room where we'd started making Christmas packages to mail—probably late—to family members. As long as I sat there, my fantasy piano might still be on the other side of that wall. I didn't want to change the subject. I wanted to cry about it. So I did.

I feel funny crying in front of the kids. Turning them into adult friends. Making Mary cry and say she is scared. They hug me and I comfort them while they comfort me. They crowd each other and bump heads on my chest. Soon they'll argue. I make my crying stop.

It's time to go into the other room and play Santa Claus.

I walk straight past the presents and the boxes, and land on the couch. "Just give me five more minutes to cry about my piano. Then I'll be ready to do the presents." I bury my head and sob. Asking myself if the piano is what I am crying about.

(Writing this, I stop at the word "sob" and sob some more, asking myself the same question.)

Mary waltzes into the living room and demands, "When are we *ever* going to wrap the presents?"

"Five minutes," says Daniel. "She wants to cry for five more minutes about her piano."

MONDAY, DECEMBER 19, 1988

My dad. Slurry, drunken, manic, angry, would say we prefer him to be depressed, no matter how it feels for him. That made us nervous and uncomfortable because it was true. When he was depressed, we knew what he'd do. He wouldn't badger us and accuse us of being ourselves. Whatsammatter? Can't you take a joke? It's like being goosed in a crowded bar. Did anyone see what just happened to me? Nope.

People ask, "Isn't it hard to be away from your family over the holidays?"

TUESDAY, DECEMBER 20, 1988

Reliving things Robb did. Reliving the pain and the rage. My punishment now for not admitting it then. What aren't I admitting now?

WEDNESDAY, DECEMBER 21, 1988

Today. What a day. Another day.

Babysitting. Carol dropped Drew off at 8:15.

When I want to hurry down the sidewalk and get things done, another kid is different. More work. More patience. He's not trained to respond to my cues the way Daniel and Mary are, especially when the cue is, "Stay in orbit around me, give me lots of room, pay attention, and don't need anything."

Downtown to the vitamin store to send the xmas stuff UPS. Four inches of snow last night. Five blocks. Six boxes to carry, four of which were made by cutting up bigger boxes and taping the pieces back to-gether. I knew I bought some better tape the night we went shopping for crayons. At least I remember fingering it. It was a week after Thanksgiv-ing, a Friday night, the day after I got paid. Buying the tape was going to put me so on top of things. Maybe I fingered it and then procrastinated. Maybe I thought it would be cheaper somewhere else and then it slipped my mind. Maybe I brought it home and lost it. I don't know. No tape could I find.

In the doorway, Mary won't leave her kitty, a two inch Disney trinket that plays electronic Jingle Bells when you press its belly. I tell her it's too little come along. She nuzzles it against her cheek and says she wants to carry it and take care of it.

We shuffle down the unplowed sidewalks, scale the berms of snow at every corner and get to the vitamin store—where they don't sell tape. I tell the woman I'll go to the drugstore and get some, but she says, no, she has tape. I say they're really going to need a lot of tape, I'd be happy to pay for the tape. She gives me six forms to fill out.

From. To. Zip. Contents. Declared value? As little as possible. $50, I put. What a joke. A lousy little jar of apple butter and one of the Christ-mas ornaments Robb's Mom made that I want to get rid of. They flew from her hands like flower petals. She mailed them to the four winds. *Oh, it is so cute,* they will write back in their timely thank-you notes, telling me which branch of the Christmas tree they hung it on.

There's a single bench to sit on. Three dripping kids in snowsuits. Give me room. Don't touch me. Don't talk to me. Don't breathe on me. Don't watch me. Be good. Be quiet. Be invisible. Don't make me deal with you in any way.

Somebody jiggles, the stack of boxes tumbles, and four of the com-pleted forms spill to the floor behind the bench where there is a puddle of melting snow.

I jump up to retrieve them, but Daniel is standing in front of me and doesn't immediately anticipate the direction I want to go. "Move," I order, but he seems short-circuited, playing statue or something. "Move," I re-peat with a tad more how-dare-you intensity, and poke him impatiently in the ribs with my fingers. He steps back, and stands still while I retrieve the papers. It's claustrophobic. They want to take their snowsuits off.

"I'm sweaty," complains Mary.

"I need a tissue," says Drew.

"I don't have one," I retort. Don't you see how talking to me is fruitless and not fun? Jerk a different chain. Nothing for you here. Christmas is hard enough. There's no room in the inn.

Daniel is motionless behind me. I lean over and kiss the top of his head, tell him I'm sorry I poked him.

"You hurt me," he accuses.

Oh bullshit, says the voice of exasperation. It wasn't polite. It wasn't nice. It was even uncalled for, but it didn't hurt. It's not right to hurt your children.

Finally ready, I'm still ashamed of my boxes. The woman checks a list and tells me they won't make it by Christmas. I don't care. I'm doing my job by sending them out. I have to resist telling her I don't even like the people I'm sending them to. I keep apologizing for the boxes, how she has to use so much tape. I ask her if she gets to keep the dollar handling charge. She does, but it barely covers the price of the forms and the tape. I apologize again for the ugly, unwieldy boxes. You can see newspaper through some of the cracks. I can't get her to say it's okay.

The first one weighs two pounds and costs two dollars and twenty cents to send, plus the handling charge. This is gonna cost twenty dollars. Definitely not worth it. Should have written one of those long letters I can send off for the cost of a stamp. Too late now. What's in my checking account? I have a twenty in my wallet that's supposed to be for fun and groceries for the last week in December. I can't tell her now that I don't have enough money to send the boxes.

Reward: ice cream.

"The ice cream store will be for three kids," Mary beams, "now that Drew is here." Mary has seventy-eight cents, and the ice cream store sells 25-cent samples. With her plastic juice bottle of pennies and nickels she handles the entire transaction. She has a pink one, Drew has a brown one, and Daniel has maple nut because that's grandpa's favorite. The bonus: Drew gets to empty his green congealing boogers into a napkin.

Stop in the food co-op. I like it there. Get to talk. Worried they find me a pain in the ass for coming around so much. Rubberfeet was there. Daniel left him behind the last time we passed through. He did all the vocals to express both his delight and Rubber's at the happy reunion. We leave—then go back for Drew's mittens.

We cross Third Street at the light. There's a berm of snow down the middle of the road. Climbing over it, Mary trips and falls down. Panics. Gets up and falls again. Drew is between her and me, and my arms are laden with groceries, so I can't take her hand. She is shrieking and sobbing, falls one more time before I reach her. Trapped in the snow, in the middle of the street, in the sound of traffic—she doesn't know she's not really in danger and she is terrified.

We make it across. We cover half a block. "Where's my kitty?"

"In the grocery bag." I would've put it there if I had thought about it. I wonder if I did. I hope she forgets by the time she gets home.

The boys stop to kick at clods of snow. C'mon let's move it, move it, move it. We've been at this for two hours. Just get me home. Drew keeps lagging behind. He's the same age as Mary, but she and Daniel have made this hike a lot.

Home. Mittens. Boots. Snowsuits. Icy clinkers of snow melting into everyone's socks. Fix some kind of lunch.

"It's not in the grocery bag," Mary cries out. She flings herself into my arms, wailing. She needs to feel what she feels. I know she's tired, too. And hungry. Will food and rest mitigate this? "How about some lunch? Will that make you feel better? Hot chocolate?"

Nope. She wants to wail. OK, I'll hold her while she wails. Daniel sticks his face into mine and tells me he's *hungry*. I tell Mary I know how terribly sad she is, because I have felt the same way about my piano.

We make it to the kitchen. We carefully take everything out of the bag. She's cheerful and hopeful—until we don't find it and she wails all the more.

She gets a realization: "If I dropped it when I fell down, then cars would roll on it and make it break!" Daniel surmises that if something did run over it, the song inside would be wrecked, causing her wail to rise like a siren.

We eat and go back to look for it. Drew is asleep on his feet. I wonder why I am doing this, and at the same time I know why I'm doing this. I'm confident we won't find it, but she's so overcome with grief, I can't blow this thing off.

I want to rush down the street and back. We trudge. I park them in front of the Community Center and tell them to play in the snow while I search in the intersection. Mary insists on coming along. When the light changes, I tell her to wait on the corner. In the middle of the street, you can see the dent in the dirty snow where she fell and flailed earlier. I kick the snow around until the light changes. No kitty.

I hustle the rest of the way across the street, scan the sidewalk and the inside doorway of the co-op where we'd had our extravaganza of zippers and mittens. I can't bring myself to go all the way in and ask. I spend as much time in there looking for things we leave behind as I do buying things, and I've strewn children all along the sidewalks behind me.

When Mary, who has been watching so hopefully, sees I don't have it, she throws back her head and wails. Her little face is swollen and distorted, smeared with snot and tears. I carry her. She can't stop crying. A woman passes, smiles at me. Drew trails behind. Daniel is lugging an enormous clod of snow. "Leave that snow there. We have plenty of snow at home." That really came out of my mouth.

I know why this happened. Because she brought the damned thing with her. They would take everything they own on every trip to everywhere if I gave them half a chance. They just love to take their junk out the door. I always end up carrying it, even though I always say, "Okay you can take it, but you have to carry it." Coming home, they're always tired and bogged down. If I don't carry it all, I'll spend the rest of the day on the sidewalk.

Her sobs have quieted. Should I start an I-told-you-so lecture? See what happens when you don't listen to me? I'm so weary of this kind of thing. This isn't the time to talk about it, but when is?

Suddenly she blurts another explosion of tears. Howls. "I shouldna never brought it with me."

Somehow it all ends. When I tucked her in tonight, she informed me she won't be sleeping well at all because she doesn't have her kitty. Like it's the principle of the thing.

SUNDAY, DECEMBER 25, 1988

As in Christmas.

OK day. No tears. Took my cues from Thanksgiving—simple is special. We took off our jammies when we *felt* like it. The only downer was talking to my family.

I tell my mother I think I found someone who will take the piano hulk away. She asks if it's still on the porch, and I think she's concerned about moisture damage in case the pieces are useful to someone. I start to explain why I'm sure it's dry, and she interrupts, "But doesn't it look awful junky? That's such a nice street…"

I volunteer to my dad that we had pizza for dinner because that's what the kids wanted. "Pizza!" he hollers. Then snorts. "Don't you think you are carrying this vegetable thing too far?" Over-enunciating.

How do I refuse to play this game? I don't know. I try to be pleasant and wait for it to be over. Just like I used to do with Robb.

What an epitaph: She waited for it to be over.

Monday, December 26, 1988

Christmas is done! All that's left is the aftermath—play with the presents, play with the kids.

Tuesday, January 3, 1989

Ooh, is it winter. A foot of snow overnight.

Tulips on the tables in Café Spudnik. Daffodils, too. Reminding me of spring. It will come. I will feel different in the spring.

Saturday, January 7, 1989

Dream.

Outside the Old House waiting for some people to arrive. The car comes, passes, and stops. This is according to the plan. I'm to follow them in the old truck. First, I have to turn around, a lot of clumsy maneuvering between the snow berm and the edge of the bank. The engine is cold, gears grind. I work at it. The inside of the truck is too roomy for me. I have to hang from the steering wheel to reach the clutch. I've almost turned around when, at the edge of the bank, I accelerate, but I've forgotten somehow to put it in reverse. I slam my feet into the clutch and the brake, hang one-armed from the top of the wheel while my right arm flails for reverse. It's too late. I've tipped over the bank and am slowly rolling, then plummeting towards the creek. Having given up hope of stopping, I concentrate on not rolling over. I flash on the process of pulling the truck out of the creek with a chain attached to some large, steady, well-treaded rig, probably Delbert's. I don't have any worry for bodily injury or damage to the truck. I'm keeping a cool head to prevent that. I hit a big bump and for a holy, slow-motion instant, I am airborne, flying towards the road on the other side. Could I really reach the far bank? As soon as the tires make contact, I accelerate, and sure enough, I spin up from the snow, onto the gravel, and out of danger.

Wasn't that something? I can't wait to tell Robb all about it. But now the road is steep, and I'm picking up speed. It's icy, too. I'm not in low gear. If I brake or downshift, I'll skid.

A word about that other car. It's red, shiny and well-kept, a California car, the kind that passes in the summertime with the windows all rolled up because it has air conditioning. The passengers are unaware of the dust, the heat, and they are dressed in clean, new clothes, too warm for the season. If they got out, or if the window opened even a crack, they would melt. If I were to get into their car, I would look like a turd on a china plate.

WEDNESDAY, JANUARY 18, 1989

While the kids picked out the books they wanted me to read, I went into the office, buried my face in my hands and tried to shit out some sobs. Uh-unh-unh. They came, sort of, a scraping off the surface. I grabbed a pen and wrote, "I am in pain" and taped the paper to the wall. There. It's real.

THURSDAY, JANUARY 19, 1989

Fears I have: of not being loved, of not being cared for, of never being appreciated for the person I am inside for as long as I live.

MONDAY, JANUARY 23, 1989

A house blessing for Annalee from the women's group. We were to visit every room, beginning with her son Adam's. Obviously he'd been coached ahead of time, but the party atmosphere, the visiting kids and all the tension in his life made him wild and giggly instead of spiritual and profound in a childlike way. When it came time to play the song he had chosen, he wanted to change it. Annalee tried to wrangle him with reason, but he rolled on his back and spoke nonsense.

"What do you want for yourself in this room, Adam?"

"Slime!"

"What about privacy? Comfort? A place to play and be happy. Be safe and be yourself."

"I already *have* that in here!" he shouts.

In the living room, Bill remains on the couch, snuggled against a lanky beauty named Nina with bottled raven hair. She holds his hand and fondles his head lopped against her shoulder. Surreptitious glances don't afford enough detail to know if this is comfort or making out. Annalee has been planning her new life since October when she announced, radiant, "Bill and I are going to separate after the holidays." Bill, an economist, doesn't believe there is a spiritual aspect to anything, a position that is stifling Annalee.

In the spare bedroom Annalee is manifesting what she talked about all fall. "I just can't wait until I have a whole room dedicated solely to the spiritual." Talismanic-looking stuff is arranged on a low table in the middle of the room. We join hands around it. Nina slips into the room to recite the prayer that came to her today. "Breathe," it begins. All eyes are cast down. I fart. Hot and steamy. Black beans. The odor saturates the room. I guess I "breathed."

Next all six of us crowd into the bathroom. Annalee introduces the space where she will come to cleanse herself, reflect, and be good to her body. We gather around the sink. I keep stealing glances at the poor forgotten toilet. What about elimination? Would that be the ceremonial word? It wouldn't make us picture Annalee grunting, shitting, running out of toilet paper or yanking out a suction-stuck tampon. Another fart. Deadly.

At departure time, Bill leaves first, but not before Nina clamps him into an embrace. Full body spiritual communication. Except the marriage is ending because Bill doesn't go for that jazz. They cling, and cling. And cling. When he is gone, the rest of us get our coats. All but Nina, who stays.

TUESDAY, JANUARY 24, 1989

I remember a restaurant. It was a darkish place—booths with high-backed benches and heavy wooden tables. I was visiting my family the summer after I left Dominic. *Let's go out for lunch.*

I couldn't take bites out of my hamburger because I was crying so much. When the waitress came by, we were all embarrassed because I couldn't hold it together long enough for her to ask if the food was okay. Of the whole inquisition, I only remember one thing. My dad pressing me about how I told my mother that before getting a divorce, I would go to counseling with Dominic.

"Did you say you'd do that? Did you? Did you?"

"Well, yes, but—"

"And did you do that?"

"Well, no, but—"

My mother breaks in: "See. She lies."

My father, who might not have thought I was a liar, then learned the miserable truth about me. That's how it always goes. She had hoped to spare him. If I wasn't such a creep, maybe he wouldn't be so depressed all the time.

Nice trap. He never spoke one goddamned word to me after I was five years old, other than to criticize—bumbling father stuff out of TV or movie scripts. Like pointing to the only A-minus on my report card and asking, "What happened here?" Or measuring with a ruler to see how far above my knee a skirt was and sending me upstairs to change before school. A lousy all-girls Catholic school where we could've all run around naked and no male eye would have been cast upon the goods. He never had anything friendly to say. Nothing positive. Nothing good. Nothing interesting.

Never? Am I being mean? Can I not think of one lousy time in my life he was ever simply nice to me? Nope. I refuse. I couldn't remember one now if I wanted to. Can I remember a time when he wasn't at work, depressed, manic, drunk, or asleep?

And yet. A part of me is still willing to buy into the notion that he would have admired me if he hadn't been repeatedly devastated by the things I did.

WEDNESDAY, JANUARY 25, 1989

The minister guy asked me if I would come to his church and talk on Valentine's Day. For his program on all the aspects of love. He has a gay couple, an over-sixty couple, teenyboppers, and he needs someone to talk about the pain of love. He hands me a tape of this wonderful song he has to go with what I'll say.

Made me so mad.

My problems with love don't begin and end with my relationship with Robb. It's not a simple story of getting my heart and my furniture broken one day. Our relationship was the long slow playing out of a situation I'd already been in for 30 years.

If I was gonna talk about love on Valentine's day, I would talk about how the love I didn't even know I was missing has shaped my life. Instead of singing some whiny song that begins (can you believe it?) "Breathe," I would sing a lullaby. The one I sing when I curl me up and rock me and search for that crying child who shouldn't be ashamed of herself. I try to hold her and sing to her, love her and heal her. Not only am I the only one who cares enough to do it. I'm the only one anymore who can.

Stand me up in front of your congregation to tell a story I can't tell without crying. Watch me bravely hold back the dry heaves of the soul. Great sharing, Nancy. Thanks for impaling yourself in front of us. Now we can go home and give thanks we're not a mess like you.

The good part was the fact that I'll be gone that week. No discussion after I'd said no.

FRIDAY, FEBRUARY 3, 1989

Women's group last night. As the conversation shifted to children, I was washed in anxiety and guilt about my own.

I have been reading *Grandchildren of Alcoholics*. When I saw the title I thought it was funny. How about second cousins and next-door neighbors?

I can't get my mind around the idea that my dad is an alcoholic. He didn't do the outrageous things they put in the books children of alcoholics read to understand their damage. What's the harm in a dad who comes home, drinks 3 martinis and falls asleep in his chair? Isn't that what dads do?

My grandfather, however, is a different story. They always say he died of pneumonia, but there's a whispered understanding that it had something to do with binge drinking, how he'd sleep on the street and be gone for days at a time. A real alcoholic. I always picture him passed out, freezing to death in a rain-soaked gutter. Grandchildren of alcoholics? I qualify.

Turns out the book didn't make me think any harder about that grandfather who died before I was born. It made me see the patterns operating right here in my life, right now, in my household. The central theme is the idea that if you were brought up in a family that was confusing and damaging to you, and you don't want to raise your children like that—well you're just going to have a real hard time because you don't know how to do what nobody did for you. You don't even know what it is that's not being done.

You're willing to work so hard. You work as hard as one human can on the things you understand. The rest, the part you don't see, is enough to make your kids as confused as you once were, make them grow up knowing they don't want to raise kids the way you raised them. The book say all this in a compassionate way, makes it seem like figuring out the things you don't understand about a healthy family life doesn't have to be just one more eloquent way to list your defects. It can be an interesting daily puzzle, where you try to notice what you ordinarily miss.

The book suggests that there are household rules for what can and can't be talked about, even if you think there aren't. That isn't necessarily a problem, unless someone in the household needs to talk about one of the "forbidden" topics.

When Daniel said every time he stands in front of the toilet and pees he is sad because he can't look up at the sky and see tamarack trees, tears brimmed up out of my chest so fast I could hardly see, and I pretended I was so engrossed in my bustling that I hadn't heard. What a morass it makes for him when I steer him from telling me what makes him sad because hearing it will made me sad. What was I supposed to do? Fill the bathtub with tears, sobbing, "Me, too. Me, too."

The book says just to start by noticing what the forbidden topics of conversation are. Keep paying attention and eventually you'll notice ways to let them into your household calmly and safely. Pay attention without trying to change things, and overall communication will improve. Pay attention and learn.

Monday, February 6, 1989

Robb says he's moving to Central America and never paying another cent of child support. Because he can't stand to see his kids playing with my bi-sexual, syphilitic, clap-ridden friends.

Wednesday, February 8, 1989

Another exhausting round last night.

Daniel was being contrary and negative. A squabble looking for a place to erupt. I snapped at him to quit being so rude or he would have to go to bed. (How many awful feelings has this bewildered boy had to stuff and suffer alone in his bed?) I found him with his face buried in the couch pillows.

"How do you feel?"

"Mad."

"Do you know why you feel mad?"

(Nods.)

He was mad because I had talked rude to him when he was upset. I told him I was wrong to be rude, especially because I was trying to teach him not to be rude.

"Were you already upset when I talked to you rude?"

(Nods.)

"Did something happen to make you upset?"

(Nods.)

"Do you remember what it was?"

"Mary got 2 cherries in her hot chocolate and I only got one."

"Well, you could have said then that you felt upset because Mary got 2 cherries and you only got one."

"I did that."

"Then what happened?

"Nothing. Nobody ever listens to me." (Important piece of data.)

"I get the idea you don't feel very special." He snuggles closer and closer to me, buries his face next to my lap. I am amazed at how his body language is the same I use when someone is trying to know what I think, but I am confused by it and think it's either unimportant, dumb, or bad.

"So what could make you feel more special?"

"If I had 2 things and Mary only had one."

"How about if you had 2 things and Mary had none?"

(Nods.)

I bring him two dates.

He said he's thought about it some more and knows what would make him feel special. "Make a special book. Just for me."

"We can do that. Not tonight, though," I say. It's pretty late to start that." (So, did I say no?)

THURSDAY, FEBRUARY 9, 1989

Daniel: A long time ago, so long ago that nobody can even remember, horses didn't have *hooves*, they had *toes*.

Mary: So did people have hooves, then?

FRIDAY, FEBRUARY 10, 1989

Hard day. Heavy time at the women's group—business as usual, I guess. Janet talked about why she thought maybe she should leave the group. Said when she signed up for it she was told it was for talking about normal women's issues, and that's not the kinds of problems that have been coming up. She talked a long time, round in circles.

"What I hear you saying, " I finally said, "is that you didn't come here to listen to details of domestic violence and that women who have been abused are so screwed up that you don't want to expend any energy to have a friendship with any of them."

"That's pretty much it."

While the rest of them had a fine intellectual conversation about her "inability to give support," I cried. Not demonstrably. Just settled into the corner of the couch and leaked. It was almost relaxing.

I was trying to make Janet squirm when I said that. I hated her for being like all of the people who didn't want to know I was in trouble. I hated her, too, for being like the part of me that didn't want to know that I was in trouble. She plugged straight into my fear that nobody would want to be my friend if they knew how bad my life was fucked up. And my fear that my life is so fucked up now I will never recover.

I've wanted to cry for days. I guess that couch was the safest place I've been all week. I left without saying a word to anyone.

Sunday, February 12, 1989

Last night, I was in the back yard when Robb brought the kids home. By the time I got into the living room, he was peeing in the bathroom. Once he was out the door and onto the porch, I asked him not to come into my house uninvited. Even said "please." Asked him three times. Got three responses:

Don't get me wrong, I hate it here…

You don't want some guy peeing on your lawn, do you?

Can't you ever meet me half way?

Wednesday, February 15, 1989

We walk down to Friendship Square and wait for Robb. Mary runs and spins and jumps down the street so extravagantly I am afraid she is going to whirl into traffic. Daniel drags. He has such a dismal, slack face.

We get to the square 10 minutes early. They head for the climbing toys, but soon Daniel is slumping slowly towards me, wearing the saddest of looks.

"You need some lovin' and lap time?" I ask.

He nods, crawls onto my lap and settles like a limp noodle. I hold him. He tells me the sad thing that happened to him today is that he called Robb and he's not going to take him to the toy store tonight. The conversation wends a lot of places. Essential parts—

"Do you think maybe your dad doesn't love you and care about you?"

"I *know* he loves me and cares about me."

"Sometimes you can *know* something is true and still not feel like it. Do you *feel like* he loves you?"

He shakes his head. "But I *know* he loves me because he buys me treats and even lets me eat them before dinner."

In another part…

"He has only told us one story since the divorce."

I try to talk in simple language about his losses. "You used to have a dad in your house who did lots of fun and special things with you. You painted pictures and sang songs. He told you stories. Now he's not like that and that's really *sad.*"

"Don't say those things. You are going to make me cry."

"People cry when they're sad."

He sucks his thumb and buries his head against my chest. When Robb rounds the corner, he slithers from my lap and bounds over to him, all excitement and smiles.

I would cry all the way to yoga if it wasn't such a public walk. Feeling so incompetent to deal with all the sadness in these sweet children I love so much.

My garbage pile is so deep and so tall. I fear I am powerless against it.

SATURDAY, FEBRUARY 18, 1989

I am growing every day. Just like Mary and Daniel are—changing bit by imperceptible bit. I have lots of areas in process at once—family issues, my kids, my circle of friends, my job, my house, my body, making things, playing music...

I am somewhat competent at all of them. Progress has been made on all fronts. When I focus on one and give it the energy and concentration to move forward, the whole rest of my life doesn't fall apart.

I had a wonderful day. Made a basket in the sun, was outdoors for the twilight birdsong. A backyard campfire with the kids. What could be a better way to play be-here-now than staring into a fire, sometimes cuddling, sometimes burning up sticks? They told me things.

Daniel told me I didn't see the tears on his face as we drove away from the Old House. He and Mary used to stay awake after Brahms Lullaby to see if there would be a fight. Fights always made Mary scared and she cried.

I told them I was so very, very sorry. Said it's a sad and terrible thing to lie in your bed at night and be scared or listen to a fight and I never wanted that to happen to them again.

They have both been hugging me so much lately...

MONDAY, FEBRUARY 20, 1989

We have been talking about a project of making flowers to put on our window and decorate the door. So I thought we could eat out and get that together.

They were all wound up, giggly, jumpy, unable to sit still, unable to eat. We loaded all the food into a styrofoam container and went off to make day-glo photocopies of the shapes of flower parts we had drawn the day before. Back home, we started cutting the shapes out. Started. This whole project was probably more my idea than theirs. The cutting-out was big, big work for little hands and kid scissors.

Carol called to make arrangements for Thursday night. Mary and Drew got on the line shouting and babbling at each other. I wanted to scream at her. Tell her to make conversation, make sense, use telephone etiquette or shut up. (Under other circumstances, I call this behavior 'wordplay'.) Why can't you be a normal subdued kid? Ok, you don't even have to be normal, just be subdued. I want calm around me.

Here I am working so hard to create a situation where they are free to talk and act according to the way they feel, and when they do, I can't stand to be around it. I end up talking to Carol for half an hour instead of just 5 minutes and I get off the phone because the kids are starting to fight.

We settle back down in the living room and get back to cutting flower shapes. I realize I will need to cut most of them, which is okay. It's mindless and somewhat soothing.

I can't remember in what order things happen next. It wasn't orderly.

Tired of cutting, I force myself to continue. I am forever taking my last reserve of energy and dumping it down some rat hole. It's like using enthusiasm instead of aim to hit a target. Sitting on the living room floor with a scissors, carving out hot pink petals, I'm crying. I can't believe what starts to come out of my mouth. "This whole idea is stupid. Making these stupid flowers. Here I thought you wanted to do it and you don't." If I let all the way loose, I would call them stupid, too. Helpless little snots. I hate their needs and dependency. What they really are is tired and faced with an overwhelming task of manual dexterity. I know this, but at the same time, I am gone, falling, falling into a cavern. There's no clawing back onto solid ground with mere awareness, only watching myself go. Knowing what the mistakes are doesn't stop the damage. Little round faces, fat cheeks, and innocent eyes don't know what I might deliver next. It's not fair for them to be vulnerable to all of the garbage in me.

I keep crying, harder and harder. "I try and try and try so hard," I sob. I remember saying that. I want to throw the scissors and paper, shred it, burn it and scream. But I don't. I have limits. So did Robb. Once you cross them, it's a free-for-all.

"I feel like nobody loves me," I say. It's true. We're getting to the heart of the matter? But this kind of stream-of-conscious self-exploration isn't rated G as pre-bedtime entertainment.

Overwhelmed, I just put the stuff down, go into the office, lie down on the floor and cry. Mary starts to cry in the living room, saying she is scared. I want to kick and pound the floor, but I don't. I want to scream bloody murder, but I don't. (The neighbors would come over straight-away. Just a little after-dinner screaming, I would say. Nobody's breaking furniture.)

Somehow I get it together. I tell them the divorce makes me really upset sometimes, and it's not their fault. We read, do PJs, cuddle, and decide the flowers are still a good idea. A good idea for something to do tomorrow.

If nobody catches me, how can I catch these kids?

TUESDAY, FEBRUARY 21, 1989

I spent the day with a crushing weight on my chest. What do I feel? I have no idea. Incompetent? Is that a feeling or just my latest adjective?

This chest is a house for the soul's moan.

WEDNESDAY, FEBRUARY 22, 1989

Robb seems so together and I am having such a hard time. I refuse to be fooled. I, too, meet the criteria of being dressed and standing up.

SATURDAY, FEBRUARY 25, 1989

I pick up the kids from Robb's yesterday, and they're crabby. I tell them to play outside while I start dinner. From the kitchen I can hear them fighting over which snow belongs to who. I make two fists and roar. Why can't it be sane and straightforward? Why do we have to preface every "nice evening" with some kind of hassle?

The counter is stacked high with clean dishes. I put my head on the formica. For as hard as I want to pound my fists, I will only bruise my hands. I remember what I tell the kids to do when they are angry. I can't get my shoes and glasses off fast enough, run upstairs and fling myself on my bed. I roll and thrash and kick and scream bloody murder into the pillows.

I am merely sobbing when Daniel comes in to look for me and tell me the clothesline is knocked down. I want him to hug me, but don't ask. It's not his job to be my comforter. I tell him I took the clothesline down so they could deliver the firewood. He goes downstairs. I hear Mary come in.

"Where is she?"

"Upstairs."

"Oh, she's crying about her piano?"

"No, she's crying about the clothesline."

Mary brings me a teddy bear. Daniel brings vitamin C. I cry until I am done. It takes another 15 minutes or so. They wait it out next to me, sucking their thumbs. Together we start dinner.

While we eat, I tell them I started thinking about all the things that make me sad at once and they made me cry and cry. We started talking about the things that make me sad—my piano, the divorce, not living at the Old House anymore… They volunteer a lot. They know. They talk about the things that make them sad. We talk about the things we have to be happy about.

Tearwater Tea.

It's over. It's okay.

Sunday, February 26, 1989

I am weary of anger and pain. Beaten-down weary. I don't want it any more. I don't want it, and I have it. The first four cups from a fifty-five gallon drum have washed over me and I hate it. It either washes over me and I feel it, or I stuff it and it will drive me, creating more of the same. Legacies. I hate it.

No I don't. It's my life. I refuse to hate my life. I refuse to dump this garbage on my kids.

Manipulate your surroundings in a concrete and positive way and you will feel better. Translation: hang up the laundry.

Monday, February 27, 1989

Breakthrough notion: I feel bad a lot of the time—anger and pain to the point of physical illness. These are simply responses to rotten things that have been done to me.

This morning I awoke with a headache, stiff all over, nauseous—and was disappointed with myself for failing to take good enough care of myself. No, no, no! I'm not going to blame myself for making me feel the way I feel. I still need to care for my body. I can't just blame other people for everything.

BUT: A lot of bad things have happened to me. I am learning to "protect myself" from the insensitivities of others to which I am vulnerable. That's how I take responsibility for not gathering up more pain. I still have a backlog to deal with here, and in dealing with it, I am setting myself free—remaking the parts of myself that are form-fit for the traps.

I'm not lost in a stupid slog at the bottom of a mud pit.

TUESDAY, FEBRUARY 28, 1989

An all-time assertive triumph last night. Robb dropped off the kids at nine o'clock, said, "I gotta talk to you," brushed past me and walked into the living room. He started up with how we can't be holding grudges in a small town, how we need to make a plan for getting along in this situation—for the sake of the kids.

"All I want to work out with you is what time and where to meet with the kids," I answered. "The rest—it doesn't matter anymore."

"Now there you go. Getting all mad and starting a hassle. You want a hassle?"

"No. I only need to be clear about what time and where with the kids on Saturday."

"Boy have you got a lot of anger."

"I sure do."

"Wow, you have a serious problem."

"I'm not interested in your opinion of me."

"But you have to validate my feelings."

"I don't care about your feelings."

"You *have* to validate my feelings."

"I'm done with your feelings."

"Well, that's *your* problem, then."

I shrug. "Maybe so. But what I need to know is if you want to pick up the kids on Saturday or if I should bring them down. And what time." I zip the lips.

He says what a sick situation this is and what serious problems I have. He paces around and I don't say anything, just use body language to herd him out the door. He manages to growl that I should bring them down at nine on Saturday and is still muttering and shaking his head when he hits the sidewalk.

If you're stuck in an argument with an asshole—go for the second-to-the-last word.

The best part was how I didn't boil and burn about all the things he said that were so wrong. He lards his monologues with half-truths in hopes I'll step in to contradict them and get caught in the shredder. Using the vocabulary of openness—oh such a mature person!—he wants me to "validate his feeling" that I am all fucked up and my problems stand in the way of our kids being happy.

It can be safe to swim here if you don't take the bait.

FRIDAY, MARCH 3, 1989

Daniel had collected up all the straws from the tables at the Garden Lounge when the kids were there last night with Robb. He sold one to Mary for a dime and rented one to me for free. We set off down the street for home in the dark. It was snowing hard, cold, after eight o'clock, but somehow, for a change, I didn't want to rush them home on some agenda that hurried them through the door and into their beds. I didn't care if we walked slow.

"These things are good for catching snowflakes," says Daniel, and turns a straw upward. "When one falls in, you suck it down fast so it lands in your mouth before it melts." He and Mary run ahead, chirping delightedly up the sidewalk, their snowflake catchers held high. I marvel at their ability to play.

Some children who grow up in strained and serious homes don't learn to play. Can they learn when they are older? The problem with the snowflake-catcher is that from my adult perspectives of science, engineering, and dignity, it's a useless and unnecessary endeavor. These are cocktail straws, not milkshake ones. Walking around on a winter night with a straw protruding straight up from your lips? I would look so stupid. Do I look less stupid when I cry?

"Okay, Mommy, now walk all the way home with your tongue sticking out and snowflakes will fall on it," Mary orders. My tongue would be stick-dry if I left it out in the air for three blocks. When Mary does it, she shrieks at every snowflake that lands on her tongue, as well as every one that *might*.

"You aren't catching any snowflakes," complains Daniel, pointing to my down-hanging straw. My excuse is that it's too stupid? How could anything that brings up those liquid ripples of their beautiful laughter be stupid? So I raise my straw, hope no one is looking, and give it a try. No freezing pinpoints fall on my tongue. When I think I've done it long enough, I quit. They race ahead, crouching on the sidewalk, straws up.

"If you pick out a snowflake and watch it, you can get it under control," says Daniel. "If it gets out from under control, just get another one instead." He is so enthused—such a smile, such confidence in his understanding of what's to be done. This beautiful boy, drenched in delight—I want to scoop him up, keep him and this moment forever. Yet what I want to scoop is as elusive as the sunshine in the water coursing over my hands in the Old House. The simple act of taking him in my arms would chase it away. If I were to hold him, to try to absorb some of whatever it is he has, he would have to stop dancing.

Daniel's method works, though. You look up into the wide field of snowflakes rushing at you like time-travel universes, and choose one. Wait for it. Watch—and—sip it out of the night. A zip of cold air on your tongue, and *(flick!)* the sliver of ice. It's funny. It's fun. But I can't quite *have* fun. Every time I catch a snowflake, I don't know if I'll catch another one. Why raise an empty straw to the sky again? Checking to see if it's fun makes the fun disappear, and I want to hurl myself onto the snowdrifted sidewalk, thrash, and cry.

I remember thinking all that. I remember the white galactic sky and the delirious light in their faces. I remember catching snowflakes.

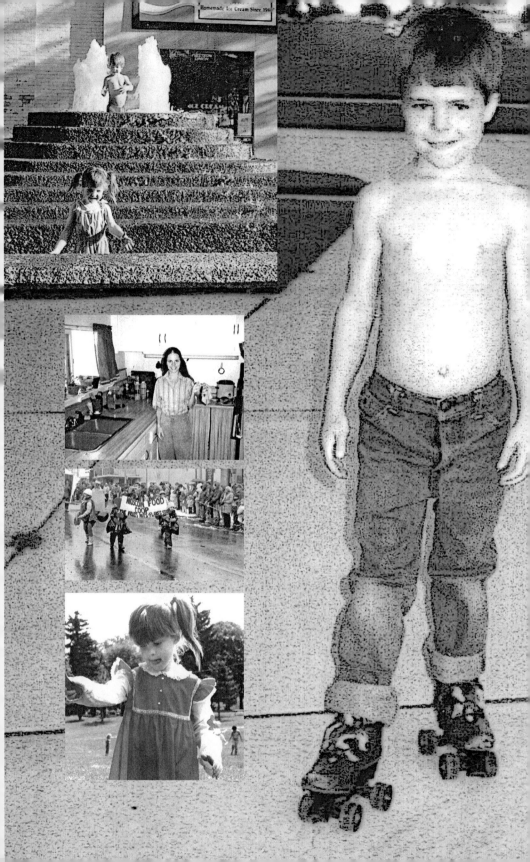

For Keeps

And it should be,
it should be,
it SHOULD be like that!
Because Horton was faithful.
He sat and he sat.
—*Horton Hatches the Egg* by Dr. Seuss

SUNDAY, MARCH 18, 1990

Oh, the sounds here. Fire on a quiet night. The strike of a match, the lick of flame catching the lantern wick. Cast-iron clatter of the stove lids, industrial squeak of the oven damper. The individual and recognizable creak of each porch step, chirps and whispers of every hinge. A rig on the road, grouse drumming, water from the spigot. Drips in the basement. I am at the bread counter. The cookstove ticks as it cools.

Clayton's ubiquitous dead chickens have become a joke. Every time I find a new one, I laugh out loud. They are as tiresome and jarring as Daniel's and Mary's poop jokes. Specialty of the house: bucket of chicken.

A long stroll this afternoon, beginning with an examination of Clayton's below-the-road handiwork. The level of industry in these botched projects is prodigious. His pig lot, fenced with tin—the tin that wouldn't die. The tin Robb salvaged from the burned-down barn at the pig farm. It covered woodpiles and hay before Charlie used it on a shed that subsequently burned down. Now it's here. I look at these pig barns of Clayton's and see we've come full circle—animal sheds moldering into the creek. There's enough plywood in them to board this place up. I peek into one of the low enclosures—simple and square, pig shit on the floor, and in the corner—a dead chicken.

I walk down through the cedars and take the trail towards Clayton's old place, which I see he has transformed into a masterpiece of wire mesh stretched over partitions and poles. It looks like a human-size psychology experiment. I couldn't find the way in, so I felt like part of the experiment. Then I imagined being trapped in there, and didn't want to go in anymore.

I climb onto the flat roof of the hay barn and laugh at how I had wondered before I came out of the trees if there might still be some hay in it. I could use some old hay—about a half-ton, I think, to cover the shit and carcasses everywhere. Behind the building is a wall of rabbit cages. I peek inside each one—rabbit shit in the cage bottoms, and in the corner of one of them—a dead chicken.

Friday, when I first got here, chatting with Stan and Marsha in the wood room, up to my ankles in chicken shit, spilled feed, and scrap wood, I noticed a big sack of carrots with a chicken foot lying next to it. Later, shoveling up the orange, rotten glop the carrots have become, I saw that the chicken foot was stuck to the whole rest of a dead chicken.

What's with these chickens? They're pretty intact, but dead long enough that you don't want to do autopsies. Canine chicken rampage? Weasels? Did Clayton shoot them? Did he use them for target practice, and only take to windows and water tanks after he ran out of moving things? A boy of Daniel's curiosity and development grown into a man's body... I don't want to think so hard about Clayton that I enter his mind.

I awoke this morning, how? Happy, interested, eager to continue with the great mucking-out. Awash in how much I like myself and am proud of myself. I have worked so hard.

I built a fire, and while the coffee water heated, started to sweep. *Oh, my body around this motion.* From the corner of the living room, outward around the chimney and on toward the kitchen door, down the red porch steps, past the greenhouse to the porch door. Twice a day I did that. At least.

Everything here, all the struggles, not only with Robb, or the general struggles that come with this lifestyle, but the struggles with myself. Trying to be so perfect that Robb wouldn't abuse me was a road to nowhere—but I still get to keep the improvements. The tra-la attitude in the letters I wrote wasn't a lie—it drew from a happiness rooted in me here. Amazing what I learned to do—make soap, butcher bears, be a mother. OK, so my course with Robb quickly became an unrelenting string of hurts and disappointments. But under the shadow of all those incidents and insults, I was still committed, believing, working, and I derived a lot of joy from that. No private joy could have countered what Robb did to me, the way I shrank, but that doesn't mean I can't reach back, touch the happiness that was there, and keep it.

It's so fun to be here, free of Robb, free of Clayton, undisturbed in the pleasures of my former world. Sure, there's a huge mess to scrape away, burn, and haul to the dump. I'm peeling the place back down to what matters to me. This isn't just the shell of some broken dream. It gives testimony to a gutsy and courageous experiment. I tried.

At the end of sweeping the floor this afternoon, I hooked the door open and leaned on the frame, drinking the soft spring air and the racing creeksounds. It was as though everything that had been good about my life in this place was rushing up from the past, offering itself to me. For keeps.

I shift the lantern so the shadow of my hand doesn't fall where the pen will go. My pigtails still get caught between the sticks of stove wood I load across my forearm. Yesterday I tossed a tin can into the spot where the wastebasket stood. Every time my hands get wet, I turn to where the towel used to hang. Has it been so long since a moth fried itself in a lantern?

It's the sounds most of all. They embrace me like a lost mother. This sound: me alone, pen scritching, doing what I choose.

Acknowledgements

So many people to thank for their help, encouragement and affection on the journey to Second Street, and beyond.

My children. Foremost and deepest.

Paula Coomer, who said the words that made the book possible, then offered her skills and encouragement to see it through.

Many friends, especially Dale Young, Maria Maggi, Elizabeth Taylor, Josiane Magloire, B.J. Hargrove, Arlene Falcon, Carla Osborne, Andrea Masom, Miriam Kent, Laurie Cortright, Karen Young, and Helen Nugent.

Readers who provided honest, constructive feedback: Lois Blackburn, Pam Bettis, Louise-Marie Dandurand, Marsha Schoeffler, and Gary Williams. For help and comments on the very earliest version of the story: Mary Blew, Jill Dacey, and Tina Foriyes.

Much appreciation to Alternatives to Violence of the Palouse and RadioFreeMoscow for providing opportunities that changed my life.

Thank you Erik and Robert Jacobson for lending your artistic sensibility and two generations of design experience to this project.

Special thanks to BookPeople of Moscow for 30 years of celebrating the written word.

CPSIA information can be obtained at www.ICGtesting.com
Printed in the USA
BVOW031625120911

270907BV00004B/5/P